Pain So Deep

Shon Sheffey
with Leslie A. Lawrence

Copyright 2020 by Shon Sheffey

All rights reserved. No part of this publication may be reproduced, distributed, or transmitted in any form or by any means, including photocopying, recording, or other electronic or mechanical methods, without the prior written permission of the publisher or author, except in the case of brief quotations embodied in critical reviews and certain other noncommercial uses permitted by copyright law.

cover Art: Stilo Da vinci

Killian King Legacy Sheffey. This book and everything I own will go to you! Daddy And Mommy Love you! And even when our hearts go cold, We still got you!

Rest In Paradise to the Following:

Freddie Jean "Pee Wee" Washington
Tre Dyer
Robert "Teddy" Noble
Rosie Trout
Matty "Roll-a-fatty" Hammond
Yorry Timley
Travonta smith
Jerome "Rome" Noble
Ian Jones
LeDondre Raimey
Josh Philipps
Brandon Muncy
David Garrett
Elliott Spikes
Oscar "Choco" Vera
Antionette Ratcliffe
Roderick Alan Coffee
William Cooper Sr.
Neil "Bunk" Lawrence

To the people with a story to tell, the people who didn't get a chance to tell their story, and to the people with post traumatic stress that will never share their story.

- Leslie A. Lawrence

This book was created how I remember it. I acknowledge that others may have conflicting memories that are different from my own.

Contents

Introduction ix

Chapter One: Childhood Memories 1

Chapter Two: Growing up in Painesville 6

Chapter Three: Paintball Backfire 10

Chapter Four: Fading Sports 16

Chapter Five: Off the Porch! 21

Chapter Six: Run in with the law 29

Chapter Seven: Don't Fall In 41

Chapter Eight: Juvie 45

Chapter Nine: Juvie Part 2 48

Chapter Ten: Shipped Out 53

Chapter Eleven: CCF 59

Chapter Twelve: CCF Part 2 62

Chapter Thirteen: Level Two 67

Chapter Fourteen: Victims 70

Chapter Fifteen: Level Three 72

Chapter Sixteen: Level Three Part 2 74

Chapter Seventeen: Back Home 79

Chapter Eighteen: The Fire 84

Chapter Nineteen: Raid 93

Chapter Twenty: Cincinnati 95

Chapter Twenty One: Summer 2011 98

Chapter Twenty Two: The Play 104

Chapter Twenty Three: Night before the lick.. 108

Chapter Twenty Four: The lick 110

Chapter Twenty Five: Count Up! 112

Chapter Twenty Six: Cash Out!.. 121

Chapter Twenty Seven: Party Bus... 127

Chapter Twenty Eight: Snakes.. 133

Chapter Twenty Nine: Good Cop, Bad Cop 136

Chapter Thirty: County.. 144

Chapter Thirty One: 6 Years no tears 151

Chapter Thirty Two: Disrespectful and Disgusting.................................... 159

Chapter Thirty Three: Marion Correctional Institution 178

Chapter Thirty Four: Life Inside 181

Chapter Thirty Five: O'Block 190

Chapter Thirty Six: 23-1.. 204

Chapter Thirty Seven: Gangland 208

Chapter Thirty Eight: Barber School 243

Chapter Thirty Nine: Walking out Not looking Back!! 259

Chapter Forty: Family!! 264

INTRODUCTION

November 16, 2011

It's three o'clock in the morning. I hear my phone ring. I roll over in bed and look over to my phone and my heart drops. *I just need to smoke and go to sleep! I can't even think straight right now*, I thought. I kept telling myself, "One more day Shon... one more day."

Half-asleep and half-lit from the smoke, I nervously answer the phone. No answer! I'm curious but anxious. I hang up and realize that in these last few days, it feels like everything and everyone is closing in on me!

The night was quiet, until I heard a key jiggling in the hotel door. There was a push and I realized the door was locked! My head pops up, to my dismay, there was another push, and I could see the door coming off the hinges. My heart dropped to my shoes. I know it's over. There's nowhere to run and nowhere to escape.

For a brief moment, I was lost in time. My palms were sweating, and my heart began to race. I felt like there was an elephant sitting on my chest. My mind was racing a million thoughts per second. But the only thought that stuck was, *Fuck! I'm caught! I'm about to lose my freedom and I won't see it again for a long time.*

What happened next was a strike of lighting that would change my entire life. The flashlights! The riot gear! Guns out ready to shoot if I make one wrong move! I remember someone shouting, "Get on the floor!" Police rush in flipping the mattress demanding to know where the guns are. In my head, I know that there are no guns in this room. But there were so many cops, everyone was staring at me, and at this time, I knew I was stuck!

Everyone wants to know what really happened. Everyone wants to know how it all went down.

Here is my story, pure and uncut!

Chapter One:
CHILDHOOD MEMORIES

Knock! Knock! Knock! The door swings open. I look up and there's an elder woman who was short and dark-skinned. She stood with one hand on her hip and the other on the door. "Well, you got something to ask me, since you're knocking on my damn door?" I stood still for a moment.

"Is G home?" I asked without breaking eye contact.

"Yeah… he lives here!" You could feel the attitude radiating off her small frame.

"Can he come out and play?" It was her turn to stare me down.

Then she turned around and yelled, "Greg! Get your ass outside and play for a little bit! Got these damn kids knocking at my door at all times of the day!" Then, she added, "And your room better be clean! I'm not playing with your little ass!"

In my head, I was proud because I had stood my ground. In my head, I had gained the respect of my childhood friend's mother. I would come to her house every day to ask if her son could come outside and play. Some days, she said yes, and other days, she said no. Occasionally, I'd get a, "He's GROUNDED! Now go play!" Whatever her answer was, I was fine with it.

Pee Wee Washington, may she rest in peace, was my second mother. She earned that title because to this day, her son has been my friend since the sandbox days. Even today, he has never switched up on me, and has always been there when I need him.

Greg, also known as "G," was my dog growing up! As long as I can remember, he and I have been friends, running around our "hood" shamrock. From eight years old to this very day, he's never switched up on me.

G was different in many ways, but his loyalty was golden! Right or wrong, G would stand next to me proudly, ready for the consequences. He knew that when it was my turn to show my loyalty, there was never a question. I always stood front and center!

Thinking back, I got a lot of ass whooping's for G. I know you're probably wondering that how I got MY ass whooped for another kid. My mother was NOT into me playing with G at such a young age. G was a couple of years older than me and very advanced. However, to some, he was bad as hell! He was small but mischievous, and everybody knew his little ass was always up to something.

My mom tried everything to keep me out of trouble. She tried to get me to make different friends, keep busy in activities, and tried to keep me from hanging around G. In her eyes, she was protecting me, but this was a friend that I couldn't shake. This friend later turned into my brother.

My mom was a single mother. A strong, independent, white woman with six kids. I still don't know how she made it happen, but she did! There were many hungry nights. There were nights I watched her cry herself to sleep because she had no one to help her. There were nights she cried because she couldn't pay the electricity bill, so we would have to light the house with candles. Despite all the adversity, I have never met a woman as determined and motivated as my mother. Failing was not an option! Making sure we had food was not an option! She always made sure we came first, no matter what.

With six kids and barely any help, my mother could've easily quit or gave up on us. It happens every day. Except, she couldn't. It's never been in her to just give up. In fact, she did the exact opposite. She made sure her kids had food to eat, a roof over our head, and clothes on our back every night possible. I will always respect her because that's a true mother. Her kids were always first, even if that meant putting herself last. She's a woman that would go hungry so her kids could eat. Every day, there was a new sacrifice that she made for her children, and for that, she will never lose my respect.

To my family, I'm known sometimes as Anthony, which is my middle name. I remember hearing my mom shout, "Anthony!"

And me replying, "Yes?"

"Turn your ass around and look up at that light! What do you see? What's the problem with this picture?" I was confused. I looked at my mom and shrugged my shoulders.

"Uhm... I don't know," I responded.

Her voice was like thunder, "Them street lights are on and that means that you are coming into my house LATE! That's a problem! Now don't let it happen again!" I felt small.

"Okay, sorry, mom." She looked and me and gave me a smirk.

"Mhm, don't give me those eyes boy. Now get cleaned up and ready for dinner."

You see, my mom was definitely not your average white mother. Like I said, she was a single mom of six kids. She was blessed with three boys and three girls. Some nights, our house could be a zoo, and on others, we made close bonds because of our family struggle. Making it out of the struggle made our family stronger.

There was no choice but to be hands on with us, and that's exactly what my mother did. She made sure we knew right from wrong. And when we got out of line, there was never any, "Aww it's okay, just go sit in time out," or any slaps on the wrist.

CRACK! CRACK! CRACK! Running around the corner, I see my oldest brother outside of the apartment, picking branches off a nearby bush. I didn't understand what he was doing or why he was doing it, so I just watched. "Get your ass in here and let me see what you picked!" I knew the voice all too well, it was my mother. He dragged himself into the house. Slowly, I tiptoe to the door to see what's going on. I know that if I get caught, then that's my ass on the line too, because if I get caught, that automatically means I'm next. I quietly watch.

"Christopher!" my mom yells.

He replies, "Yes mom."

"You're the oldest in this house, correct?"

Once again, he replied, "Yes mom, I am."

"So, when I'm not here, who's in charge? And when I'm not watching your brothers and sisters because I'm at school or work, who is supposed to watch them?"

My brother started moving around nervously. "I am mom."

"EXACTLY. So why is your homework not done, dishes not done, and someone colored on my Damn, wall? I need answers and they better come QUICK."

Confused and upset my brother knows that he fucked up. He knows that he can't blame anyone for this one. He was in charge and this is a lesson he learned quickly. We all learned quickly!

"Don't look like that now! Take your pants off!" You can see the agony burning in his face. *Smack, smack, smack!* Christopher tried to pull his pants up, but he was no match for my mother. *Smack, smack, smack!* "Now go finish those dishes and do your homework, NOW!"

I heard her yell again, "Anthony!" Running from the door as I just watched my brother get his ass tore out the frame, I'm trying not to be next. When my mom calls me by my middle, or full name, that usually means I'm in trouble.

"What did I do? Am I next?" I asked anxiously.

"Get in here and let me see that homework!" I grinned because I knew that meant this time, I was safe.

Ass whoopings were a real thing growing up for my family and me. A very real thing! I keep bringing up that my mother was white so you can understand that she had black tendencies. My mother never sugarcoated or babied us. She had to put her foot down so we would know when she was serious and meant business.

When my dad was seventeen, he moved to Ohio from Pittsburgh. With no resources and barely knowing anyone, my dad created his own lane and his own beautiful family. He's a true hustler and provider! Grow-ing up, my dad taught me a lot. He taught me even more through the lessons I had to learn on my own, you know, *the hard way*. My dad moved in a peculiar way. Some people liked it, and some didn't, but one thing is certain, he always kept it real with me and still does to this day.

A simple decision can change your life. We face decisions every day. We face temptations every day. Unintentionally, our decisions can hurt other people in the process. This is called the ripple effect, when one de-cision affects multiple people without the intention of hurting anyone. When I was six years old, my father was released from federal prison…

Chapter Two:
GROWING UP IN PAINESVILLE

At six years old, I didn't know anything about prison. At such a young age, how could I? However, as I got older, he told me himself, all the things he had going on at that time. I have always respected my father for doing that and it's also something I plan on doing with my own son. To this day, my father has not been back to federal prison and words can't express how proud of him I am for that.

Ever since my father was released from federal prison, he's been grinding. He is a man who puts in blood, sweat, and tears for his family. I can't reiterate enough that he is a true provider. While I was growing up my father had his hand in everything. He opened business after business, crossing the different worlds of different businesses. For as long as I can remember, I recall him constantly making profit and creating jobs for people. Ironically, when I was a child, he owned a barbershop, way before I ever picked up a clipper. It's crazy how life works, right? Who would've guessed that twenty years later I would be blessed with the opportunity to cut hair?

His hustle was unique and relentless. Hustle came to him like breath does to lungs. He was a serial entrepreneur, constantly creating new businesses. There was the barbershop, the carwash, and the kickback. All of them were never just ideas to my father. They were ideas that were put in to action! A wise man once said, "A goal written down and not put in to action is just a DREAM."

Beyond his hustle, my father was always low key and smooth. Not only was his personality smooth, but he was a smooth lady's man. (*cough cough* I guess you can say it runs in the family). He could be studious and well-dressed if the occasion called for it but he also was never afraid to get dirty, and I loved that about him. Even if he thought, we weren't paying attention or that we weren't watching him we always were. And he taught us so much. I remember being younger, he told me, "If you want something, you have to get it, son. DO NOT expect anyone to hand you or help you get anything. If you do that then they will try and throw it in your face!"

Watching my father as I got older, he never gave up on us. He always made sure we were provided for, even if he and my mother weren't on dating terms. That is something he will always have my respect for. He truly values family, so much, that it cannot be described with words.

Once my father came home from prison, he got right to it with us like he never skipped a beat. He wasn't an, "I'm going to do me, and I'll see you when I see you" type of guy. He's a real stand-up man. I know a man came into my life and wasn't like any other man, so he had to be my dad. He fed me, kept clothes on my back, and made sure my mom was happy! This was him, and I didn't care that he would be the one that I'd be watching and learning from.

Life is full of lessons. There are small lessons like when you're not touching the stove, but you see it turn red and decide to touch it. And there are big lessons, like going to prison because you think you know everything. My father taught me a lot both directly and indirectly. There were many lessons that came from riding shotgun with my dad. I couldn't see over the dashboard, but my little ass always hopped up front and put that seatbelt on!

Don't get me wrong, me and my father had more than our share of head butts. Of course, a lot of the fault was on my end because I was hard-headed and was a young boy growing up in a city where it was quiet to most, but to me it was LIT! So as a young boy, I would lie, steal, and always think that I was slicker than my dad. And each time I would end up looking silly because he was ALWAYS a step ahead of me. My dad is a short, five feet six-inch brown-skinned man but he was built SOLID.

It was that he wasn't super cocky or that he was the most "in shape" man in the city, but he was solid, and he knew his strength. He had his own way of dealing with his children, but we are his children, so that is the end of that!

"Hit the floor! You think I'm dumb, don't you? I keep telling your ass that you are not smarter than me!" Sweating, I thought, *Damn, how did he know?* "Hit the floor" is a term my father used, meaning that we had to get down and do push-ups until he said you could get up. It was a physical workout, which built character, mental strength, and toughness.

My dad had this special way of making you tell your story multiple times and catching each error in your story. I still haven't met anyone else who teaches like this! Whenever I got in trouble, he would ask me, "Slim, what's up, what happened?" and made sure he added a, "Look me in my eyes when I'm talking to you!"

I can hear him saying, "You're going to learn that lying is harder to keep up with than the truth, now do those pushups until I get back from cleaning the dog cages!" My mind was blown! I had thought that I covered all of my tracks. How did I end up doing pushups until he comes back from cleaning the dog cages? When he walked back to the room I was dripping from sweat and my arms were shaking. "Keep pushing!" he said. "It hurts doesn't it? Now imagine someone lying to you in your face! That's how I feel. I tried my hardest to concentrate and not listen to my father while he was lecturing me. "Now get up and get in the shower… LOOK AT ME!" Slowly getting up, my shirt was drenched in sweat like I had been running suicide drills for an hour. I looked him dead in his eyes. "You are not smarter than me; I've been doing what you try to do, give it up! Next time your mom calls me and tells me that your ass has been acting up in class, I'm going to PER-SONALLY pull up to the damn school. Are we on the same page?" By this time, I was sniffling, crying, and wiping my runny nose. I answered him yes and headed to the shower.

My parents frequently disagreed about his parenting techniques, but he never backed down. I know that my mom understood that he only meant to teach my brothers and I, nothing more and nothing less.

I never questioned my dad's discipline techniques. They were like any other ass whoopings that I got. I didn't expect for my mom and dad to treat me the same. As I got older and was too much for my mother to handle, my father was there to make sure my ass was dealt with. Any time my mother called my father about one of us, he would come with no questions asked. My parents used teamwork and have always had a mutual respect, which they still do to this day.

There was my dad who didn't do the "you're grounded" talks but was hands on. And there was my mother who was quick to put my ass on lockdown because she knew what I loved the most was to be outside and active. Whooping my ass only worked for so long, and then I started being grounded AND an ass whooping. What can I say is that, I was mischievous.

Chapter Three:
PAINTBALL BACKFIRE

One of the worst ass whoopings I ever had was a result of getting my first paint ball gun for Christmas. I remember this Christmas as if it was yesterday. I couldn't wait to open my gifts!

Everyone was in the living room. My siblings: Chris, Jayden, Tati, Amaree, and Jordyn, my mother, and my grandmother all gathered to celebrate. My father never has, and probably never will, celebrate Christmas. Another peculiar thing about him is the way that he celebrates holidays. In fact, he doesn't. For him, holidays were made by religion and fake meanings that he refuses to stand by.

It's Christmas morning and I smell my mother's food beginning to cook. The smell of greens and mac and cheese filled my nose. Again, she's not your average white woman; she can throw down in the kitchen! It's soul food at its best! I walked in the kitchen just in time to see her open the oven. The macaroni and cheese had cheese dripping down the side! I saw yams on the stove after peeling back it's aluminum foil into a cloud of pure love! I take a deep breath and I swear I can taste every ingredient in her desserts.

"Okay everybody! Come in here and let's open these gifts!" my mom yells. Everyone gathers in the living room as we all take turns opening gifts.

The night before Christmas, my brother Chris and I stayed up late, trying to sneak and see what our parents got us. We were curious and couldn't wait any longer! We had a small window of opportunity to pull it off. He told me to watch the window while he looked. "I can't see, it's double bagged!" he told me.

"Uh… we have a problem," I replied. "They're on their way in with more bags and we have to go now!"

All the gifts were gone, and everyone was satisfied. Everyone was smiling, but my mom had the biggest smile. "Shon, go get that last gift upstairs, it was too heavy for mommy to carry." I dashed up the stairs and busted open the door! I can't believe what I'm seeing. She really got it for me! The exact same one I wanted! Same color and everything! The paintball gun! I flew back down the stairs to give her the biggest hug ever. "Thanks mom! I love you sooooo much!" I had gotten the paintball gun that I had wanted for so long; I was pumped to shoot it off! "Now you and your brother don't have to share one," she said with a smile. It was my favorite gift, until the day I wish I never asked for it.

My mom was at the grocery store and my brother and I were cleaning out our paintball guns and switching out the barrels. We had two completely different guns. So the barrels looked different, and even better on different guns. Earlier in the day, we had been shooting off the guns.

Mom took everyone to the store with her except Chris, Amaree, and me. This day, Amaree was so energetic! She had been running through the house all day. Well that day I decided that I was going to scare her the next time she runs downstairs.

When you shoot a paintball gun while it doesn't have any paintballs in there, carbon dioxide shoots out and can scare the person you're shooting at. My brother and I have done it plenty of times before. That was my plan, and man did that plan backfire.

I yelled out to Amaree, "Amaree! Come find me!" and she ran down the stairs. I jump out and squeeze the trigger expecting to hear air… But I don't hear air. As soon as I hear it, I know something is wrong! I heard the sound of a paintball coming out! I couldn't understand how that could be; I thought there were no paintballs in my gun! There was only supposed to be air coming out. I instantly felt sick to my stomach. What did I do? What happened? All of these questions shooting through my head before I can even take a look at my sister.

Chris runs into the room, "What are you doing bro?"

Before I could answer him, he snatches my paintball gun out of my hands. "I was just supposed to scare her!" I yell back.

"You know, like we do! You remember how we do?"

He looks at me and at this moment, he knows I'm scared, and he knows my ass is grass if mom figures out what happens.

This is the first time my brother stuck his neck out for me! We cleaned my sister up and tried convincing her to tell mom that she was running in the house and hit her nose on the edge of the couch. THIS WAS OUR LIE! Looking back, I can't believe it. We ran the lie back to each other multiple times so when my mom comes home, we would all be on the same page.

I turned to Amaree, "I'm so sorry, I just wanted to scare you…if you don't tell mom, I'll give you candy and do all your chores." Amaree was sniffling and just barely keeping it together, but Eventually, she said okay and agreed not to tell mom.

The next thing I heard was Chris yelling, "She's here!" When my mother walked inside, she saw my sister's face and she immediately knew something was not right. "What's wrong with your face?" I could feel my heart drop. My mind raced around wondering what my sister would say.

Amaree looks at me, then looked at Chris, and the next thing you know she starts crying crocodile tears. My mother shot Chris a look of death. She was steaming with fury. "What happened to your sister's face? I want to know, and I want to know NOW."

Chris stepped up to her. "She was running around the house and Shon scared her and she tripped. She hit her nose on the edge of the couch."

Then my mom looks over at me. "Shon, is that true?"

"Yes, it's true!" I answered. "That's how it happened!" As soon as the words left my lips, I knew I fucked up.

My mom knows this is not the story. She calls Amaree over and starts to view her face. Amaree is crying and trying to talk at the same time. My mom tells her to calm down and tell her what happened. She touches her cheek, "It's okay, tell mom what happened baby." Then she touched her nose and my sister loses her cool! Her nose hurts so bad from the impact of the painful shot to the face she just took not even 20 minutes ago. My mom pushes her nose up like she's looking for boogers only to pull a shell of a paintball from my sisters' nose. As she's doing this, my skin is crawling. *IT'S OVER, IM DEAD*, I thought. She is going to try and kill me.

She looks right at me! "She tripped and fell on a paintball? Is that the dumb ass lie that you're going to tell me next?" She's steaming and I can feel her energy. Her jaw is clenching she's furious, face red she yolks me up! "What did you do?"

Chris tries to intervene, "Mom she tripped!"

Mom lets me go and snatches Chris up, rips his pants down, and open hand whoops my brother's ass. *Smack! Smack!* "I told you about lying to me…" *Smack! Smack!* She whooped his ass for what seemed like eternity! I could only imagine what my ass whooping was going to be like after seeing his. She whooped him for lying and showing me that it was okay to lie to her.

When she finally finished and it's dead silent. I can only hear my heartbeat. "Take your pants off," she tells me. My ears hurt when I hear these words! My hair on my neck stands up as I know it's my turn and this is the GRAND FINALE!

She walks toward me and I start to back up. Bring your ass here! Her hands are worn out from my oldest brother. He ran to his bed after his ass whooping. The only thing he wanted to do was go to sleep.

Time slows for a second as I look at my little sister as she stands in front of me in shock. Her eyes were watering, and her hands were shaking. She doesn't know what happened, but she knows I fucked up because I look HORRIFIED! I know I fucked up big this time and my ass was on the line. I knew for sure that I was getting my ass whooped, I just didn't know how bad.

She grabs me by my arm and with her free hand, she lets loose, she's so quick and accurate. *Whack. Whack. Whack.* I yell at the top of my lungs because it stings. Every stroke and every hit feels like it's getting stronger and stronger! How is she so strong? Why did I underestimate my mom? *WHACK. Whack. Whack.* "You shot your sister in the Face! You won't ever see that gun again!" *WHACK. WHACK. WHACK.* Now go apologize to your sister and then go to bed!

Finally, it's over! I thought, but this was only the beginning!

As I'm getting out of the shower, I open the door only to have my heart drop again. MY DAD IS HERE! What did I do? He takes his belt off and waits no time! He snatches my towel and lets me have it. Still wet from the shower every blow from the belt stings and is piercing my skin. *Hold in there! The worst is almost over!* I kept telling myself.

"Now you can take your ass to bed. Oh yeah, and you're grounded for the SUMMER!" Every word my mom just said hit me harder and harder as I repeated it. Grounded for the summer.

Can they do that? I try to convince myself they didn't mean the whole summer. I've been grounded before, but NEVER for a whole summer.

I still remember posting up in my window, looking down on all the kids play outside after school on those hot summer days. They'd be laughing, playing tag, and football, meanwhile all I could do was watch. *Damn, I fucked up bad this time,* I'd think to myself. I really was sorry though. I really didn't mean to shoot her, but I know it wouldn't take it back.

NOTHING would take that back, I love my sister and we grew even closer and laugh about it even now. But those ass whoopings and being grounded for the summer just almost killed me!

Chapter Four:
FADING SPORTS

Summer time used to be my favorite time of the year, hands down. Growing up, I lived outside. I absolutely HATED being in the house. Whether we were playing football with the older kids or playing BB gun wars, there was always something to do outside, especially in my neck of the woods.

My city is pretty small. The population currently is only 19,881; I grew up on the north side. NORTH STATE! SHAMROCK!

That's my stomping grounds! My grandma lived in the same complex that my family was raised in for 30-plus years. SHE THE OG OF SHAMROCK! Anyone who is really from there knows that.

My Block was connected to another block called Argonne arms. We did everything with them. They were like our hood rivals. Basketball games, football games, paintball wars, BB gun wars, man hunt, fights… ARGONNE VS SHAMROCK WAS LIT!

With no basketball hoop, we used a crate. We nailed it up to this blue shed and held our own basketball games. We used to use the side of the buildings to play dodgeball. Any age was invited. If you could walk, you could play!

To play football was played diagonally from corner of courtyard in the opposite corner! This same yard was used for baseball and Kickball. It went down in the yard.

For baseball, we used the standing trees as 1st, 2nd, and 3rd base, and we used a hat for the home base. We used what we had work and I loved it.

Growing up in Shamrock, we weren't rich. Some of us were better off than others, but we still came together as a whole and made sure everyone was taken care of and having fun. In Shamrock, we were a family.

I met a lot of good friends and family from growing up on my side of town. My little cousin Delmar was known for popping wheelies, not just riding them a short distance, but up and down streets, and around complexes. Our childhood was amazing. We had bikes for days. Old school bikes, sports bikes, it didn't matter because we had them all!

One summer started a bike chop shop. G, Delmar, and I all had a new bike flipped over spray painting. This was our way of having fun before we ever hit a lick or touched a gun.

Sports were always a big thing in our house. Basketball, football, track, softball, and cheerleading. My entire family was very athletic and very in-tune with our athletic talents. My oldest brother, Chris, was my motivation in sports. He was always a fucking dog! He was fast as fuck and quick on his toes. Playing football against him was something I always saw as a big test.

He was older, stronger, and smarter, but I was still shooting my shot and not giving up no matter what. He pushed me to work hard, and we Eventually, ended up playing football together for teams. He was the running back and I was the quarterback. Believe me we had our way.

It was the summer of 2002. *Buzz, Smack, Buzz, Smack*. It's 90 degrees, which feels like 100 degrees with these football pads on. I'm hot and irritated from the bugs that were trying to get inside my football helmet. I was the quarterback and my brother was running the ball. It's the end of the game and we are backed up on our own one-yard line. The other teams coach loaded the lineup and there was no way my brother could run the ball.

The coach called a timeout. "Shon, fake run to Chris and bootleg it. Then, run it for your life because they will be expecting your brother to get the ball." I hear the play and it registers, my heart starts beating faster and faster. *Break*! We walk back to the field and line up to run the play.

Ready! I scan the field and do a fake audible! Their line shifts confused! I look at my brother and I see their lineman getting excited like they know what's coming next. *Set! Hike!* I fake the handoff to my brother he sells it perfectly! Running to the left, I cuff the ball.

They follow my brother, and I take off to the left from the one-yard line. I'm running, and suddenly, it feels like every player is shifting across the field closing in on me! Shake one player, shake the second! I see my brother blocking up the sideline… I can hear him talking to me with his eyes. *Follow my block little bro.* I can hear him say it… I run as fast as I can to his block.

My adrenaline was pumping because that touchdown won the game!

I hear my mother screaming her heart out, "GO BABY, GO BABY! Run! Run! You're almost there!" My brother was blocking for me up the sideline as my coach right beside on the sideline.

I hear the announcer, "Oh my gosh, he did it, how did he do that!" Sprinting up the field, to the 50, 40, 30… Another block from my brother. Breathing heavy I tell myself, *"Get your ass in the end zone."* 20, 10 TOUCHDOWN THE BUCKEYES WIN THE GAME!

I remember my brother knocking me over he was so pumped at what his little brother just did. *Good Job Bro! We did it!*

We raised our helmets in the air because we had won. For me, there was nothing better than having my older brother proud of me and playing a sport we both love.

My mother was crying at the end of the game. She was always so supportive of us all when it came to anything we did, especially sports. I looked at my mother with a puzzled look, "Mom we did it, why are you crying?"

"You did great baby, mommy's just happy for you and your brother! Let's go to the snack line."

I accepted her answer and replied, "Okay," then told her, "I love you."

As much as I loved the game, and as much as I loved playing the game, one day, everything changed. My brother was my go-to guy on the football field. One game changed my view of the game one play changed everything.

I had been hit late and taken out for a play; I didn't want to leave the game. To me it wasn't even that serious of a hit but it was the rule to step out for at least one play. Once they replaced me, I felt that something was off. Something wasn't sitting right, but I was hoping they would just run the ball. Wishful thinking. They called a pass play to my brother.

Hike! The quarterback drops back and I watch my brother take off, and in my head I'm saying, *Throw the ball, what are you waiting for?* He under throws my brother causing him to slow down! He jumps for the ball. I've never seen him jump this high! He's too high! My stomach tightens as I see the defender go under his legs! I remember thinking, *Oh my God he's fall on his neck.* Not him! Not my brother. Not the one person I love to play this sport for.

It happened exactly like I called it. As he laid there, I instantly knew that something was wrong. I sprint down to him kneel by him. I can see the pain on his face. Gasping for air and grabbing his back, I am in complete shock. I have rarely seen my brother cry. He was screaming at the top of his lungs.

As far as what to do next, I was lost. I felt like there was something that I was supposed to be doing to help. But there was nothing I could do about it to help and that's what hurt.

My feelings for the game dramatically switched. Even my mother could sense it. I just didn't love the game anymore. That hit made me look at the sport differently. My brother was so strong. How could he play the game so well and still get hurt like this? I didn't understand. I felt guilty. I felt like if I were in the game then that hit wouldn't have happened.

I played football until my freshman year of high school. At that point, I finally said that I was done with it. Those years in between, I was trying to fill a void. I loved playing with my brother, but him getting hurt didn't slow him up, he ended up going to college to play football. What was it that made me stop playing? The streets filled that void. I found something that I liked doing better than playing a sport I no longer had love for. Nobody could understand why I was skipping practice. They didn't understand that I didn't want to play anymore. We grew up playing this sport and this was our way of life… but in my heart, I was done.

I stopped taking sports seriously and my younger brother picked the ball up. I loved watching that little boy grow up playing sports. Every sport he played he gave so much pure effort and raw talent. He sat back when he was younger watching his older brothers play football and the whole time was soaking the game up.

Jayden was a combination of me and my older brother Chris. Because of his talent, there was no limit for this kid. His speed and agility were off the charts. I loved the game so much that I started helping him grow with the sport; I couldn't just let the game go like that. I sat back and watched my little brother turn into a savage on the field AND on the basketball court. He progressed and grew in age.

I was blind to what was going on though. Blind to the fact that I was thinking I was grown and doing shit on what I *thought* was sneaky. But believe all that shit came and bit me in the ass later. The streets had me off the first taste like a dope fiend taking their first blast. What did I just do? Why was it so easy? Why does it make me feel like this? I felt free. I felt untouchable.

Chapter Five:

OFF THE PORCH!

It was the summer of 2007. I was a freshman in high school finding my own ways; I was walking and talking differently. Slowly, I was becoming a man.

Skipping class became a sport in Harvey High School, the high school that I went to. It was too easy, which proved not to be a good thing for me later on. My high school friends consisted of classmates and sports players I either played with before I quit playing or just knew from around the city. I wasn't the most popular, but I was definitely known.

There were a few specific people I kicked it with outside of school. There was Mike, Terrance, and Zay. We became really close over the years of high school. We all played some sport together whether it was football, basketball, or track. We all enjoyed doing the same things. Dancing, skipping class, smoking, girls… we were all on the same page.

Mike was like my brother. We grew up together and had the same brother. Chris has the same dad as Mike, so we were always around each other for as long as we both can remember. Mike definitely wasn't the best influence growing up but I wasn't looking for guidance. I was trying to kick it and live life because I was 15 years old. With sports slowly fading away, I became more mischievous, always into something. Mike's house was the "go to" when we skipped school. His mother was always at work, so we would sneak into the house while she was at work and then leave before she got back.

Terrance was my right-hand man at this time! We went everywhere together. He lived with me at this time because he had personal things going on in his life. This was the first person my mom actually let me bring around and help. My mom treated him as one of her own children, and I respected that because instead of letting him just go without, she welcomed him into her home.

He was definitely a smooth talker. He got me out of a lot of shit, but I knew what he was good at so I would let him do all the talking.

By this time, I had started smoking weed and drinking alcohol. I was also getting deeper and deeper into the streets. In hindsight, I don't know how I didn't see what was going on. *How can I not see myself slipping into this trap? Why is it so fun right now?* I felt so free. This is my safe zone. I get dropped off at school and I'm free until I get home after "practice."

You see, even though I wasn't into sports, I still used it as an excuse to be out of the house. The Streets is where I wanted to be, partying, making money, and having sex. Let's get to all that right? In due time… we will get to all of that, but right now, I want you to understand how life was changing for my family and me. I began skipping class which is what I believe gave me a sense of confidence. This confidence later leads into bigger decisions and bigger consequences.

It's lunch time, 4th period… I meet with everyone at the table, it's Wednesday, so pizza it is. I turn to my friends Zay, Mike, and Terrance. "Yo, I'm out after they ring the bell."

Zay laughed, "What do you mean you're out?"

Then Mike chimed in, "Fuck it I'm out too."

Terrance shot back, "Hell no, coach will catch me."

I turned to Zay, "I mean, I'm walking out the back door by the study hall when they hit the bell, all the upper class do it and they slow as fuck can't be that hard."

Zay couldn't believe what he was hearing. "Never, you're tripping bro."

Then Terrance hit us with the, "Y'all be safe." I told Mike to meet me by the study hall room after the bell run so we could leave. He told me that we were going to go to his mom's house.

We talk and finish our food as the bell rings. Everyone in the cafeteria files out and heads to their lockers before their next class. It's loud, all you hear is girls laughing, shoes squeaking on the floor, and lockers opening and shutting. The halls are packed wall to wall. This is the perfect time and now I see why the upper class does it like this. I head to the spot to meet Mike, I notice him following up behind me. We get to the spot and my chest is beating loud and fast! I know Mike can hear it beating out of my chest. I'm nervous, this is the very first skip, and with time starting to run out, the bell rings for halls to clear and people to get to class. This is our moment. As we walk up to the door, I feel my adrenaline pump, I look to see if Mike is ready and he is.

Boom! I push the back door open and we step out walking fast and quickly. There is a bike trail behind the school we make it there and we are safe... at least I thought. We didn't see anyone, but did anyone see US is the question! We step onto the bike trail, that was easy... we start walking and laughing, just talking shit about how Zay and Terrance should've quit being so scary and Came with us.

I heard tires rolling on rocks... I slow my pace up as I feel my heart drop. *What the fuck is that sound and why does it feel like we are in slow motion?* Do I turn my head and look, or do I just take off running? I need to make a decision and quick.

I turn my head only to see the school cop officer, Ponder, driving his car onto the bike trail. Fuck! The way he is driving, he knows kids are on the trail as there's no casual driving here. He floors it, I hear his engine rev. We run to the left through bushes and into backyards... all I feel is tree branches smacking my arms as I hold them in front of my face running as fast as I can out of these woods!

We make it to the street but that's exactly what Ponders wanted... and we know that. We sprint to Mike's house, cutting through back roads and in and out of people's back yards. I can only imagine how crazy we looked running in broad daylight! But this was our first time skipping and we were not going down. That was out of the question! Finally, we make it to Mike's house and we are out of breath, but we are safe. Now we can chill, smoke, and eat. This beats sitting in class all day in my mind. *It won't hurt to skip school once or twice.* Personally, I never saw what I was doing wrong until it was already too late.

Skipping class turned into an addiction. A thrill. A test! Could I get it off? How many times? I LOVED skipping class! Even when my friends said that we were going to stay in school and not skip. I would leave them in school and skip class on my own. Harvey Eventually, turned missing class into after school hours. Each missed class added up to hours that you paid back after school in a detention style class. I hated it, so I skipped out on that too.

My grades were slipping and quick. I wasn't focused on anything but kicking it and doing me. With sports fading, the streets, and my friends becoming clearer, I thought I knew what I wanted in life and slowly my life started to get crazy.

Once I started skipping school more, I began smoking more weed. I loved how it made me feel. I was so calm and relaxed, I felt like I could be my true self. But to everyone else, I'm changing, especially to my mom.

My mom noticed everything I did was different. She knew I was growing into a young man and I was soon going to have to learn lessons, either with my dad punishing me or life lessons on my own. The ass whoopings have worn down on me, being grounded became regular. What's next?

I could get away in my head, not from other people, talking about other people, I could easily block out if they're not speaking my language or what I want to hear. See, at this age, I'm starting to think that I know shit. I'm about to learn a couple things and learn them *quick*.

Laid back and quiet was the title I always got from people. Sneaky was an understatement. But to me, I was living, and this was normal. Soon, skipping class, smoking weed, and stealing, consumed me like quick sand. Slowly, I felt myself losing control.

I began to get closer to my friends and I started to hang with my friends more than my family. I was so lost and blind.

Eventually, sex did nothing but elevate my confidence. Especially the way I lost my virginity. Growing up in Painesville, we had flavor on the female side. Painesville is literally a "Melting Pot." People from all over come here, it's always been like that! Spanish girls, sisters, white girls, mixed girls! We had them all.

A lot of times, growing up girls were faster than the boys. That's why mothers used to say stay away from "that little fast ass girl." Surprisingly, my friends always said I was a prude. I didn't lose my virginity till I was 15. My other classmates had been turned that page, some of them already was turning into parents. One thing I didn't want to do was get a girl pregnant off the first time. That was my biggest fear along with getting in there and not knowing what I was doing. I just remember everyone telling me, "There's nothing like your first time." What did that mean though? I'm sure it feels good and will feel good next time, right?
Terrance calls my phone. *RING. RING. RING.* "What's up bro?" he replied right away. "What's up, you trying to kick it? I got the spot for us. It's official no bullshit. And I got a surprise for you!" I took the phone off my ear. *You got a surprise for me?* I had to make sure I wasn't tripping. "Yeah, just pull up on me I'm bout shoot you the address."

My phone vibrated and the address came through. I didn't recognize the address, but fuck it, I went anyway. I pull up to the house as I shoot him the text, *'unlock door I'm pulling up'*. I walk in as our friend Bean daps me up.

"What's up baby boy?"

"What's up bro?" He told me to come inside because everyone was chilling.

"Who *is everyone?*"

"Relax, bro, it's cool."

I walk into the living room and I see her chilling on the couch, I walk in and say what's up as I sit on opposite side of her (remember I'm shy around females still, this is my first time). She says hi and waves. Terrance sits in middle of everyone and starts playing music. I feel her looking at me and from the heat on my face; I can feel her staring through me. I lean back on the couch and get comfortable. Terrance tells her, "Sit on his lap." She does! Before she sits down, he grabs her ass and smacks it showing me how thick she is. Both hands were full of ass. He shakes it and she giggles, looking at me biting her lip. I look up at her and she winks, I'm shocked as to what is going on. She sits down on his lap.

She starts dancing to the music, ass clapping in his face. He's getting a lap dance, but the whole time she's biting her lip looking at me! I didn't understand what that meant. And why is my heartbeat starting to get faster?

Terrance says, "I'll be back bro." He gets up and walks her into the room. With the door slightly cracked, still I hear *clap, clap, clap,* and moaning following it. *What the hell are they doing in there?*

It gets louder. *Smack. Smack.* The bed hits the wall. Me being curious, I walk quietly to the door making sure NOBODY hears or sees me at the door. I put my eye to the opening of the door to see what is going on then I see it. I've seen this before. I instantly get happy as to why I know why my bro called me over and what the surprise was. I watch her. The way she's bent over the bed with him behind her. *Clap. Clap*

I go back to the couch. Damn, now I know why he's always over here. He comes out smiling, walks up to me, and daps me up like he knows I've seen what just went down. When he daps me up, he tells me to go in the room! *GO IN THE ROOM,* echoes in my head for what seems like five minutes.

I walk up to the door and push it open. She's there, laying across the bed, naked and comfortable. She's smiling and biting her lip when she calls me over! She pulls my pants down and I immediately feel a tingling sensation. I never felt this before. I closed my eyes and it felt so warm but so good. I opened my eyes to see her whole mouth wrapped around my dick. My eyes grew and I felt them bulging. She stops because she notices me; I'm not use to what is going on. She knows this is my first time. I wasn't embarrassed. I was glad she knew. Then I could really relax.

She stood up and I followed her lead. She placed my hands on her hips and turned around, so her back was facing me. I smelled her perfume on her neck. She got on the bed, ass in the air she waved her ass back and forth looking me in my eyes and taunting me. "Come here." My heart is pounding, it feels so good… I want more!

I stood behind her as she moved to the edge of the bed. She knew she was in control but wanted me to lead. Using her hand, she guided me. *It's so warm and wet.*

She puts the condom on me. The time is here. When I touch her, she grabbed me.

With the tip inside of her, I started to tense up. I slide all the way inside her and she gasps for air, flinging her head back. I put my nose in the sky. It felt so good, but that was only the beginning. As we continued, it got hotter and our breathing sped up. I'm going off what I've seen in movies, that's all I know.

Clap, clap, clap. She moans and I grab her hair because it felt so good. *What have I been sleeping on? Why haven't I done this sooner?* I start smacking her ass. *Smack. SMACK.* She moans. I pick up the speed and force. She moans louder! We are both are into it! Squeezing her ass, I feel my dick start warming up. It feels good but different. I sped up and as I speed up the feeling intensifies. *Oh, shit this feels good.* I hear her moan and see her grabbing the sheets. I give her two more strokes, *deep strokes. Clap. Clap.*

My knees almost buckle from the next feeling. I feel my whole body jerk. I continue to stroke, and my dick explodes with pleasure. She puts her head in the bed in exhaustion. All I could do was smile.

She lays there naked, with breathing heavy, she looks at me and bites her lip as she playfully kicks me with her foot. I smack her ass and pull my pants up.

Terrance walked in with a big smile across his face. He knew the play he just set up. Walking home that night, I felt my self-esteem and my self-confidence rise. Sex made me feel more like a man. Some might say how I lost my virginity wasn't the "correct" way, but fuck it, that's how it went.

Things started to take a turn after that night. Like I said, I began thinking I knew more than what I really did. I began thinking I had a grasp on life but deep down, I was losing control fast.

Chapter Six:

RUN IN WITH THE LAW

"Your car's dirty as hell," I tell Katie. Katie was this white girl from Cali, who moved out to Painesville with her family. She was going to Riverside, the "rival" of Harvey. She had blonde hair and bright, blue eyes, which were cold as ice. She was short, thick, and had braces. Katie drove a Lexus truck. Me, Terrance, Jordan, and another friend of mine, rode with Katie to the car wash. I told her to pull into the automatic car wash. There is a car in front of us, so we vacuumed the car out first. I went to the air freshener machine to buy some good smell for the truck. I put a $5 bill in the machine but nothing came out. I press the buttons but with no avail this time, so at that point, I get mad. I hit the machine twice and then Jordan walks over to me and says, "What's up, why you spazzing?"
I snapped back, "This dumbass machine just ate my money bro."

I walk to the side of the building to talk to the manager of the shop. The door was cracked open. I push the door open and call out to see if anybody is there. When no one answered, a thought popped my head inside, *Nobody is here. I'm getting my money back, they got me fucked up!*

I tell Jordan to watch out for me. He asks what's up. I tell him to just watch and just trust me. He does as I asked. I look inside and scan the room. On the counter, I see stacks of $1 bills and $5 bills. I grab the cash, stuffing it in both of my pockets. My adrenaline was pumping because I know I am not supposed to be in here and DEFINITELY wasn't supposed to be taking the money! I look under the counter and I see 4 buckets of quarters. It had to be over $1,000 in quarters. I stuffed two hands in the buckets, and you can hear the quarters splashing up the sides of the bucket. Four pockets full of quarters, my pants are sagging as I leave and tell Jordan it's his turn. He switches spots with me and does the same thing. When he finished, we jumped in the car. *KATIE DRIVE!* She looks back at us and we say GO!

She pulls out of the driveway not knowing anything that just happened. We go to the coin exchange and cash in. The adrenaline was extreme! That feeling, the rush of taking the money and not getting caught made me hungry. I was addicted. This was only the beginning, a small taste.

As I continued school, my grades fell and I continued to skip class. It got to the point where the principal called my mom and set up a conference. I was shook. I hated when my mom came into school.

"Ms. Bowler", she looked my mom in her eyes, "Your son has 100 hours of missing classes." My mom looks at me with the look of fury, "100 Hours? Are you fucking kidding me? How do you miss 100 hours of class Shon? Look at me when I'm talking to you!" I look up at my mom and immedi-ately shake my head. There's nothing I could say. I was caught. "Get your ass to class I'll be here to pick you up. Sports is over for you!"

Fuck! That was my way of kicking it after school. Saying I was going to practice but really skipping out. Now I have to go straight back to one of my parents' house after school.

My dad had this woman he dated for a long time and they are still together and happy. Maureen was golden in my eyes! Her heart was pure, and she would give you the shirt off her back to see you smile! She was the head nurse at Lake East Hospital, a local hospital in Lake County. I remember one day, she let me see her work check before she deposited it. "Why so many zeros? Don't you want numbers instead of zeros?"

She laughed and said, "You got a lot to learn little man."
She always looked out for me and took care of all of my dad's children like they were her very own. Anything we needed, she was there to help with it. She's a true rider. No matter what, she had my dad's back. She loved this man from jump and never stopped loving him. She remains by

his side and ready to do whatever he needs from her. A solid woman, if I've ever seen one.

My dad and Maureen lived right around the corner from my high school. This came in clutch as I progressed. Growing up my dad always showed us ways on how to save money. He had this change jar where he would drop his change. All loose change went in this jar. Bills under $20 and all coins! I've constantly seen my dad adding money to this jar. I remember counting all the change up with Maureen, separating all the dimes, pennies, and quarters, rolling them up in to change sleeves. We'd count all the bills $1 bills over here, $5 over there, $10 over there... All night counting up! When I was ten, that jar paid for us to go to Disney World!

As I got older, I became bolder and more mischievous. I started turning into someone else, but it felt normal to me. I felt like I was really living, and whoever didn't agree was holding me back.

Even my mother noticed me change. I would come home and go straight in to my room. She noticed that I became anti-social and hurt people close to me, even I didn't realize it.

Skipping school was easy! Going to my dad's house to pick up money made it even more addicting. I started skipping school and going to my dad's house to eat, grab money, and then leave before anyone would notice I was there. I knew where the spare key was at, because coming over and feeding the dogs in the past. I would skip school, get the spare key, and let myself in making sure no one was home, quickly making myself something to eat. In my eyes, if my dad pulled up and asked what I was doing, I'd just say grabbing lunch. I finished making my food and I was ready to leave. I looked at this tall, stand up change jar. Staring it down, I walked up to it. I looked around one more time before I went for it. I squeezed my skinny arm down into this jar open handed. Whatever I could fit in my hand when I closed it was coming with me! Change or bills, I need it! With two hands every time, I stopped over his house. This money paid for food, shoes, and weed for me and all my friends. When I ate, they ate.

After going and doing this over a certain amount of time, I felt like my dad would notice. That's what caused me to do what I did next. This next decision caused me so much pain in the long run. I hurt so many people with just this one decision.

A ripple effect! Not thinking and being young-minded, I made a decision. The jar was extremely low. Low enough to notice. I decided to set my dad's house up to look like someone robbed it! I broke a window in the back to make it look like someone had broken in. I had tossed the couch pillows on the floor, emptied the jar of change into my duffel bag, and left the jar on the floor. Leaving out the back door, I ran to the bike trail. *What did I just do?* I had to do it, if I didn't do this, he would find out later and want to kill me. *Did I go too far?* It's too late to turn back now. Telling on myself wasn't an option either... I head to my brother Mike's house!

I called Terrance and told him meet me at Mike's house because I had something for him. He comes to the house and I tell him what happened! He looks at me like he's just seen a ghost. "Bro, what the fuck did you just do? We are fucked! He's going to find out, your dad always finds out bro, FUCK!"

"Bro, I had to the jar was getting low I was taking too much out and not putting nothing back. I know I fucked up, just act like you don't know shit."

A day goes by, and I'm riding in the car with my mom to school in the morning. Normally, I ride in the back and let someone else sit in front but today I sit in front seat. Her phone rings and she answers, "Hey what's up... Yeah he's right here..."

I look in the mirror and see confusion on her face! *"Okay... he will be there!"* My heart drops, I want to jump out of the car and take off running. HE KNOWS! My mom hangs her phone up and looks at me.

"SOMEONE broke into your father's house; did you hear anything about that?" Did I hear what I think I just heard? I look out the window then look at her. Nah, I haven't heard anything. That's crazy. My heart is thumping, and I don't even know how I'm keeping a straight face without showing any emotion. I have to keep a POKER FACE! She says, "OK, we will see." I asked her what does that mean? She shakes her head and says you better be right. She pulls up to my dad's house and I immediately ask what we are doing here.

She tells me to get out of the car! Walking up to the house, she shows me the shoe print in the mud. It's an Air Force One and it's my size! She looks at me and says, "This look familiar?" Again, I say no. "Looks like a shoe print to me." She says OK, and points to the car, "Let's go. I'm taking you to school." We pull up to school I can't wait to get out the car. "Bye, love you," I say. She says good luck as I stand there confused.

I walk into the schoolhouse and I feel relieved. A sense of comfort. It's like I at least have a few hours to collect myself. Walking to 1st period, I remember going to class and seeing Terrance. His face was flushed, and he was sick to his stomach. The money wasn't worth this! The money wasn't the principle though, being scared to death that my dad was going to find out I was pinching his change jar was scary to me and I panicked. I decided to make it look like a robbery. *What I thought looked like a robbery.* I get to class, sit down, and the bell rings. Teacher shuts door and begins to take attendance.

Knock. Knock. Knock! The teacher answers the door and received a slip of paper. She looks it over and closes the door. Turning around, she heads toward me. I sit up in my chair confused as she hands me the paper, "I look at it." What the FUCK? It's an early release and on the top of the paper, it says '*DAD!*'

I'm sick! Heart pounding, palms sweating. *Why is my dad getting me out of school?* He literally had NEVER done this before. I'm caught for sure. *How did he know?* I walk to the car for what seems like a marathon.

I open the back doors to the school and see his car. Heading to this car felt like death on earth! *What was I to expect? Should I run? Or man up and tell him what happened?* Nah, I'll stick with my story! I don't know what happened and I'm sticking to that!

>I walk up to car and my heart is in my throat now as I reach for the door. I open the door and get inside. We take off! He's driving faster than normal and aggressive. You can tell my dad is furious! Mad as fuck! We bend corners as I look out the window. He breaks the silence.
>
>"Slim, you got something you need to tell me?"
>
>"No, I don't have nothing to say."
>
>"One thing I never did was do you wrong. So, when did you think it was OK to STEAL from me?" (He drives faster and starts shaking his head. I was shocked at how blunt he was).
>
>"I didn't..."
>
>"Shut the fuck up when I'm talking! If you didn't steal from me, then you know who did, so what is it? You tough now huh? You're grown now. You're stealing from me, so you don't need me."

He pulled on to the freeway. My throat tightens. Where are we going? I don't know what to say. I'm caught but I'm NOT admitting I stole from him. I can't... he will kill me! *Why hasn't he already?*

We drive on the freeway in silence. *Who will break it?* The tension is in the air. He's heated. I remember seeing his hands tighten on the steering wheel. My jaw clinched, expecting to get hit eventually.

He says, "I'm going to ask you one more time Slim, who stole from me? Look me in my eyes and tell me who stole from me? Man up if you stole it man up and stand on it! You tough enough to steal so be tough enough to admit it."

It's decision time! *What do I do?* Tell him the truth that I had been going in the jar, taking change to buy things I wanted? Even though I could have asked for those same things, I was young and dumb. One of my biggest mistakes up until this time is stealing from my dad. I was 15 or 16 at this time and lost as fuck! I know you're wondering, *What mind state do you have to be in to steal from your family?* EXACTLY WHAT I WANT YOU TO UNDERSTAND. I was sick in the head and thinking what I was doing was okay. I thought that I wouldn't get caught. I thought that I was smarter than my dad! I thought that my WANTS were bigger than the RESPECT OF MY FAMILY.

I looked my dad in his face and said, "I don't know who stole from you dad and that's the truth!" He looked me in my eyes, shook his head, and pulled the car over to the side of the freeway. What he says next cuts deep... I feel every word piercing my heart and ears. His tone in his voice... the hurt! The disrespect! He was hurt. I CROSSED THE LINE. What the fuck did I really do? Whom did I hurt in the long run? Thinking about myself and being selfish is what I was doing.

"DONT YOU EVER SPEAK TO ME OR MY FAMILY AGAIN. YOU STOLE FROM US. YOU DON'T NEED US. NOW GET THE FUCK OUT OF MY CAR!"

On the freeway, I step out of his car and he skurts off in his car never looking or coming back. I start walking back the way we just came from. Cars whizzing past me, head down, I continue to walk. A cop pulls up on me and asks what I am doing walking on the freeway.

"You know that it's school hours and it's illegal to walk on the freeway?"

"Yea, I had a pass out of school to go to dentist."

"Your school will confirm that right?"

"Yeah."

"OK, sit tight… Okay get in, I'm taking you to Willowick police station were your mom will pick you up from."

Getting in the car, he pulls off. "Now what happened? Why are you walking on freeway?" I need to think quick because telling on my dad is a dead option. I'm definitely not taking that route. *Think! Think!*

"Me and my girl were arguing, and she kicked me out. I didn't want to get in trouble, so I just got out of her car and started walking, officer." *I hope he buys it.*

He looks at me in the mirror as I'm shaking my head. I got him; I see it in his face. Lying and manipulating became something that grew on me. He says, "Well, you're going to have to have your mom come get you, is she at work?"

"No! I tell him. She can come get me!"

My mom picks me up from the police station. Mad, we ride in silence. When we pull up to the house, she loses it! "What the fuck is wrong with you? What has gotten into you? That's your father? He loves you, we love you! How could you?"

I'm sick to my stomach! I didn't want to hurt or disrespect anyone. I didn't want this punishment, not this one. *Why did I take it there! How can I fix this?*

We go in the house and my oldest brother is in the house waiting. He wants to put hands on me after hearing what happened, but my mom won't let him. He tells her to move and she doesn't. "No, I handled it and his father handled it leave it alone Chris!"

I was glad my mom was holding my brother back. I went to my room and packed my bag. Crying tears of anger, I pack my little duffel bag.

My little brother Jayden asked me what I'm doing. I told him I was leaving. He begged me not to go. At this point, my little brother and I were really close. He loved me and I was big bro. With my oldest brother being in college, I was whom he looked up to. Crying, I hug him and tell him that I have to go. I never ended up leaving that night but it definitely crossed my mind.

I never talked to my dad again, until later on, when I made another fucked up decision...

After I stole from my dad, shit really went downhill. School was a blur! I started getting dropped off at school and leaving after they took my attendance in 1st period. I knew they wouldn't call my mom if I had checked into 1st period. I thought I was so smooth.

With my money supply cut at my dad's, I turned to a guaranteed money spot I knew of; the car wash! I had hit a lick here once before, and I know I can do it again. I'm 16 now. I call Terrance and he answers. "What's up? Pick me up I got a play for us!"

He picks me up with a couple of his friends. We ride off and he says, "Where are we going?" I tell him the car wash. He looked at me and I nod my head. We head to the car wash.

I walk up to the car wash door and knocked twice that hoping no one was there. *Knock! Knock!* No answer. "Hello?" I pop my little head around the door. "No one is here! BINGO!" I turn around to make sure Terrance is watch-ing for police. I grab two handfuls of money! And I grab two big buckets of full of quarters. These buckets were bigger than I was! These gallon buckets were damn, near filled! I waddle down the car wash and I hear someone yell, "HEY, STOP."

I turn around to an older white man running at me. At 16, I was scared and shocked. I dropped the buckets of quarters and ran. Luckily, I had the money in my pocket! We pulled off.

Laughing, we thought we made it safe and were free. We drove to a mutual friends' house to get some smoke. As we leave the house, right when we pull off, I see red and blue lights. I sink down in my seat. *I know they didn't just catch us buying smoke... fuck.*

I toss the bag to Terrance and he cuffs it. They approach the car and I see the guy from the car wash. "What the fuck? Did he follow us?" He walks up to car and says, "Yes that's him… he tried stealing from my shop."

The police cuff me and take me to the station. They put the cuffs on me tight as fuck. OUCH! Cop looks at me and says, "Shouldn't be stealing, we wouldn't have this problem."

I get in the backseat of this cop car and it's tight as fuck. I'm tall, and I've always been tall. My knees are crammed in this back seat. *Why is it so tight back here? Why are these seats hard plastic? Why does it smell so stiff back here?* The air is tight and smells funny. I hate it here! Hurry up, get me to the station.

I put my head against the window. *Damn, my mom going to flip when she hears this one.* I get to the station and they question me. I play stupid, "I wasn't even there! I don't know what y'all are talking about. You didn't even pick us up from there!" My mom walks in and my heart stops beating on sight. She doesn't step another foot in the room. She stopped dead in her tracks. She stared at me deep into my soul. I feel her eyes glaring down on me and I know I'm in trouble.

This was another type of trouble now. See this wasn't just an ass whooping or getting grounded. This was TROUBLE WITH THE LAW!

She finally sits down and talks to the cops. They tell her what happened and let her know that I'm leaving with her. Half of me wants to leave NOW. The other half wants to leave, just not in her car!

I know I'm about to get an ear full and most likely get my ass beaten and be grounded! I knew this one warranted the whole package. That's how I had to be dealt with at that time because I was doing too much.

We leave and go home. The entire ride was silent. I mean neither of us made a peep.

At this time, my mom feels like she is starting to lose me to the streets. My grades are falling, after-school hours are adding up, and my friends are getting more of my time than family. That cuts her deep! My mother only wants me on the right track. She just wanted her baby to play sports and make it out. We clearly had two different visions.

I was blind to the fact that I was being selfish and didn't care who felt some type of way about it. I need to have fun and live life the way I know how. *Why can't people just see life how I see it?*

Stealing turned into robbing when I turned 16. This was a new high! This was a feeling I fell in love with. From the first lick, something sparked inside of me. I felt different. Like this was what I was supposed to be doing. Robbing became second nature. My dad used to always tell me, "Son, there's better ways to get money than the way you are getting money. But you're grown, you will learn!"

I wasn't trying to hear any of that. I was trying to go rob someone and use their money to pay for my wants and needs. I became grimy! I began stealing and robbing instead of hustling and asking.
Why ask when I can take? That is how I was thinking. *Lick money is free money, never spend your own money,* that was my motto. A code I loved. A code I lived by.

It didn't matter who you were when I started spiraling out of control. Anyone was up for grabs! If you weren't with me or sliding with me then your ass was over with.

I need it. All of it. Standing there frozen, I look this man in his eyes as I see the fear trembling through his body. The forty-caliber looked bigger than me! No words, just eye contact as he reaches in his pocket and ups his fold of cash. Not budging, not blinking, I snatch the money from his cold hand. "Turn around." He does as I say.

I took off running. My heart was pounding, and my adrenaline was off the charts, but I felt so good. I felt untouchable. So easy, so much money, so quick!

I'm hooked. I'm addicted. In school, thinking about robbing! *Whom can I get next?* Mind scrambling as I sit in study hall plotting.

At this time, I became more rebellious, so my friends grew. I became more popular and more dangerous. The females came and went. This lifestyle was so damaging. So exhausting. But in that moment, I was living it up and showing no remorse. No feelings were ever involved. Even with the girls, we never had relationships, were just having sex. As my friends grew, so did my ego.

Chapter Seven:
DON'T FALL IN

"Rosie and Iysha really love y'all," my mom said as she walks into the house. "They're paying for both of y'all to go white water rafting and then to Cedar Point. If they hadn't paid for it already, your ass wouldn't even be going! So, you're lucky, because you definitely don't deserve it. At all! Now y'all go clean that room up," my mother said to Terrance and me as we sprint upstairs to pack our bags and clean the room.

"Bro she's letting me go! Let's go!"

"Bro, you know I got her to let you go." (He always wants his credit, ha). Rosie and Iysha were sisters. We did everything with them. Rosie, may God rest her soul, was a loving and beautiful soul. She really was a true friend. She loved Terrance and me. She would do anything for us. As you can see, she paid for us to go on a summer vacation with her and her sister. Iysha was the older and more mature sister, always trying to look out for little sis. Of course, they'd bumped heads, but what family doesn't? At the end of the day, they loved each other and never wanted anything bad to happen to one another. Funny is a quality that ANYONE will tell you Rosie had for sure. She was hilarious!

Destinee was another friend. We had also grown up together. Our friendship was different from everyone else's friendship by a long shot. When I met Rosie and Iysha, I also met another great friend named Taylor. You add Mike, Terrance, Zay, Greg, Katie and a few others and you have my main group of friends. We loved each other. Our bond was un-breakable! All of us rode for each other. Right or wrong, we stuck by each other side. Daily, we would kick it with each other or end up at someone in our circles house... like clockwork! We were all on the same page. Having fun and living life. We all smoked, we all drank.

With the bags all packed, my mom helped Terrance and I load the car up with our bags. We pulled up to Rosie and Iysha's Church and they run up to the car and gives us hugs. These are our best friends at this time. Our circle was! Taylor was already on the bus waiting for us. We hugged and kissed my mom and told her we love her. She told us we had better be good.

We got on the bus and saw everyone. We drove to a campground about an hour away and when we got there, all we saw were cabins. There were five cabins and kids everywhere! We played sports, games, traveled through paths in the woods, and had activities with the church. We also ate good, many good memories in that camp!

The next day, we went white water rafting! This was new for us, as we never did anything like this. Honestly, we were a little scared. *What if I hit a rock? Them bitches are sharp!* We had split up into groups of six and I heard someone yell, "Grab a Raft... let's move!"

Without hesitation, I grab the people I know we get in a group and get by our raft. It was me, Taylor, Rosie, Terrance, Iysha, and a friend of Iysha. "Set your raft in the water but don't get inside yet!" The water's cold. *I am determined not to fall in the water once we get rolling. I'm holding on for my life.* I watch everyone get inside their rafts and head down the lake!

We hit wave after wave. *Splash! Splash! Splash!* The water is freezing, even though it's summer time. There were birds chirping, kids laughing, dogs barking! The waves got bigger and more sharp rocks started to appear the get further downstream. The rocks stuck out of the water look like huge-ass icebergs.

All I could think of is, *DONT FALL OUT THIS RAFT*! The raft rocks to the left. We hit a rock and spun in a circle. We all screamed and laughed. We watch as other rafts went through the same spin we went through. I can see a big dip coming up, so I yell, "HOLD ON TIGHT!"

Everyone grabbed their handles and prepared for the impact. The water pushed us up stream fast! We hit two small rocks one on each side that spun us towards "the big dip." Without a warning or hesitation, the raft shook viciously! We smacked a rock! The girls screamed.

While we were spinning around the front of our raft tips forward, Iysha's friend falls into water. She can't really swim, and you can tell she's terrified at what is happening. All I heard was the water crashing against the rocks and people screaming, "Help her!" The three guys jump in the water without hesitation.

As soon as we come up for air, I heard someone yelling at top of their lungs, "What the fuck is going on?"

Taylor yells, "My foot, I think I cut my fucking foot!" His pain is throbbing in my ears. We just need everyone to get back into the raft.

We continue in the water, sliding down dips and almost crashing bone-to-bone into these huge rocks. *Why are these rocks so damn big anyway?* We go down one more bend and finally get to a calm path to help people back into the rafts. We made it!

Tired from all the swimming, I was breathing hard once we got back in the boat. I looked at Terrance, he looked at me, and we busted out laughing. "Man we said we wasn't getting in that water!" Then everyone joined in on the laugh! We headed back to the bus and Taylor had to be helped.

He split his big toe on a rock! Split it wide open. The crazy thing is we were going to Cedar Point the next day. Taylor was pissed. He was ready to turn up at Cedar Point and now he's going be on crutches eating and watching us ride all the rides.

We went to Cedar Point the next day and we all had a blast. Good times with Good people…

Amongst all, the fun and friends I was around, robbing was itching in my head constantly. It was a sickness. No matter what, I was going to take someone up top for that cash AS SOON AS WE GET BACK.

Ecstasy was a drug that took over my group of friends back in 2007-2009. This drug was something I had never experienced before, something I needed to experience repeatedly. I didn't have it nearly as bad as some of my friends, but I definitely had an addiction.

Chapter Eight:
JUVIE

Summer of '08 was something special, anyone who was around that time and in the loop would tell you. Ecstasy and robbing went hand in hand for me! There was no losing when I had Ecstasy, it was my way, and that was that. I wouldn't even listen to my friends if they told me not to do something. It was a mindset of *"either you come with me, or I go by myself."* I became hungry with thirst. It was a game, a gamble, and I LOVED the risk!

"Lay yo ass down! Bitch don't move!" My 40 cal and I were a unit! Especially when it got dark outside. Laying in bushes and popping out was nothing out of the ordinary for me. There was a lot of times I hit "plays" on my own, I didn't want to hear people try to talk me out of a lick. I hated when people tried to ruin my fun.

"Run those pockets, you know how it's laying; I don't want to hear shit…. I'll smack yo ass with this 40, keep playing with me!"

At the age of 17, how did I become so violently cold? It was me or them, and I always chose me. I wanted money and if you had it and you wasn't with me then you were a target, and I hit all my targets.

Doostie was a friend I met through a house we had on Mentor Ave. This house was lit as fuck at ALL TIMES! 550 Mentor Avenue was the jump off! Partying, robbing, alcohol, drugs we… got it popping! A lot of raids from the police and a lot of people on the run. This house had it all and truthfully, I'm surprised it lasted as long as it did.

My friend, Greg, had called me and told me that he was about to come to pick me up. When he picked me up, a blunt marathon is going on as soon as I jumped in the car. Blunts were everywhere. As I coughed from the smoke, I asked him where we were going. I had to yell over the music for him to hear me. He tells me that we were about to go to this party. I sit back and listen to the music as I hit the blunt.

We finally get to the spot. Because the lights were on, you can see people partying and dancing through the living room curtains. When we walked in, I had never seen some of these people before. But I knew some of the girls there a few people I played sports with. A white guy with tattoos walks up to Greg and me. They dapped each other up and Greg introduced us, "Bro this Dootsie."

This was a real-life fraternity house right in Painesville. We made so much money out of that house. We threw many parties in this house and the police came multiple times only to be left knocking on the door.

"Turn the lights off, nobody move they're here! Shut the fuck up. Everyone shut up for five minutes till these cops leave!" As long as we didn't make noise or open the door, we were okay. I was in shock the first time I saw them do it. Won't the police kick the door in? How do we get out? My mind started racing as I scanned the room quickly looking for an exit.

The police knock for what seems like twenty minutes on three different doors. Everyone had their hands over their mouths trying to hold in their laughs. We felt young and free. Eventually, the police would get the point and leave. Once the police left, we would turn the music back up. When I walked through the house, I saw craziness everywhere. Beer pong tables, music and more clouds! There were girls dancing everywhere, the whole house looked like something straight out of a movie scene. This was an all-summer event. You could pull up to the house on any day and catch someone in there getting to it.

Sex was the only reason you were upstairs. The down stairs and basement was the kick it, but upstairs was another level. If you went up there, then it was for a reason. And if someone saw you go up there, we respected it without hating or sneak dissing.

The summer was wearing down... and we began to get more and more thirstier to rob people. It was like a monster that I kept feeding.

Everytime I robbed someone, I added to this monster. Everyone I was around was into what I was and that was robbing or stealing. I was catching whatever someone threw at me, and addicted was an understatement. I was all in with or without my friends and they knew it. My friends and I made a "chalk board." We were young and wild and had all day to do what we liked to do. A list was put together of people we knew in our city who were up and getting money on the chalkboard. Those were the targets! We hit every target that was on that board. We had our way, and everyone ate was well taken care of.

Some people's greed got in the way and we didn't always see eye-to-eye. Some people took their own paths, some people got locked up, and some just grew up and matured. Maturing happened later for me but right now, I'll explain how I catch my very first case. A case that landed me in a place so cold and different. For some it was hard physically, but for me it was a pure mental pressure. It was a place of disgust but ulti-mately, a place that I put myself in.

Chapter Nine:
JUVIE PART 2

"I got a lick bro are y'all trying to come or not?" I looked at Terrance and Black, a guy we played football with. They both ask what it was for and what they would be getting.

I turned around to them both, "Look, all I know is this the spot. I'm not saying what's in there because if it's not then I'm going to look stupid. But they said there's money, weed, and pills in there, so what are y'all on? SHOOT or DRIBBLE, the ball is in your court. I'm going regardless!"

They look at each other and said, "Fuck it, let's go."

The day started off like any other day. I tried to make it feel as normal as possible, even though I knew what I was carrying in my Nike duffel bag. *Stay calm and don't let anyone touch your bag*, that was the only thought that I had in my mind.

My mom dropped me off at school that morning. She looked at me and said, "Your ass better stay in school Shon." I say OK and shut the door. Knowing that I wasn't going to stay in class was one thing, but what I was going to do next, I *know* she didn't expect.

I walked into the school. Everything that was going on around me was a blur because there was only one thing on my mind. It was one goal for me! I had tunnel vision. All I knew what that I was going to get this money. I walked to my locker and placed the duffel bag in the locker. I saw Terrance and Black walk up.

"So, what's the plan?" I told them to meet me at the back door after first period. The bell rings, and first period has started, the teacher talks but I didn't hear anyone or anything. My mind is in one spot and isn't budging... I just want to leave already I'm thirsty to hit this lick!

"Shon! Shon! Shon!" I snap out of it and hear my teacher calling my name. I looked up at my teacher. She said, "I'm doing attendance can you pay attention please…"

I say, "I'm here, my bad."

Class is over and I walk into the hallway. I look to the left and kids were piling out of their classes. Look to the right and see the football jocks book checking people and laughing. *Corny ass dudes.* I walk to my locker grab my duffel bag and walk to the meet up. I know I had to look crazy walking away from class with a duffel bag. Eventually, a teacher asks why I had a duffel bag. "I have a lot of books I need to carry from my next class, so I need a little help." He took the bait! My heart was racing because I thought that he was going to open my bag and see what I had inside.

I see Terrance and Black at the door the bell rings again and without hesitation I push the doors open and we run to the bike trail. We jogged at a steady pace all the way to Mike's house in unison for what seemed like a mile! No talking, just jogging. We all played sports and were in shape so running wasn't hurting us.

Breathing through my nose, jaw clenched, all I can think about is kicking in the door, and taking what I wanted, I was so violent, not giving a fuck who was in my way. I was on a downward spiral in life and right here life was about to change.

We got to Mike's. He already skipped school. I made sure he was home before we left. He answers the door and we walk in. In Mike's room, we smoke and talk about the plan. I lay it out for them, plain and simple, and they understand. I stand up, I look everyone in their eyes! I say, "If for any reason the police come, RUN! And you don't know me." They shake their head and show understanding as to what I'm saying.

Let's get this money! I unzip my duffel bag finally revealing what I had hidden for so long. Zip ties! Rubber gloves! Black hoodie and a .38 special!

I pass everyone gloves and a stack of zip ties. Their eyes don't budge. They are focused on one thing, The GUN! They want to hold and touch it. "Is it real? What do we need that for?"

"Yes, it's real, and y'all don't need it, I got it for me. Now let's go get this money." Mike stays back and me, Terrance and Black head out.

Walking to "the lick," we took all the back roads. Wearing all black was good during the night but it was daytime. Walking in all black, the three of us were ready to go and get this money. Young and reckless...

My heart was pounding. "We're almost there, just a little closer." We approach the apartment building. I walk around to the apartment we are supposed to be going in. I can't see inside because the window is too high. Black gets down and I stand on his back. I look into the apartment, but I don't see anything but children's toys. This is NOT the right spot... it can't be... This doesn't look anything like a trap house or what I'm used to. I'm confused and frustrated, and then in it gets worse.

OH SHIT. My heart drops to my feet, as I know something is off. WE GOT COMPANY! An undercover cop car pulls up. A cop jumps out and yells, "Get on the ground!" with a gun in his hands. "GET DOWN! Don't fucking MOVE!"

They freeze in their spots, it's slow motion. *Why aren't they running?* In my head, I want to scream, *RUN*. With their hands up, they laid down on the ground. I took off running! I told them specifically to run! *Why would they stop and lay down like that?*

Cop cars are pulling in left and right, flying down the street with their sirens on. It starts raining. I run to the left out of the complex and with my duffel bag across my body, I sprint. They follow and there too many. I cut back the opposite way and I lose some of them, but they still see me. I need to make a couple cuts. *Backyards I go... fence!*

I jump the fence with ease. I hear them behind me. I hear footsteps and walkie-talkies going off. There are sirens in the distance, and they are EVERYWHERE. Every cop in the precinct had to be chasing me.

I pick up the speed, trying to lose the few that are on feet chasing me. Another fence is coming up. This one is a little bigger and I feel it because it takes wind out of my body once I get to other side. I'm starting to fatigue. *DO NOT STOP! MIKE'S HOUSE IS THE DESTINATION AND YOU ARE ALMOST THERE.* Adrenaline is the only thing keeping me running. Cutting through people's back yards, I dump my duffel bag with the gun inside into a trashcan. Now I felt that I was free as long as they don't catch me with the gun, I'm good. Well in my head, it sounded good. *Keep going you're almost there.* It rains harder. My jacket is drenched as I pull the drawstrings tight and tie them. I think, *DAMN, I GOTTA MAKE IT TO MIKE'S! Run faster, run across the railroad tracks!*

"Stop! Police! We will shoot! STOP!" I dig deep within me and sprint across the tracks as I feel myself getting tired. *I have to keep going...* I sprint into someone's backyard and I see what looks like a wall. Fuck!

This fence is huge. I know from first look, it will take a lot out of me to jump this one. But Mike's house is just over the fence. If I can make it past this last obstacle, I can make home safe.

I take a deep breath and in stride, I run up to the fence and reach as high as I can. My hands smack the top of the fence almost gripping the top. It's slippery and my hands are soaked. *I have to get past this fence. Where are they? Do they know I'm back here?* With my heart pounding and adrenaline pumping, I take a few extra steps back and attempt it again. I run up the fence and my hands grab the top. Smack! I can't grip it; my hands are slipping... fuck! I slide down the wall. *Can I try one more time? I can get it if I can get one more chance.* I turn around to go back and take another attempt. Then, there he is... GET DOWN NOW!

He had his gun in his hand. Rain was hitting my face as I was breathing heavy to catch my breath. Disgusted at what I'm looking at, my stomach is flipping! DONT TAKE ANOTHER STEP! I see how serious he is in his face and tone of voice. He isn't budging. More cops run up! The backyard is flooded with cops as they take me to the ground. I remember how it felt when they knocked me to the ground!

With knees in my back and grown men applying pressure, I also feel someone else's knee in the back of my neck. Don't move! Hands behind my back, they zip tie my hands AND HANDCUFFED ME! The cuffs are tight. I remember they were so tight!

I know I have a scar on my hand. Bending my arms behind my back, I look in the grass as I see the red and blue lights flashing in the green grass. Rain was splashing in my face, as I lay there CAUGHT! Stuck! Nowhere to go! This time I know I fucked up big.

Sitting in the back of the cop car, I rest my head against the window. I still hear police sirens. It's raining harder now. We ride to the police station. I see a group of people I know on their porch. I shake my head, it's over this time!

Chapter Ten:
SHIPPED OUT

Waiting to get booked in I sit in the cop car wet, cold, shaking, and shivering. I just want to get out of these clothes and go to sleep. I didn't care about my consequences! The cop lets me out. "Let's Go!" I walk into this room and I'm lost, I don't know where I am or what this place is called. I learned really quickly what this cold place is called and what it stands for... I walk to the desk. *Name? Social? Step to the left... Flash! To the Right... FLASH! FLASH!* My eyes burn from the flashes. *Why did she take my pictures? When can I leave? Just call my mom so she can pick me up.* Little do I know she's not saving me from this one.

I walked through a door and that lead into shower room. I slow my steps not knowing what was going on or where I was going. Two officers tell me to strip and shower. I have to put a lice shampoo in my hair before being booked.

The shower is cold. When it heats up, the stream of water was slim to none. A piss stream compared to the shower I was used to. *What the fuck?* I finish the shower and the officers walked four other kids in to shower. They all got in and shower without question. They don't look mad, they look comfortable. I couldn't understand why. *Do they like it here? How long have they been here?* They escort me to my room. Walking up to my room, I look around not knowing anything about the place I am in, my head was on a swivel.

I only knew what I've seen on movies but I'm not letting anyone play me! I see kids sitting in groups of four to a group. They were writing, laughing, and a section of the room was facing a TV, kids' eyes were glued to the screen. Not budging, just glued to the television like they've never seen a TV before. *Where am I? What did I do?*

They unlocked my door and I stepped inside. The floor was freezing! The sink was connected to the toilet and a blue plastic mattress laid on the concrete. *Where the fuck am I?* They slammed my door shut… *BOOM!* I jumped and looked at the guard through the slot of glass they give you as a window. Sitting in my room is a sheet set, a uniform, a pair of socks, and a pair of boxers. These boxers and socks were definitely NOT MINE. *Do they think I'm wearing someone else's boxers? Or socks?* I put the outfit on and leave the boxers and socks on the floor. I make my bed. I grabbed the thin and worn out mattress with barely any cotton inside. I wrapped my sheet around the mattress, and I noticed there were no blankets or pillow. I knock on the door… no response. I knock on the door again harder… no response. I press the *'call in'* button two times. I was tired and cold, and I just wanted to go to sleep because I hoped when I woke up, I would be released.

Finally an answer, "Hello!" I responded, "Yeah… can I get some blankets? It's cold as fuck in here. The C.O told me to watch my mouth, and that he'd be by shortly. I was mad it's cold and I was tired. *Why would they put me in here with no blanket anyways?*

The C.O comes and opens my door, throws a pillow, a sheet, and a blanket on my bed. He didn't say anything, just shut the door. I make my bed and lay down… looking up at the ceiling, I can only think. I can't leave, plus nobody I know was there. I hoped it was a dream, that I'd wake up tomorrow and I'd be going home.

In my dream, I heard a buzzing sound. *Click. Click…* Bright lights… I woke up to the lights in my eyes. I was blinded, *why the fuck are these lights so bright?*

I hear a C.O coming around opening doors and waking people up. "BREAKFAST TIME! Wake up and get your hygiene together, let's go!" I wiped the sleep out of my eyes and sat up in my bed with my feet touching the cold cell floor. I walked to the door. I saw everyone waking up and getting dressed.

Every morning, the third shift, C.O puts a new pair of clothes out for the inmates to change in to in the morning. I looked at everyone wearing blue uniforms, blue pants, and blue sweaters. *This is juvi*? I felt lost. I looked down at my clothes only to see a gray outfit. *Why gray? What does it mean? Why am I the only one with grey on? I hate standing out and being center of attention!* I got dressed anyway.

Breakfast was served in a "chow hall," meaning a cafeteria. I've never seen this room in juvi! I see everyone line up, so I line about with everyone else. The C.O said, "Line up! High security, you guys are eating in your rooms!"

Who is high security and what does that mean? I stood still in line, not knowing they were talking about me! A C.O walked up to me and told me to step out of line. I step out; they escort the others to the chow hall! I sit at a table where they bring me my food, tell me to go in my room and close the door. I thought to myself, *Why is there no one else in this room? Why are they secluding me? What does high security mean? How long before I can be regular?* The C.O comes to the door to collect my tray. I asked him what the gray sweater and high security meant. He said, "It's simple, YOU EAT IN YOUR ROOM FOR EVERY MEAL."

"YOU WEAR SHACKLES WHEN YOU GO OUTSIDE. AND ALL YOUR VISITS WILL BE MONITORED IN A SPECIAL ROOM." I asked him why. He responded back that he didn't make the rules, he only enforced them.

"Mr. Sheffey, your attorney is here to see you." I walked into the room and see my mom and a guy I've never met before. My mom's face is red, and her eyes were swollen from crying. All I could do was look at her. She stood up and hugged me. Her hug was so strong! Her hug is so meaningful. I can tell that she loves me and only wants best for me. But this, I have to learn on *my own*.

"What were you thinking? You could have asked me for anything but instead you do this?" She put her head in her hands, "I thought I taught you better than this!" I was sick to my stomach that my mom was in here crying her eyes out when she deserves to be happy. I felt like I had swallowed a frog. *What should I say? What can I say?* I was frustrated that I couldn't leave. Looking back, I know I wasn't thinking the right way. I needed time to get myself together.

The attorney talked to us and tries to get me to say where I got the gun. "Just tell us a name and we can make this all go away," I told him that I couldn't do that. My mom looked at me and said, "Why the fuck not?"

I told her that it was mine and she knew that I was lying. "Tell them where you got it!" I stared blankly at her. The attorney tells me I'm going to be charged with attempted burglary with a gun specification, which is a felony of the third degree.

She looks at him when he says felony. I thought she was going to pass out. *What does that mean? She's acting like it's the end of the world...* They let us visit and my mom loses it. "Your grandma is going to lose it when she hears this, I hope you're happy! Is that what you want? To kill your grandma!" I immediately said, "NO!" She looked back at me and said, "Then what the fuck are you doing? Look where you are!" The visit comes to an end and she gives me a hug I feel deep down in my stomach. "I'll be at your next court date..."

After every visit, you have to get strip searched to make sure no illegals are coming into the facility you are at. This is one of the most degrading moments. "Let's go, we don't have all day!" *Strip, squat, and cough!*

There were six of us in this little room, and everyone started getting undressed. The C.O stood in front of us, making sure no one was trying to smuggle drugs. We all finished the routine and got dressed.

The next day, I had court. I woke up bright and early, hoping that they would release me today. I went to my arraignment and they told me I had a $20,000 bond! My eyes popped at the number they gave me. Who the fuck going to pay that type of money to get me out! Not my parents, they want me to learn my lesson and as bad as it sounds, jail is what I needed. I looked at my mom when they said that and I asked my attorney if I had to pay it all.

He told 10% of $20,000 would get me out of there. "For $2,000 you can be a free man again…" I shook my head. The cops walked me back in to my room. In my room, I was furious at so many things! *Why did they set bond so high? Why am I the only one I see in here? When can I leave?* Not for a long time. Days turned into weeks, and weeks turned into months!

Physical workout is part of the daily Schedule in "DH" (Detention Home). I became stronger as I knew I wasn't leaving, so I might as well had got my body right. And I did! I was in the DH for four months before I got sentenced. Four months of eating alone in my room, four months of wearing shackles outside, four months of seeing my family for 20 minutes at a time… I was ready to go.

I knew I was going away, just not sure for how long. I walked into the courtroom and saw my entire family sitting there, crying. I felt lost. I sat next to my attorney and he told me the recommendations. "It's either DYS for a year or CCF for 5-9 Months." An easy pick for me. I'll take the CCF for 5-9 months. I told myself that I would be home soon. I told my attorney what I wanted to do and he relayed the message. Court ends and they say I will be going to CCF. CCF is a DYS facility built for rehabilitation. Therefore, I couldn't go home without completing their program.

This facility is in Sandusky, Ohio. It was too far to get visits on the regular like the DH.

I had one more visit before I left. The judge allowed me to have a group family visit since I was getting shipped out. They let me see my family for an hour in a private room.

We talked, laughed, and of course, we cried. We knew this would be the last time I've seen my family for a while, so we cherished the moment!

I gave all my brothers and sisters hugs and kisses and told them I love them… and just like that, they were gone. Phone calls and handwritten letters would be our only communication for a while.

I spent a few more days in the DH before they shipped me out to Sandusky. I worked out heavily in my room, not knowing what I would be facing at the next destination. I remember hearing people ride past and honk their horns. Not being able to see out of our windows made me mad. Whoever was riding past and honking was yelling, "FREE PYRO!" I heard it once but I think I'm tripping. An hour later, I hear it again with the car horn. *Beeeeep! Beeeeep!* "FREE Pyro!" Pyro was a nickname I was given early in life, but would become an ironic name for me later.

They woke me up at seven o'clock in the morning! It was early as fuck and all I want to do was sleep my time away. *"Let me sleep!"* The lights shined bright in my eyes. Even with the blankets on, it was freezing. The blankets. I got up and got dressed.

I was the only person riding out on this particular day. They shackled me up and loaded me into an all-white van. There was more room than a cop car, but I still felt crammed and lost. *Where am I going now? What will I be faced with? Is it like the movies?*

The ride was long and boring. The two officers were escorting me into the van as they talked amongst themselves. I saw them load their guns and check them. We got on van and began to leave out. They turned the radio to country music. I sighed because I knew this was going to be a long ride.

Chapter Eleven:
CCF

We drove for what seemed like hours. City by city, we drove across the state. No pit stops, just driving to our destination. I looked out of the window passing freedom by. *What did I do this time? I really fucked up!* We arrive... SANDUSKY, Ohio!

I read the sign again. The only time I had ever been out to Sandusky was for the amusement park, Cedar Point. It was NOT a Cedar Point trip. We pulled up to the facility. We needed a passcode to pass security gate. They typed the code in and I watched as the gate slowly gives us access. We drove through the gate. I see kids outside playing basketball as they load the van into the loading dock. Finally, I see life. Kids my age playing basketball and having some kind of fun. The cops escorting me opened the van door. As the door squeaks open, I can hear one of the cops yelling, "Let's go!" I hopped out of the van with my legs shackled and hands cuffed. My hands and feet were bound together like a slave. It wasn't like there was a way I could get away from these two cops anyways. I walked into the building.

Two officers sat at the front desk. They set my property on the counter. "SHEFFEY?" I stood closer and replied, "Yes?" They directed me into the changing room. I walked in and there was one officer already in the room. I saw him putting gloves on and opening something, but I couldn't tell what.

"Old Clothes over there!" I look to where he points. He turned around and looked at me. "Don't just stand there, time is ticking!" I got undressed. "Step to the yellow line." I did as he said. **"SQUAT! COUGH!"**... *I hate it here*!

He told me to get dressed and handed me a cup. "Urine sample!"

"Why? I'm already locked up."

"To make sure we know what drugs you were on. And for your information, anytime you leave here or come back you will take urine sample. Even if you are going to see a doctor. We always are watching over you! You aren't smarter than any of us, so let's get that understanding now!" I gave him a poker face and took the cup to the bathroom.

I walked into the bathroom and went to close the door. He grabbed the door before it could close. "Nah. OFFICERS are the only people closing doors around here." I rolled my eyes and asked if I could get some privacy. "No, I'll be standing right here. Now fill the cup." How am I going to pee with another man less than two feet away from me? He looked at me and said, "Figure it out!"

I hate taking urine tests. Especially, when someone has to watch. What kind of man wants to do this job? *He's weird! They're all are weird!* I struggle to fill the cup. Pushing myself, I was in deep thought. He ignorantly tapped his foot. I thought harder. *Damn, I need to hurry up.* Finally, I fill the cup, hand it to the officer and we left the room.

They tested my urine on the spot and found out that I had marijuana in my system. They walked me into another room. There were plastic mats lined up on one wall and pillows on the opposite. "Sheffey! Grab one of each!" We continued to walk into another room. This room had blankets, sheets, and pillowcases. On the opposite wall, there were uniforms and towels.

As we walked, the officers handed us the mandatory clothing and bedding. With my hands full, I follow the lead. I felt strange and out of place. *Is there anyone I know here? I doubt it.* Walking down the hallway, I can feel people's stares piercing my body. "New person on the block!" I walk to the end of the hallway and I see it. Three pods connected with glass windows. A station in the middle of the room is where the C.O's sit.

Pod A is the beginning stage for this program. This facility is set up in three stages. They called them levels. Each level depends on your behavior, meaning you can move from each level in 60 days or 120 days, it's up to you.

Pod A wore tan pants and a green polo. Pod B wore a green polo and you can wear your own pants, which your family brought in when they come to visit. Pod C could wear all their own clothing. This was the level you get home passes and more privileges as you get closer to going home!

I walked into Pod A and see people my age sitting in groups playing cards and watching TV. Some people are writing letters, someone else is on the phone... C.O sitting at his desk, they walk me to my room... using a key, he unlocks my door... Room 9! I walk in and set my things down... Metal toilet and sink connects together.

Bookshelf to the left... Hard plastic is where I laid my mat... *Smack!* I slam it down... Looking around the room, I look at the mirror, it is dirty and scratched, I can barely see myself... Looking out the window was barely an option; the windows were slim and not wide enough to see anything out of... Why would they not want us to look outside? That's the only peace we have in here! I'm confused.... How long will I really be here?

Chapter Twelve:
CCF Part 2

I walked into the day room and sat down. I looked around and noticed that I didn't know anyone there. I've always been a quiet person when it comes to not knowing people. If I don't know you, I will be quiet around you until I get to know you better.

I laid back quietly. I just observed everyone around me. There was white, black, hispanic… I had to watch my own back regardless of race, so I kept everyone at a distance. I sat and talked with a group of people I felt like I can vibe with. (There were A LOT of strange people there.) I pick the *"coolest"* ones and we locked in.

My boy E was from Mansfield. Loved playin' with guns. Got into a shootout over his sister so he was sent here! I had no choice but to respect it. We locked in and grew close. He was a hoope,r and my biggest competition on the compound the whole time I was there. Nobody else came close, But he and I went head-to-head daily. It became a routine.

We built each other up on that court. And we talked plenty of shit, but at the end of the day we both wanted to win. If we ran full court, he was a captain, and I was a captain. There was no playing on same team! That was my guy though, he was solid. Wes was my boy from Ashland; he was a solid white boy who took no shit! He was my workout partner. He stayed, comin' up with extreme workouts!

There were one or two more people I really got cool with while in Pod A. We played cards, did pushups, and talked shit to each other, it passed time! There were people from all over, Mansfield, Cleveland, Lorain, Lima, Akron and of course, I put Painesville in there.

Where's Painesville? Laughing, Wes says "what, y'all grow, corn out there"? A couple others laughs. I shot back, "Ahhh, yo goofy-looking ass got jokes, nah we get to it in my city! Stop playing with me". Laughing, I aim my hand like a gun at him!

An officer walks up and sees me, he immediately gets serious and shuts down the behavior I am showing, otherwise the others will think it's okay. "What are you doing? You think you are at home, don't you? We don't act like that around here, and you can leave if you don't like it!"

I'm shocked he said I could leave. I didn't get it. I stand there and look at him confused… he walked away. I wonder how long these kids been in here for. I ask a kid watching TV. His name was Mike and he loved basketball.

"What's up bro…?" "Wat up, bro" (he's into the TV show that's on). I ask him how long he's been here, and how long they sentenced him too. He looked at me and a cold look went over his face and he immediately got pumped. He turns his chair to face me and I can tell from his body language that he has something to get off his chest. He says, "Tell me, does this make sense, bro…" He goes on to say that the program is supposed to be five-to-nine months! "BULLSHIT! There's no way possible to do any less than a year in here!" I look him in his face to see if there's some kind of joke or bluff but there is none… he's dead serious!

"I've been here for 16 fucking months, bro! They told me that I would do six months and be back with my son! I have to get out of here before I hurt someone." He looks at me again after getting his composure, I don't know you bro, but keeping it real, expect to do a year or more. Shaking his head, I tap his shoulder and say, "I'm getting out of here in eight months bro, I bet I don't do longer than eight months!" He looks at me with disgust as I just disrespected everything he was saying. "Didn't you just hear me, bro?" he says! I look him in his eyes and say watch me work.

Each level, you had to take a test to graduate on to the next level. If you fail the test, you had to wait a certain number of weeks before you could try to take the test again. The test was built up of multiple-choice questions over topics we talked about in groups such as AA and NA and Thinking for a Change classes to help you mentally think and figure out your problems. Problem solving, they called it. Fifty questions for each level, all different tests and answers. Each test is different for each individual. The guidance counselor of the unit also does an evaluation and adds personal questions to go inside of that fifty-question test. Two questions geared toward your recovery and mental build up.

At first, I didn't know what the hell these people were talking about... a victim?" I don't have a victim, nobody got hurt" I say when my turn comes in group... "Today, we are talking about victims and who all we hurt! Everyone has a victim," the counselor chimes in. I say how? She loves the quick question I shoot back to her because I help her explain that *everyone who makes a negative decision has a victim.*

"Nobody thinks, *oh I want a victim, but I don't want more than three victims"* The counselor gives as an example. Meaning you can have a direct victim and an indirect victim, and you can have multiple victims.

" Even though nobody physically got hurt in your case, many people suffered indirect."

"Damn; I never looked at it like that," I say aloud...

This also goes hand in hand with the next topic she brings up... the ripple effect.

A lot of times in life, we see ourselves doing no wrong. We become so involved in our day-to-day living, our lifestyle, that we don't see the pain or hurt we put others through. A ripple effect is a chain reaction to your bad decisions. Thinking you hurt no one in your case is as ignorant someone always gets hurts. You see, a ripple effect goes a long way. It can start directly with your victim or it can start with yourself.

Many of times we forget that we are supposed to love ourselves. The ripple effect is like dropping a rock into a pond. After it splashes, it leaves multiple circles and layers... each of those layers are people that you hurt.

For example, I was about to rob someone's house, and for the case, I went to juvie. No one was home and got hurt directly, but indirectly, I hurt plenty of people, starting with myself. I put myself in a tough position and it was time I start really looking into my addictions and my negative lifestyle decisions.

My mom and family are the next closest people in the ripple effect to get hurt. They feel the pain of me not being home! They know where I am at and know they personally can't bring me home. Brothers hurt; sisters hurt! What did I do? Were they really looking up to me?

The next people on the ripple effect are friends. They are affected because I am no longer home, so they also feel a gap missing, and things are not the same without me. The community is the next layer. I know you're wondering how the community is affected… they were scared! In a city so small, this rarely was happening, but something that was on the rise. Robbing and hitting houses was a thing for me and some of the people I knew growing up. It was our hustle!

The community suffers because they have to pay tax dollars when we fuck up and decide to go to jail. The community tax dollars pay to house and feed inmates. And as the ripple gets bigger, more and more people can be hurt and added.

I never fully understood this until I sat in my room and drew it out. Starting with a small circle, I start to write and see who all I really hurt. One circle, two circles, four circles… six circle.! Six layers ended up in my ripple effect and I was shocked at how I filled it with people's names so quickly. The paper is filled, and I look at it like I had seen a ghost. *How all these people could be hurt over this one decision?* People I didn't even know were affected by something I wanted to do. Not NEEDED to do but wanted to do. I learned a lot from this lesson, and I will always pass it on to the younger group of people… or anyone looking to switch lanes and make something better of themselves.

At first, going into these groups, I stayed quiet to get a feel for how they ran, but I always paid attention and took notes, even if they were just mental notes. They were a little awkward at first because I'm not a big speaker. I don't like talking in front of people. I have always been like that. So often, I would pass my turn because I would feel uncomfortable in group. Eventually, as I grew comfortable with the counselors and other kids, I spoke up on certain things. I still didn't care about anyone's case or how they were getting home. My main goal was getting home as soon as possible!

So, I would ask questions and I began to learn myself. Deep down, I know I wasn't supposed to be stealing and definitely wasn't supposed to have that gun, but I did and I'm here. Now, I have to make it back home and start all over. I hadn't seen my mom or family in a couple months. They had lives to live and I couldn't hold them up.

I called when I could and I wrote constantly! Back and forth, week to week, we sent letters and they answered phone calls. Time passed and I progressed in the program.

Chapter Thirteen:
LEVEL TWO

I made it that first test was a breeze. Less than 60 days in and I was halfway through the program. But the second level is one of the longest levels, because they really make you work. make you think… test you… On this level, I learned the system a little better. Now I was getting comfortable and learning what I can and can't get away with.

Before I got locked up for this case, my grade point average was a .071. I know it looks crazy because it is. I missed so much class, I failed out of everything, literally. *What was I thinking? How did I become so hooked on skipping class and living life my way that I didn't see all of this coming*? Bad decisions for sure. My high school sent my work to the facility for me to do and they had online courses for everyone. Day in and day out, I worked on my schoolwork. I knew I had to bring those grades up to walk the stage and graduate.   It would be cutting it close but if I time it right, I wanted to get out of there by April 2010 and walk the stage in June 2010. Class after class, I passed and put good numbers up in those classes. I began to work out and get my mind right. My body was in shape and my mind was getting there.

After four months on level two, I'm ready to take my test. The night before, we went to the gym for "Rec" (term for recreation or exercise). Me and E were playing basketball, trying to dunk. Attempt after attempt, we kept trying. The officer was pumping us up to keep trying and one officer gave us tips. He used to play basketball back in his day. He gave me a couple of tips and I tried them out.

First attempt, nothing. E shoots a three. He's not as serious as I am about dunking, but at this time, I'm close to six foot, if I wasn't six foot already. Second attempt, it's close! E stops and looks at me. He starts grinning and says, "You're not about to dunk before me". He attempts but he is short! Not much taller than E, I throw myself an alley oop. I shoot it in the air from the point line. I put a little air under it, so I can get the dunk off of one bounce. It's coming down slowly, and as I time it up, it bounces! I run and jump; catching the ball in the air, I slam my hand to the basket! It goes! FLUSH!

I'm shocked… With my adrenaline pumping, I jump in the air. My first dunk! E looks at me with a grin. He dapped me up! He says, "you can't dunk on me though"! Me being in the moment… "Shit, get under the hoop then!"

He looks at me and says, "You really think you can dunk on me"! He gets under the hoop and waits on me. I start from the three-point line. Running, I jump in the air he jumps with me, the ball is cuffed in my right hand and ready to dunk… smack all I see is red… I feel my mouth throbbing… what happened? We both land back down on the ground… I immediately touch my mouth, as it feels cold and raw… blood!

The officer looks at me and rushes over. "We have to get you back to the pod! You have to go to the Emergency Room!" I remember walking up the hall, holding my mouth with a paper towel I see it started to fill with blood. Other officers looked on and I can tell from the look on their faces it was bad!

Finally, I get to my room to clean myself up, and I see it! A huge hole in my lip… my tooth went through! I taste the blood and it tastes like metal. I spit in my sink. Blood, all blood.. I use my tongue to see how big the hole is, my tongue goes through the hole! *What the fuck*? I need stitches ASAP! The officer walked me to the sally port. They hand cuff and shackle me and we left. Walking into the doctor's office, I felt like an animal. In handcuffs and shackles, I slowly walked to the doors. No one hid the fact that they were looking at me, staring.

I sat in the waiting room sticking out like a sore thumb in a jumpsuit and shackles, with my mouth throbbing. *When is the doctor going to see me? Damn, between my mouth hurting and the people staring at me I'm ready to go!* Finally, the doctor comes. They gave me three stitches throughout my top lip. We left and headed back to the facility! Of course, upon entering, I have to go through the routine. **SQUAT! COUGH! Urine Test! I hate it here!**

Chapter Fourteen:
VICTIMS

Being away from my family for so long and not seeing them taught me the value of family. They stayed by my side no matter what wrong I did... they didn't baby me but they were there.

It's test day! I go through all of my notes and recite the twelve steps. Knowing the twelve steps were mandatory for each test; you couldn't pass if you couldn't write all twelve steps out. Studying for what seems like forever, I'm ready for the test. I've been studying in my room on lockdown and during the rec time. I remember saying the twelve steps to myself and then writing them out multiple times. I wondered if the second test was going to be harder than the first. I sat back and thought for a second, giving my mind a break.

I run the scene back in my head... the rain, the cops... deep breathing. Stop! Keep running... Don't stop! Cuffs! Sirens! Jail door slams behind me!

Shaking my head, I try to refocus!

Focus bro you got a test to pass! I regain focus and get back into my notes...

In this facility and in this program; they were strategic and had a way of getting a point to you. "Offenders" or "Inmates," whatever you wanted to call us... we all were assigned a three-ring binder! This binder was what they called our "victim". The only place this binder was not allowed in was your room. Other than that, you got in trouble for not carrying your victim.

The concept is that you never stop carrying you victim around with you. You would have repercussions if you forgot your victim laying around or in another room. Never leave behind your victim. A BIG NO-NO! Especially if an officer found it, they would make a big scene and call you to the front and embarrass you. I never left my victim behind…

The victim definitely grew on me and as I got farther in the program. I really grasped the concept that they were trying to teach us all from the jump. Your victim is a weight you will always carry… you choose to make a bad decision and in turn get a victim. The pain of that victim is undeserving and indescribable. You may never know how deep you truly cut someone because of a bad decision. I sat in my room plenty of nights thinking how I hurt my family. At this point, it was proving to my family that I was sorry, and I had matured. But I was doing it wrong; it was supposed to be a program working on ME FIRST! Build yourself up then prove to others you have changed. This bit me in the ass later on.

Chapter Fifteen:
LEVEL THREE

Taking my test in to an empty classroom, I had been waiting on this test for so long. I studied long nights. I did pushups in my room while reciting the twelve steps in between sets. Any free time had I was in my notes. I was on my way! I was on a mission. Getting home in eight months was my goal and I was going to hit that goal.

Needing an 85% to pass and move on to the last level of this program, the counselor calls me to the front desk. My heart was pounding. I walked out the pod door to the hallway. She told me that my results were in. I looked at her and immediately got anxious. *I had to pass!* All that studying, reciting those AA steps, I knew them like the back of my hand. She continues speaking, "You needed an 85% to move to level three. You scored a..." She plays around with my results and pauses for what seems like forever. I grin, waiting on her response staring only at her lips. I wanted to know my results. I read her lips before I even hear her say it... 87%! I did it! I sprint around the officer's desk in excitement! I go back in the pod and jump up and down. "I'm on my way home! One more step!" Gathering my things in my room, E and Wes come up to talk to me. "You passed bruh," E says. I dap him up and say, "Yeah, bro, it's going!"

Wes shook his head. "Damn, I have got to get on my shit, you passed me up." Laughing, he jokes with me but I know deep down, he feels some type of wa.! As I straighten my room, the officers get my room ready in the next pod... Level 3, Pod C! I made it. I take a deep breath as I set my things down in my new room. We weren't allowed to have pictures, so I only could go from memory of how my family looked when I left. I didn't expect my mom to cater to me and come see me once a week or month, but I can't lie not seeing her and my family struck me deep.

It wasn't their fault or responsibility for why I'm in the situation I am in and that makes me even more hungry to get home. I let them down. I'll fix it soon enough though.

Chapter Sixteen:
LEVEL THREE PART 2

As I said before, level 3 was the step before being released. This level, you wear your own clothes that you buy on your home passes or clothes your family brings you when they came to visit.

Being on Level 3 and so quick, I could feel the hate coming from other people around me. they switched up because I passed their slow asses up. I told them from the jump, I'm getting home in eight months. I've been here for seven months now and I'll be released as long as I keep my cool and stay focused. They set you to a higher standard now… you have to set an example.

Grinding hard I finished all my schoolwork and I tested out. My grade point average?

3.7! I fucking did it! I was so happy with myself, I write home and let them know I'll be graduating. I'll be getting my high school diploma! I felt on top of the world.

I used the program to my advantage, but I didn't use the program to the best of my ability. I mean that I ran through it. I didn't take my time on each level; it was just a race to me. The quicker they let me out of this spot and back home, the better. Even if I had to fake it to make it, I was getting home.

My mother came to see me a couple weeks later, the last phase before I can get my home passes is a phase I was regretting for a long time. It came in two steps. The first step is that I have to tell everyone in the room about my case. Detailed and explain why I did what I did and why it was wrong. The second step is coming face-to-face with a victim. One of your choice.

Following these steps, you receive home passes. These passes start off with two 8-hour passes. Two overnight passes, one weekend pass, and a 10-day pass at this time you sign out and are finished with the program, not returning.

The first step was difficult for me. I hated talking in front of people with a passion, everyone staring at me! People whispering! *What are they saying? Do they believe me?*

I explain my case, and everyone is in shock at the detail! They ask questions at the end… *how did you feel when you got caught? Who was your victim/victims? How have you changed?* I answer all questions and am surprised by how well I do.

They schedule my second step for the following day… my victim? MY DAD!

This is one of the hardest steps of the whole program for me and I have been dreading it for the longest. I have to sit in a room and face my dad! I haven't seen him since he kicked me out of his car on the freeway. Damn, this is going to be hard! Facing your victim is something the program was big on! That's why they make you do it before you go home, clear conscious! Clean slate! Fresh start!

They call me to the officer's desk, "Are you ready?" I say, "Yes," and we head to the sally port. They cuff me and shackle my feet. Sitting in the back of this van, I feel a mix of emotions. I'm anxious to get this over with and nervous to see my dad! Scared for his reaction… *How will all of this go down! Will he forgive me? Will Maureen forgive me? Damn*, I hope they do, I love them so much… I think to myself as I look out the window. Passing city-to-city, we finally arrive and I immediately feel safe… Painesville, Ohio! Home!

They took me to the Justice Center and walked me and the counselor escorted by police into a conference room. The officers stepped out and my counselor was face-to-face with me giving me words of encouragement. You got this… You OK? Remember it's in the past even if he doesn't forgive you… YOU HAVE TO FORGIVE YOURSELF BEFORE YOU CAN MOVE ON IN LIFE… Your mother is here… She walks in… Mom! I haven't seen here in feels like six months… my heart races… I'm excited to see her but I still am in the back of my mind waiting on my dad to walk through that door… what will he say?

Me, my mom, and my counselor talk for a while and then I hear a knock on the door, it opens, and my dad walks in! My heart hits my feet and shoots back up… adrenaline pumping, I look him in his eyes! I see the pain! The disrespect! Maureen follows his lead! I look her in her eyes as well… damn, I really hurt my family! I think in my head, *I hope they forgive me…*

They hug my mom, say hi, and sit down. My dad and counselor meet, and he introduces Maureen to the counselor.

Now to business, the counselor says… dead silence in the room… there's tension and you can cut it with a knife! Cold staring at me, I look my dad in his eyes… I can't for long, because I know I fucked up! The counselor explains the process of me coming home and what needs to be done… she looks at me and touches my shoulder, "You're a good kid, you just made some bad decisions, don't let those decisions hold you back in life…" Good words from a good woman! I look her in the eyes and nod my head, starting to feel my eyes water, I tell myself to man up… she explains to my dad that I need to face my victim and put my past behind me. I need to be able to forgive myself and hopefully my family will forgive me as well… then she lets me take the floor.

I took two coughs… throat scratchy and tight… it feels like I'm being choked tightly. MIND RACING, this is the moment I have been anxious for. I NEED TO DO THIS FOR ME! And for MY FAMILY! I begin to speak… I tell them how it all happened… how I set it up and how I got scared because I was taking too much. I knew that eventually, I would get caught, so I tried to make it look like someone else did it. Being weak and a coward at the time, I have changed, I let them know… I let them

Pain So Deep

know I had a lot of time to sit and think about what I did... what I want to do... my plans... how things would be different.

I explain with detail and emotion as I start to cry from spilling out emotion. At 17, being locked away for a year did a lot to me... changed me in multiple ways... my dad knew I was sorry and knew I fucked up... THEY FORGAVE ME! We all hugged, and they said they wish me the best and will always be family! They stood by my side from a distance and I really thought I lost them! My counselor was crying as well, she explains how proud she is of me and how she has seen my growth. We drive home... back into the facility... **SQUAT! COUGH! URINE SAMPLE! I hate it here!**

I'm excited to get back to my room! I lay down to take a nap from a long exhausting day... smiling, I'm happy as my biggest fear and obstacle I just overcame. Me and my family have squashed our beef and I now have a clean slate. I made amends and now I look forward to big things.

In facility full of young teens, full of emotion, full of energy, full of testosterone! There were several fights. You could tell when a fight was getting ready to pop off! Tension in the air and like a snake attacking a mouse, it goes down... solid skin-to-skin contact, fist-to-face. I learn to understand these moments early in the DH, so seeing it here was no shock to me.

One day, a fight occurs differently though. It's weird because these two played cards together and ate at the same chow hall table regularly together. Sometimes in jail, I feel like the littlest thing can set someone to do something unexpected. I'm working out with Wes and E in the south hall. North hall has three classrooms, these classrooms can be occupied by people by leaving their "ID Tag" with an officer. All pods and rooms in and out of this facility were monitored on camera.

As we work out, we hear a loud noise... *Bang! Bang! Bang!* Officers run to the classrooms! What is going on... all the officers are at one room! Two kids are fighting, they have locked themselves and barricaded themselves into the classroom… they staged the fight to get into a spot where only one could leave… the winner walks, its simple.

They fight as you hear the grunting and fist smashing off flesh. The officers rush to try and break the fight up. Shoes squeaking across the floor sounds like gym shoes on a basketball court! The officers get in. They slam the two kids fighting and separate them. Cussing and bleeding, they both are escorted to the holding cell where they will be rode out. There is a no fight policy at this facility anyone found fighting would be kicked out without explanation!

They set us on lockdown! Officers escort us from the weight room to the pod! Walking past being nosy, we all look in the classroom they were fighting in. Blood smears the window. Hand prints on the glass, it looks like a scene from a movie. "Face forward, nothing to see here", an officer says as we pass. It's getting closer to me being done with this program and people are starting to get out of hand, I think to myself, *I'm too close to lose it, I can taste the freedom again.*

I was 17 when I walked into this facility and I'm 18 years old now, it's March and I'm waiting to do my last home pass. The people I once got close with either left the program or were under me watching me go home. I worked out every day training my mind and body to be released soon. I call home and write letting my family know my plans and goals.

Chapter Seventeen:
BACK HOME

April 2010… Today is the day! I've been waiting on this day for a LONG TIME!

I get released and when I leave with my family *this* time, I won't be coming back here. I'll be going back home! With them…

I'm up all night pacing in my room… mind racing… I'm amped… I haven't been home in a year! It's crazy to think I have been gone this long… watching the sky change colors, I tell myself to relax and get a little sleep. I close my eyes as I lay there on that plastic mat… wool blanket… grin across my face, I'm on my way!

Officers walk me to the front gate. I've never been this route my whole time being here at this facility, I been down every hallway and I never knew this existed. This hallway even had its own elevator. I'm excited, anxious, happy, and determined! I'm ready to get this life put behind me. We get on the elevator… 3…2…1…

We walk out the elevator and into a room where I sign papers saying I'm being released. They congratulate me and I walk out the door to see my mom, my grandma, my sisters Amaree, Tati, Jordyn, Jayden, Imani, Destiny (Imani and Destiny are sisters. We are related through my dad and her mom having a son… so we grew up together and always have been locked in).

They see me and I see them walking in through the glass doors to walk into facility, I can see it in their faces the love and happiness! We are reunited at last! I hug everyone we enjoy the company and take it all in for a second as we walk out I never look back…

We drive home and they ask me the first spot I want to eat. I just want to get far away from here I say! We stop at Sonic, because there isn't one in Painesville, and we eat and talk on the way home. This food definitely isn't what I'm used to as I'm full after a few bites, jail shrunk my stomach. I ended up falling asleep on the way home and they let me sleep peacefully with my head against window. We hit a bump and I wake up. Cleveland, OH, we are close I sit up and stretch! Anxious to get home but not to see anyone, I barely talked to any of my friends. The people who were getting my time more than my family! They weren't there! Why? What was the excuse? I know the visiting was out of the question, but why no letters? Why didn't anyone say anything to my mom? After all, I did for them and with them? Hurt on the inside I tuck that pain and keep my head up… I'm home now! It's my turn!

Coming home was different for me… it was like I was in another time zone! Time felt slow but in reality moved at a fast pace… Time is always moving! Time waits for no man… People I once knew were cool are beefing now. Girls that were innocent in school got kids now. Jock players fell off and smoke crack now. They are tearing buildings down. My old high school got torn down. The old hospital I was born in Lake East was torn down… A lot has changed… I had only been home a day or so when I was driving down the street and heard a Gucci Mane song being played it gets louder and louder. I turn around in the backseat of my mom's car and I see Greg!

He was driving a little blue car following us. I haven't seen him in a year, how did he know I would be at this exact spot in my mom's van? This was my only friend who communicated with my mom while I was gone. The only one who checked in with her to make sure I was OK… Could he have wrote a letter? Yes, but I was OK with checking in with my family many people couldn't even do that.

We pull over onto the side street and I get out and so does he… big smiles we dap each other up and hug. Missed you bro, missed you too dog! We exchange numbers and link up later on… but right now, I just wanted to go home and RELAX! All of this energy and love is taking a toll on my body!

Being home felt different, felt off. I hadn't been home in a year! I know I was supposed to be here, but I had to get use to life on the outside again. I had to get use to my family and friends again. At this time, it's around Easter! My first Easter home... I remember it like it was yesterday... waking up mom was so exciting for me to come home and be home for Easter she had a big meal ready as she always does! I wake up in the morning after the best night of sleep in a long time, I take a huge stretch and yawn! I smile! I can't stop smiling I'm home! I'm really back! I went from sleeping on a plastic mat to a queen size plush bed... Damn, I missed my bed... I make my bed and head to the shower... I look at everything different now! Coming from a place where it's dirty and sleeping is uncomfortable, to come to this is a blessing! Jail is the lowest of lows; I look at myself in the mirror and tell myself I made it! I clean myself up and head down to eat!

Walking down stairs, you can smell the love through the cooking... each step I take closer to opening this door, I feel like I smell a new dish! The famous mac & cheese aroma takes over... step closer, I smell the greens pounding in my nose, ahh, I can't wait to eat... I walk through the door and see all the family! I love this family! So strong, so loyal! They could have easily washed their hands with me! They didn't tho they believe in me! They want me to succeed...

We all get in a circle! This family has always been a close bonded family, on holidays we ALWAYS circle up and pray over the food... Grandma is the OG, so she leads, we bow our heads....

Church and prayers were a big thing growing up... we stayed in church literally four times a week.. it burnt us out and pushed us away from church, at least for me, that's why I fell back from attending church...

but prayers will always be a thing for me, to this day me and my girl both bow our head and pray over our food!

Dear Heavenly Father… she begins her prayer… I look around as everyone has their head down listening to my grandma pray for us, pray for our family! So much, love in one room! So much faith! … Bless this family, you Heavenly Father… thank you for bringing my grand baby back home alive and breathing… the room is filled with love and we listen on as my grandma says her prayer using words that pierce our soul and make us tear up! Amen and Amen! We all say Amen in unison…

The food is done and I am starving… NOTHING like a home-cooked meal and I haven't had one in a year, so I'm ready to get to it… I fill my plate, eyes bigger than my stomach, there's no way I can finish this plate… but I try my best! We all sit down, eat, and talk… good vibes with good family! Everyone smiling and happy!

In life, there are people who will doubt you, people who will try to disrespect you, people who will try to hold you back… it's on YOU whether you let it happen or if you rise above it… They never thought I would graduate with my class of 2010! I was in jail and people counted me out… but I COUNTED MYSELF IN! And that's all that matters, because at the end of the day, I made it home and now I'm about to beat the odds and walk the stage with my graduating class! From a grade point average of .07 to a 3.7 shocked ME much less than everyone around me… It's easy to get off track and bullshit in life. What is hard as hell to do is the thing you grew up doing. For me, I grew up skipping school and not caring in class… with no distractions when I was locked up, no weed, no ecstasy, no robbing, none of that in my face, I was able to buckle down and really apply myself. I graduated with a 3.7! I can't believe what I just did! Standing in this room with my fellow peers and people who counted me out… for some, I could see the hate and disgust knowing I was just in jail and now I'm in same position graduating as them! But there was mostly love for me and what I just overcame.

So many hugs and real conversations with people on my potential and how I deserve better than what I put myself and family through... Coaches, teachers, classmates... football players, people I knew from other graduating classes all happy for me! Damn, I got a lot of support out here I think to myself.

We walk the stage and everyone claps as every student in my class walks across the stage... From a felony to graduating with a 3.7, I take a deep breath and tell myself I can do anything! We throw our hats in the air and I watch as they fall back down to us... what a moment! And to only think if I would have just given up on MYSELF, I wouldn't even be here... instead, I dug deep down and handled my business... it paid off!

Chapter Eighteen:
THE FIRE

Summer of 2010 was lit, of course! It was my first summer back home and I had just graduated... My plans when being released from CCF was I wanted to go to college... Massage Therapy was my mission, I loved the fact that I could make my own pay and my own hours, it was a boss job! Being my own boss was always my goal! So, I went to Lakeland Community College. I attended my classes, and everything was smooth... until one day the teacher says

"You can miss seven classes without a note, after that you fail out of this class!"

That's the only thing I hear her say and something clicks... *now I know I can skip class and not get in trouble*! I tell myself this going to be a breeze. While I wasn't in class, I was hanging out with old friends, some-thing I wasn't supposed to be doing... When I first came home, I barely kicked it with anyone. I was distancing myself and feeling people out, but I noticed I slowly started hanging with old friends and things began to change... AGAIN! Of course, I didn't notice it at the moment, I never noticed until it was too late!

My mom saw it as well, she tried warning me, but I always thought I had it under control, she didn't want to argue with me or make me feel like she was clingy so she let me learn. I began partying again and it started to get bad!

Six Classes and the semester isn't half way over yet, I'm trippin', I tell myself, *get it together*! I'm addicted and it's too late though, I'm back in my old thinking patterns. A week goes by and I give myself a reason to skip class, there was no reason for me to skip so I made one, That's seven and I know it's over for me. I got my last school check and quit... I'm done! I took that check and bought my first car! A delta 88! This car was a boat! Big body! With no license, I bought the car because I could. I spent the rest of my money on weed and clothes!

Bought enough weed to hustle up some money and got myself fresh I knew I needed some income but didn't want to rob! Robbing was my last resort.

So the summer took off on a bad note. With school over for me, failing out and taking their money, I was bored and in need of money... Living my life again and not answering to anyone was a beautiful thing! I loved it! I'm grown! Mike calls my phone...

Ring! Ring! I picked it up, "What's up bro?"

He says, "Shit, wyd tonight? We about to have a bonfire at this private beach!"

I say, "swear I'm there!"

He says OK, he will pick me up and I hang up the phone... Later that night, Mike picks me up with Katie and one of her friends, we drive to the beach and walk down path, sand in between toes as I walk... where are we going? Mike says it's just a little further up this path... we continue to walk... getting dark, I finally see the spot. We walk over the girls set their purses down and sit on a fallen tree. Me and Mike get the fire started... we have a bottle of E&J brandy! Growing up this was our drink. This is the last night I ever drank E&J!

Drinking and laughing with the girls, me and Mike pass the bottle around, I wasn't sure who else was drinking but I know tonight, I wanted to get fucked up... so I drank even when nobody else would drink. The night got late and we start smoking, more people arrived... and we turn the music up!

Now we have a party, nothing too big but a nice group of people. The girls are giggling and laughing... me and Mike are joking and making people laugh, everything is good...

We start dancing and drinking more... someone yells out my nick-name, "Pyro". I go to answer when a guy next to me answers! I immediately tell him no, they were talking to me they said, "Pyro," he said. I know that's my name! To this day, I feel like this was a sign or coincidence this man was here I had never seen him before in my life... *who was he? Who invited him?*

My friends and family gave me the name PYRO growing up, it grew on me, and different people I grew up with have different reasons why they call me Pyro! For me, I was a firecracker and always doing some hot shit! Meaning I was always into something, no matter what time of day, I was ready... broad day or late at night, in the bushes, I had a rush for doing things my way and getting money the way I knew best.

This guy goes on to tell me how he got his name... he says, "I was caught in a burning building and I made it out alive. I have burns, but nothing devastating or life threatening..." he says, "An angel watched over me as I was in that burning building, to this day, I don't know HOW I MADE IT OUT THAT FIRE!" I look him in his eyes the whole time waiting to see if he is lying or just making this up... not one flinch or flaw in his body language gave that up this was a REAL STORY!

Me, Mike, and the girls get in the water and are splashing and wrestling around. It gets cold and I go to the fire and go drink some more. The liquor warms me up as I stand next to the fire... music playing, I'm starting to feel this liquor more and more, but I take one more big gulp of alcohol.

It hits the bottom of my stomach and I feel it immediately heat my entire body. I begin feeling the music more and more, I sway back and forth as if I'm swaying to the beat. I squat down to heat my hands by the fire. The heat is piping hot and I snatch my hands away at the touch.

Leaning down, I still sway to the beat in a crouched position, and then it happens…

Face first drunk and unresponsive, I lay there inside this fire! I hear the girls screaming… I hear footsteps! Water splashing against the rocks… Time is still and not moving, why can't I move? Why can't I roll out of this fire? I'm STUCK! Face melting as my face lays on a chunk of wood inside the fire. I remember smelling my flesh cook! The smell of burning skin! So intense in my nostrils. The smell of lighter fluid fills my lung. My face is numb! I can't feel anything! Laying there still in shock, I look into the fire! Red! All I see is red flames! How am I looking into a fire? How am I laying on a burning log? Why can't I move?

Finally, I am out of the fire. If I honestly could tell you, someone pulled me out of this fire, I would… that's not the case… I nor anyone that was there has a memory of how I got out of the fire! Everyone's story is different! I'm telling you from my life experiences and everything I tell you in this book is a FACT! NOBODY pulled me out of that fire! I was saved by an angel this night and that's the only answer I'm accepting.

Face on fire, I stand up! I sway back and forth, drunk and in shock! "I'm hot", I yell and I run and dive head first into the water… beach water at that! The water cools me down and I see people running into the water to pull me out! *Why are they trying to get me out of the water? Why are they girls crying? Is it that bad or are they being girls and over reacting?* Mike and Katie pull me out of the water and tell me I'm crazy! You need to go to the hospital! I immediately say, "NO! I'm NOT going to the hospital. I have 3 years prison time over my head from the last case I just was released from. If I get back into trouble the judge made sure she let me know I was going to see that time! I refuse to go to the hospital because that is a guarantee trip back to jail. And on top of that, I'm burned up… that's the last thing we are doing is taking me to the hospital."

"Get in the car, we are leaving," I hear Katie say… Greg pulls up as I'm walking from the fire! "No, he's coming with me, y'all got me fucked up" Greg says. In disbelief, he looks at my face. *Why does he look so confused?* Katie tries to explain and Greg wants to hear none of it, we ride to his girlfriend's house in Painesville... I run up the stairs to the shower... it's hot, I need to cool down! Why is it STILL so hot!

I jump in the shower and I feel cool, but I still feel hot... Greg runs up to the bathroom and tells me to get out of the shower... and my mom is here! My heart drops because I'm not sure what she will say... the thought of getting in trouble again made my stomach twist in knots. As I walk downstairs, my sister, Tati, is hitting Katie for not taking me to the hospital... I run over and break it up and let my sister know I was the one saying I wasn't going... my mom looked at me and said, "Get your shit, we are going to the hospital... go look at yourself in the mirror, maybe you might want to rethink that..." I turn around and head up the stairs... I'm tired of people makin' it seem like it's bigger than what it is... it's probably a little ass burn and they just over reacting...

Looking in the mirror I'm devastated at what I see! Half of my face is gone... it's pink! Half of my face has literally peeled off... all you see is flesh! Raw unexposed flesh! Pink and red Flesh... I immediately get furious and punch the wall... I look at myself in the mirror as I touch my face... it's stings as soon as I touch it... Fuck! How will I bounce back from this one! I really fucked up big this time! Head down, I start to cry! Tears of frustration, tears of Pain, tears of anger... why do I keep fucking up... my life seems to just always be going downhill! We leave and head to Tri Point! When talking about coincidences and people being at the wrong place at the wrong time my night doesn't get better... while getting booked into the hospital, I see one of the officers from the DH I was in. This officer knew me from face from being in the DH so long. He sees me and immediately stares! He's in shock... he himself is having a baby at the exact time I'm coming in... I hope that he doesn't say anything to my probation officer...

WRONG! He calls him the very next day! *Here we go again*, I tell myself! My probation officer comes to my house to do a house visit the following day. He sits in a chair next to me; I'm lying on the couch bandaged up and high off the meds, He goes on to say that he could violate me and send me back for three years, but seeing as I'm in so much pain and going through so much, he decides to not do that and lets me take this punishment instead. THANK GOD! I thought for sure he was sending me back.

This was one of the most painful moments in my life! The pain was unbearable, even with the prescription meds the doctor gave me wasn't enough! And doubling up wasn't an option, I'm damn sure wasn't about to turn into a pill head! After the meds wear off, it's a roller coaster ride.

The right side of my face holds 2nd degree burns! The upper-half of my right arm is burned with 2nd degree burns as well… My knee and my wrist marked with burns

ALL ON THE RIGHT SIDE OF MY BODY! I literally was laying on my right side in this fire. *How am I here? Why am I still breathing and who got me out of that fire? Who saved my life?*

The doctor walks in. When he looks at me and I can see the look of disbelief on his face! His body language, he is shocked I'm lying in front of him. He shakes my mom's hand and I hear him say, "Sorry, this happened to your son". my heart pounds faster. Damn, why do I put her through this? When will it be enough? She takes time off work to make sure I make it to these appointments when she could easily say I'm done and leave me to fend for myself… the RESPECT I HAVE FOR THIS WOMAN IS INDESCRIBABLE! Pure love is all this woman gives us, and look at me got her in here crying her eyes out… Damn, man, I go to get my shit together…

"Shon, saying you are blessed is an understatement. If you had been in that fire a second longer, you would have needed to get skin grafts from other parts of your body to cover the skin tone on your face! For example, you would have to get skin grafts from your thigh and attach it to your face through surgery" The doc breaks down what he is trying to tell me..." If you had been a skin tone lighter or darker then what you are right now, you would have needed those, but for the level of burn you have, your skin tone fits perfect to NOT NEED SKIN GRAFTS"! Did I just hear what I think I hear this man say! My mom is crying hysterically, she stands and hugs me... I love you we say in unison! Both crying in that hospital room... the doctor says, "I don't mean to stop you but there's more,"

My mom stands next to the bed, now looking confused holding my hand. The doctor goes on.... "Shon, you were laying on your right side on a burning log, I don't know how your eye is not torn apart from looking into a burning fire at that close of a distance," he pauses... takes a breath then goes on, "If you would have been in that fire another second, you would have lost your right eye! Yes... I'm saying you would have had to get a replacement... a false eye." Pure silence hits the room.... I look at my mom I see it in her red watery eyes! She drops her head... I do the same ... tears stream my face... chest breathing heavy I sit there in pain INSIDE & OUT! I'm hurt....

I just want to get away from people I keep hurting everyone that means so much to me.. Should I just leave? Isn't that a coward way? Why me? How the fuck did, I get out of that fire? My face hurts! It's on fire! More pain pills... lay down sleep it off hope the pain goes away... I lay there on the couch stuck, can't move, and only sit there taking the PAIN I caused MYSELF! *Don't make a sound take the pain you caused. It hurts so bad... Fuck...*

The cleaning and healing process of my burns was by far the most excruciating PHYSICAL pain I ever felt in my life! Every morning, I woke up, with face, arm, and knee bandaged up... I would slowly get up from the couch and make my way to the shower... sometimes, a family member would help me set up my shower gear but other times, I sucked it up and dealt with the vigorous pain myself... Thinking to myself as I grind my teeth from the pain I feel, *YOU DID THIS, YOU DESERVE THIS!*

Stripping naked, I slowly get into the shower... I can see myself in the body mirror hanging across from the shower. My face is split in half, one side is normal and the other side looks like something from a horror movie... face melted away, I wonder how this is going to turn out... I can barely get under the water as it is blistering my skin... ahh, fuck, this water is too hot! EVERYDAY I HAD TO SCRUB THE DEAD SKIN AWAY FROM MY BURN... the pain was so excruciating sometimes, I could barely hold my tears in! The pain was so physically exhausting... every day, the same routine... waking up sore and sticking to the couch from blood and burn treatment oils... Ace bandage wraps bloody... some days, I just wanted to scream as loud as I could, I was so mad and frustrated! How long would this be for? Hopefully it would be a quick healing process.

Weeks go by and a few friends come by. My friend, Dom, came to my mom, I remember it because she couldn't even speak... As soon as I came around the corner, she immediately began to cry... deep, sorrowful, and sincere crying. She genuinely cared and was hurt by what she saw! I teared up seeing her face go from a cold smile to unstoppable tears streaming down her face! When she could talk, all she could say was, "I'm so sorry, I wish I could have been there, this wouldn't be like this..." I tell her not to do that to herself... I messed up and now I'm paying for it.

My dude, Matty Roll, a fatty, called me. This was a real good friend of mine who I'll talk about more later, but he was always the type to check in on me and make sure I was cool. My white dude was always on the go and they took my guy WAY too early, but he will always be remembered... NEVER FORGOTTEN!

Weeks go by and the cream for the burns is working unremarkably fast... I follow the steps the dermatologist said to follow... I take care of my burns and barely go outside! And I bounce back! Like I never fell in a fire before. I tell people this story till this day and unless I show them my face and the outline of the burn, they don't believe me… I'm a living walking TESTIMONY… I just want y'all to hear MY STORY!

Chapter Nineteen:
RAID

Weeks go by and the summer is dying down into fall. The house on Mentor Ave is still jumping but the cops are onto us. It wasn't going to be too long before they raid it and board it up. But UNTIL then, we're in there... Drinking, gambling, and robbing took this house over. People were coming over and getting robbed before they even made it to the doorstep... it's out of control! The level of greed is getting crazy and people are running from the police and coming straight to the house! THIS SPOT IS ON FIRE!

Bang! Bang! Bang! The police knocked on the door using heavy force, police dogs barking. Flashlights pierce the dark house... everyone is laying on the ground or in some cut to where the police can't see them. This is the 2nd time coming to this house tonight. Two people are in the attic, hiding with warrants, the house is filled with drugs and alcohol, upstairs is a group of people I am hiding with. We watch more cops pull up from the upstairs window!

All of a sudden, we hear a noise in the basement. It's the down stairs basement door. They are twisting the knob, they push and we hear the door open! Fuck! They are inside now we have to hide! Looking around, I don't see anywhere to go, so I jump in the closet behind the door. I hear cops yelling and telling people what to do. Up the stairs, they come, I hear footsteps, with the floor creaking, he walks into room, someone takes off running. He grabs them up and the whole upstairs takes off. Everyone ran down stairs, exactly where the cops had everyone else at. "FUCK! EVERYONE LINE UP ON THIS WALL," the cop in charge says.

Lined up against the wall, we listen as the officer tells us that we all are to leave, either get a ride, walk or go to the station, everyone disappears! Quickly, we leave from the house, but we will be back...

They did everything to keep us out of that house. The living room had a stack of mattresses, a light on a dresser, and nothing else. The light was turned out by the police and landlord was to vacate people, but we still found a way! Breaking into this spot was a last resort, but if you needed a place to stay, the trap was there for you.

With the spot on Mentor Ave, closing up its time for a new kick it spot. Luckily, Mike saves the day! Mike always had his way with the females. Still to this day, he has his way! Mike came across a female around this time, a cool-ass female, who was older than Mike, but he ran the house! She let him have his way with pretty much anything he wanted. Their house then turned to a party house.

They had a few people who stayed as roommates, one of them being my guy, Tory. Tory was down for whatever when it came time to kick it. He had the basement of the house, so that's where we partied at! Bottles, blunts, pills, whatever we wanted, we had at this house.

I would call Mike and he already knew what I wanted... he would just answer and say, "Yeah, bring the bottle, I don't give a fuck!" And that's all the confirmation I need after that I was making calls! Party tonight hit me up! And at the end of the night, it was always a banger! This house was lit and in perfect timing because the last spot just shut down. The rest of the summer and fall we partied at Mike's!

So much alcohol was consumed in that house. So much weed was put in the air and everyone was on the same page... no bullshit, just good vibes!

Chapter Twenty:
CINCINNATI

It's January 2011! It's my birthday and I'm turning 19. This is my first birthday back home, I spend the day with the family because I know that tonight, me and a group of friends are riding down to Cincinnati to party. We have a mutual friend who goes to the college. Her name is Bri! We all meet up at the post on Mentor Ave. There were nine of us… me, Doostie, Iysha, Rosie, and my cousin, ZO, along with a few other people, were all riding out. We took the middle row of seats out and put blankets on the floor of the van! We stopped at my mom's and I swiped a bottle of goose, some blankets, tell my mom I love her, and we are off… We hit the freeway!

Blunts in the air, we smoke all the way down and all the way back! We also brought a total of seven bottles with us… all different types! Riding illegal and hot as fuck! Music blasting, we drive this minivan down to Cincinnati… Bottles go back and forth, Blunts go back and forth… girls laughing… we stop at a gas station… I'm drunk as hell right now. I feel myself slurring words and it's only eight at night! Doors open, music blasting, we hop out and start dancing… everyone in the van! In the middle of the gas, station like this was our city or we knew where we were at… not knowing what this city is really about! Not knowing what part of the city we were in got real and got real quick!

We go inside the gas station and I am just spending money on dumb shit… paying for people's food, drinks, and gas, it was my birthday… fuck it, I'll get it back when I get back to the city! Thinking to myself who I was going to rob first! Drunk, I walk to the hot dog machine, I make my food and walk out, not paying, we get in the car and leave… we drive and bend a couple corners, trying to make our way to the college… Call Bri, they say we are here… pulling up to a stop sign I dial Bri and her phone rings twice… no answer! I look at the phone, she knew we were coming, why she didn't answer? I call back to back… still no answer! What the fuck… *Bang!* My head snaps back… what the fuck was that… we jump out the car.

Everyone confused, looking around, we finally see the car… a guy rear-ended us and we wanted smoke… talking was out of the equation, three of us walk up to car, but my cousin, Zo, was the first one to the driver side window! *Smack… Smack*, he hits the driver… the man hits the gas, the engine revs.

He pulls off laughing at what I just saw and how quick it happened, my cousin Zo says, "That bitch hard headed, fucked my hand up!" I lose it… laughing uncontrollably, my stomach tightens and I can breathe! I dap him up and we get in the car… why was this so funny? Did we take it too far? Fuck, it's my birthday and we living! We can't get ahold of Bri… at this time we are leaving voicemails and one of the girls says, "Let her know I'm beating her ass, on sight!"

We park the van and everyone jumps out, we walk up to the campus doors… we about to try to walk in… We approach the doors and they are locked! Fuck! We're stuck out here and we don't know where to go… we blow her phone up… No answer! Was there too many of us? I don't get it! Mad as hell, we walk back to the car… As we walk up to the van, I see the LICENSE PLATE IS MISSING… it's not under the car or anywhere in sight… where is the license plate?

It had to have fallen off! THIS IS ALL, WE NEED MORE ATTENTION! I'm pissed, I'm ready to go home… we all agree to head home… in a city we know nothing of, we take turn after turn and lose ourselves deep in the Cincinnati streets…. red and blues hit the car…. weed and alcohol fill the van… nine passengers, no seatbelts! Open containers! Weed! It's over I tell myself! Fuck! The officers walk to the door… "License and registration!" One cop on each side of the van… the other cop takes names and socials, "Do y'all know where y'all are at?" the cop says, we all look at her and say yeah… Cincinnati… she shakes her head and tells everyone to get out of the car… We line up against the building outside, they search the car, and I know they see the liquor bottles and smell the weed… they finish and shockingly they walk back to us!

Heart pounding, I know they are calling back up and we are going down! The officers look at us and say, "Y'all need to get out of here, y'all are lost, and this is not the neighborhood you want to be lost in! You guys are five hours away and it's late, we don't want to do paperwork, otherwise I would book y'all asses," she looks at each one of us… hands us our ID's and says, "Get back home! Now!" And we don't ask any questions, we got in the van and took off… back to Painesville.

Chapter Twenty One:
SUMMER 2011

Sitting in the car with my dad as we ride, we talk and he lets me know I'm getting money the wrong way. "Son, there are more ways to get money, that robbing shit is temporary! Think about it…" I stare him in the face, then I stare into a deep gaze out the window… he always says that! This is what I know! This is what I love! Robbing is a thrill, an adrenaline rush, an addiction! This summer, I moved out of my mom's and was tryin' to do my own thing.

Living with a couple of friends I grew up with, these were real good friends to me! They came from NY when they were 10 and 13 years old! They were brothers! We grew close, so close my closest friend, Greg wanted to beat one of them up! He didn't like the fact he was getting in so close so quickly. He didn't trust him… But they put their differences behind them! They grow and get close later on but still weren't seeing eye-to-eye and I never knew why. Later on, I learn my lesson…

Party Night at Mike's, I make the announcement on Facebook and send my private messages out! Tell everyone to pull up. Me, Mike, and Tory set up for the banger. Mike and me got a lick set up and it's so smooth, it's sick! The night goes on and we get everyone to the house… more females than males was always our goal… one thing we didn't want to do was to stand in a room full of guys, so my mission was to invite people and spread the word.

Mike had an out-of-towner pull up with a girl he knew… She ran the play down to me and Mike before the party that night, texting us the address as she pulls in with him. We sneak out of the party just as it starts to get packed… The lick is 20 minutes outside our city, and we get there quick… lights off as we pull in the driveway… gloves on backpacks over the shoulders, we creep out of the van in all black. Tiptoeing to the house, the neighbor's dog barks! "Hurry up and get out of his sight so he will shut up," Mike says. We find a window and slide it open. Breathing heavy, heart racing, adrenaline pumping! I love this shit! We rush the house, flipping beds and drawers inside out, we've done this plenty of times! Flat screens off the walls and shipped outside like WE WORKED FOR A MOVING COMPANY! Anything of value was coming with us, no questions asked... we moved silent and quickly! A safe! I walk past it and catch myself in stride, I turn around, and walk up to safe it stands alone in the closet! Mike walks up, sees what I am interested in, and immediately jumps in to help! We take our time and work and work... finally, we get a corner to pop and we are in there... money, a pistol, and a few other things now are added to our collection... I drink some juice and we leave... adrenaline still pumping, we slowly ride back to the house and party we park the van in the garage and split the earnings after everyone has cleared the house... everyone is starting to wind down and leave and I'm anxious to see everything we got!

The van is filled another successful night now time to dump this shit and get paid... When robbing didn't go good for me, Cash for Gold came in clutch. A lot of times I would hit a party in the suburbs and the only focus on my mind was get the gold. I became a gold connoisseur! The weight, the type of karat, if it was fake or not... I knew it all and that was the easiest money for me to cash in.

And when cash for gold wasn't an option breaking in was ALWAYS an OPTION! Grimey and disrespectful when it came to eating, I didn't care! I needed what I needed and if you had that then I needed it!

August rolls around and we hit a party in Fairport! A couple friends and I hit the party to see what it's about; we heard it was supposed to be a banger. We pull up to the apartment and we hear how loud it is and immediately we get happy! *It's about to go...* I tell myself, ready to party and make some money! We knock on the door twice! Music shuts off, we hear talking… they unlock the door and we walk in. People packed in this little one-bedroom apartment. One way in and one way out! I hate these tight spaces! I go in the room and we meet a few girls. we introduce ourselves! "Hi, my name is Sam," I hear a girl say as she sticks her hand out! I introduce myself and shake her hand… "Cops," I hear someone say! Lights go off and people are starting to get scared… "Who turned the lights off?" someone says… another voice… "They won't turn on, I think the cops hit the breaker downstairs!"

"Fuck, they are trying to flush us out…" a couple of people leave out the window and jump off back porch! I tell them stay put till more people leave, then we can make a run for it… Sam says that she is coming with me and I say OK, she is driving at the time, so this worked out perfect… we run out of the apartment with a group of people… adrenaline pumping, I sprint across the street and they follow! We hide behind a tree as I see a cop car pass by and flash their flashlight! "DONT MOVE," I whisper to them.

The next day, a friend throws a three-day banger at his house… his parents are out of town! The first night, we smoke and chill, getting everything and everyone ready for the next two nights to come… I do my job as always and invite all the girls and made sure everyone showed up! It was going on that second night… Beer pong tables over in the kitchen… Girls boxing match in the living room! Twerk session in another room and ALOT OF SEX UPSTAIRS… I don't know why, but every party, the upstairs was THAT ZONE! Guaranteed you walking into a porno if you walk up those steps!

I brought a girl with me so I was occupied… everyone brought their own bottles and owned weed, nobody was leeching and everyone passed what they had around… good times and good vibes… me and the girl I bring go upstairs… Walking up the stairs, her hand in mine, as I lead her to the bed, all I can think is, *Damn, I'm drunk as fuck and we bout get it goin' in this room!* We get in the bed and we fuck! Drunk sex!

Both tired and sweating from the movie we just made, we lay there... out of nowhere, I start laughing and so does she... we are friends and nothing more, we get dressed and go back to the party! I continue drinkin' and playing beer pong, I feel someone staring at me... burning a hole in my back... who is staring at me something feels off... I turn around to see jet-black hair... and big, green eyes staring me right in my face, she cracks a grin and I see her braces with the color rubber bands... sexy to me at the time! I'm shocked, she is so bold as she walks up to me and says play pong with me! It sounded like a demand but had a sound of a question like she was asking me... I said yes! She was wearing a black hoody and black yoga pants! My eyes were glued when I see her turn around! *Where did she come from? What was her story? Who was she with? Why isn't anybody else talking to her?*

We play pong and laugh and talk, getting to know each other... we win! She screams with joy and we hug... longer than normal and as I'm hugging her, I grab her ass... one hand on her waist the other on her ass... it feels like a soft pillow as I squeeze I hear her giggle... just as I do that, I look up to see someone else staring at me... this time, it was a guy! Who is this nigga looking at? Does he know me because I've never seen him before? I shake it off and go back to partying... Sam grabs my arm and says do you smoke? I say yes and she pulls me to go upstairs... Walking up the stairs with this new girl I've never even seen until the other night! Where did she come from? Why am I just now seeing her? We get to the top of the stairs, she asks me where I'm sleeping, and I point... "Over there on that bed!" I say... she jumps in the bed and says, "Nope this my bed tonight!"

Knowing she is flirting, I laugh it off and say looks like we sleeping in the same bed! She looks at me in shock at what I said... I ask her if she had the weed, she said, "No, do you?" I said, "Yeah, I got some, you going to buy it?" She looks at me, smiles, and gives me $20. I roll up. Later on, she tells me that I better not ever charge her to smoke again. I still laugh about that. As I'm rolling up the same guy comes up stairs. The same guy who was staring at me in the party. He speaks to her... *damn, she knows him*, I think to myself

"So you smoke now..."

"Dude, get out of here, yes I'm smoking."

He looks at me, I shoulder shrug and he walked back downstairs.

She immediately apologizes and says, "Sorry, that's my crazy baby, daddy!" I look at her, shocked that she has a kid, now it made sense! Why he was mugging in the party! His baby momma was a done deal... she showed her interest and that's all I needed... the rest was history! She looked at me and said, "Don't mind him..."

I hit the blunt and say, "I'm not!" She smiles and we finish smoking... she gives me her number and we go back to the part! After that night, we linked and were fucking with each other ever since... Sam was a cool-ass female, younger than me, I've seen potential in her, only wanted the best for her! But my ways didn't match up with what I wanted for her! I did put her in danger multiple times being reckless! Hitting licks, robbing people put her in the way and I wasn't paying attention... Innocent girl from Fairport! She loved the new lifestyle I introduced her to! She knew I was different, and it made her want me more...

We became close and every night seemed like I gained her trust more and more! We were having fun, it came to a point where we had no title, but we both knew where we stood! She knew she wasn't fighting for a position... We were on the same page.

Her: "I'm about to come get you, I got a surprise!"

Me: "A surprise?"

Her: "Yeah, I'm here, come outside…"

Me anxious to know what she was talking about, I walked to the door and opened it up! All black, tinted windows, I see the new machine sitting in the driveway! I crack a smile so big! I walk out the house, she hops out the car and we hug, I smack her ass and she giggles. I say, "You got it!" She says, "Yea, I love it! Get in and we take a ride…"

Dodge charger! At this time, this was one of my favorite cars… Driving the new car, I push the pedal to the floor on the back streets, we max it out and push its limits… all you hear is the engine roaring… she laughs and I could tell she is excited! She screams as we push 100… "Slow down!" she says laughing… I finish playing with the new machine we got and take her home.

I had been staying with a couple of friends, trying to figure life out as an adult, not wanting to hear anyone tell me what I could or couldn't do was a sweet deal to me! Come in at whatever time I want! Leave whenever I wanted! Smoke and drink! Life was good.

Chapter Twenty Two:

THE PLAY

August - November of 2011 was a downward spiral and a huge moment in my life whenever EVERYTHING CHANGED... I became SELFISH! Time was flying, in a blur, the weeks passed by and life consists of partying and robbing to make sure I have money... day after day, this was the mission... sex, money, and drugs took over... the money was the most addictive drug though!

Something about this gun and their fear... seeing their pupils in their eyes change size when I point this .40 call down their nose... adrenaline pumps thinking about it! What a rush! What a thrill! Daily, I need it to make my day complete like a junkie with his fix.

> *"Run those pockets... Shut the fuck up, DONT say shit, just run the money... I need it All! Hurry the fuck up... you move ima smack you with this .40 and I ain't playin'! "*

A play was so smooth and so easy! It was just like playing sports in my eyes... Draw a play up and execute it! Simple! Quick money was what caught my attention! I loved it! Went to sleep thinking about it or smiling from a lick I hit that night... young and reckless! I think about all those licks and it blows my mind how grimy I was... ROBBING WAS MY ADDICTION! As you can see, I said *WAS*, this isn't a typo I beat that side of me and buried it! It will be a REAL COLD DAY IF I EVER GO BACK...

Halloween this year was different, the girls wanted to go out and I just wanted to chill in the house and party. I wasn't into going out on holidays, was just always too up tight! Sam: "Let's go to Kent State?"

Me: "What's out there? I'm tryna just chill here foreal…" I can tell she doesn't like it and wants to step out… Couple of other people are in the house and they also want to go to Kent!

Me: "What y'all wanna do?"

Them: "We tryna do something different this year let's go…" Fuck it, we to KENT!

My girl drove the charger, floating down the freeway! We played music and drank vibing… Finally, we get out there and it's packed… people walking everywhere… they are swarmed around the car as we drive two miles an hour, trying to move without hitting anyone. Finally, we get a break in the crowd and out of nowhere, my bro Murph jumps on the hood of my car! This was a good friend of mine I grew up with… a coincidence, we ended up at the same party spot!

That's not it though, as the night goes on, we meet at least 10 other people from our city. There're at least 15-20 of us now, as our numbers grew quick, males and females, it was lit! We walk from house to house! Party to party! If one spot was dead or weak, we moved to the next! Every house was a party or frat party! Guaranteed! These whole four blocks were sectioned off like it was just a known party section! We partied for what seemed like hours… Fighting was also a GUARANTEE! Liquor men and women always guaranteed a fight especially on the college scene.

I walk in the front door and it's a tight fit, pretty much elbow-to-elbow with everyone and you have to sometimes force your way through the crowd. Then the dance floor is packed, but I see gaps, meaning it's not as crowded as where I'm at, so I head to the dance floor! I look to the right and I see someone from my city, and he's drunk as fuck. He walks up to a girl as she is dancing with a guy on the wall! He stands in front of her and touches her chin… tapping it up and she smiles… the guy getting the dance gets upset and says something, I watch as it goes down… I step a little closer, feeling the tension, rising, and knowing what's coming next… she continues to dance… walking up to her again, she smiles and he touches her breast! Cupping it and giving it a slight squeeze!

The guy getting the dance tries to smack his hand away and catches two jabs to the chin… the girl gets moved out of the way! He fucked up! I watch as they land, hit after hit on his face and body… pulling his shirt over his head, I knee him to his ribs! Bitch! Bitch! Bitch! Everyone leaves the party, laughing and joking, still drinking… the night goes on and we need to sleep!

"Where are we staying at? Let's go get a room"! It's too late for all that it will be a waste of money! Fuck we to have think! We go to the gas station! Two girls walk in and Murph and his friend say that they want them… Sam and her friend say, "Y'all for real, we can get them to leave with us!" They look at them and say do it! The girls smile get out of the car and stroll into the store.

Walking back to the car, they get in and tell Murph and his friend to go talk to the girls… they do and the girls get in with them… now we are crammed in this charger, fits five and there're eight of us in a city we are not from looking for a room! We drive down the street for 30 minutes, looking for a hotel! Nothing! Where the fuck are we and why aren't there any hotels?

Finally, we pull up to what looks like a college dorm… We let someone jump out to see if it was open and one of the doors was! Bingo! We're in there! Not even knowing what this spot was, we found ourselves sleeping good for the night! As we walk in, I see a pool table, lounge chairs, and vending machines. It looks like a college dorm! We put all our drinks and snacks we bought at the gas station on the table and get comfortable!

We talk, laugh, and smoke… tired and drunk we pass out! Waking up at six, we need to get out of wherever we are at! I tap the people I'm leaving with! We leave the girls we picked up… we hit the freeway back home another successful night partying!

We get home early and take a shower and sleep for what seemed like the whole day! Need to get rest my body is beat…

I'll never forget November 2011! This month was cold and I'm not talking about the temperature outside… November was different! Everything was about to Change! Drastically….

Chapter Twenty Three:
NIGHT BEFORE THE LICK

"Bro, my girl trippin'," she said. "Y'all have to go!"

Me: "We gotta go? Nigga ain't this your house or it's hers? Last time I checked you were walking around here like this was yours, that's why I moved in!"

Him: "I know, bro, but her name is on the lease, not any of ours, so we have to do what she says…"

Me: "That's easy for you to say, you not getting kicked out!"

At this time, going back to my mom's was not an option! I was used to living a certain way and what was I going to say when I walked up. *"Momma can I come home"?* Nahhh I wasn't taking that route.

The part that fucked me up was I knew I COULD go home! I knew I could ALWAYS go back to my mom's house… to this day, I can, and she will tell you any of her kids can! But I wanted things my way and that's all I was going for anything else was going in one ear and out the other!

Jumping from house to house with my clothes and my .40, I made it work, until one day, my life changed… for what I thought was for the better!

The phone rang, It's Murph! I answer, "What up, bro!"

Him: "Shit chillin', my birthday coming up bro, I need some money, it's my 21st and I ain't got shit…"

Me: PAUSING… "What you trying to do bro, you know I got a play but you can't be on no scary shit!"

I had this lick set up but backed out prior to this phone call, because I felt the other people with me were scary! So I never went through with it… but this was different, I could hear the hunger in his voice! I could hear how serious he was!

Him: "Bro, you know I ain't never been no scary type, stop playin' with me!"

Me: "OK, bro, link soon, I need to holla at you anyway…"

Him: "You good, bro?"

Me: " I just got kicked out, can I crash there for couple of days?

Him: "You already know, bro, let me know when you on your way!"

We hang the phone up and I catch a ride to his house, we sit at the table and I run it down to him! "This the play bro…"

> "We going in masked up! No mercy, I don't give a fuck! If they move, then you deal with them!" I look him in his eyes, so I can make sure he is as serious as I am! "I do this daily, bro, I can do this all day… it's you, I wanna make sure you can handle this!" He looks at me and says, "Let's go, bro, I'm in!"

He brings a driver and I add a person who was supposed to plug us in with a gun plug… Both of these people fell victim to the feds and both of these people FUCKED this mission up…

Chapter Twenty Four:

THE LICK

I meet with the driver and Murph; we drove to set the route for the lick... I need to know everything! Our escape route has to be smooth and accurate; there can be no fuck ups! It's us or them! We drive past and circle back... there it is y'all! Pull down this street! She does! We pull in the back and I say this is where we start and I say pull out... go left... at the next light, go right and that will bring us back to the main street and we can get to the freeway from there! If we do it right and catch all green lights or at least two green lights, we should be back on the freeway within three minutes from the lick location! I wanted everything smooth! Like I said, I been had this lick set up I just never hit it... I came up on the lick so sweet.

One summer day, I was at the house, bored and talking about wanting a big lick Mike's girl, at the time, had always worked in jewelry stores since she had been 18.. I was laying down lookin' up at the ceiling, laying on the couch... ceiling fan spinning... "I just need one nice lick, bro. I swear and I'll quit!" Mike's girl chimes in, "You wouldn't hit a jewelry store, would you?
Sitting up, I ask her, "You for real or just talking shit?"

She laughs and says, "I got something for you but it's not small time! Like it's serious shit, you can't be on games!" She has my full attention at this time, it's just me, Mike, her, and Tory in the room all people I trust! This doesn't leave the room she says! I can get in serious trouble if we get caught! I give her a head nod and motion for her to keep going.

I used to work for these people, I know them like that back of my hand, she goes on to explain, "Two female and one male worker are present at all times," she says." They are old people, so it should be easy if you do it right! NO LESS THAN $20,000 will be in the CASH BOX." This is where she has my full attention! This is my main goal! I'm going in this jewelry store and I'm going to get that money! $$$$ is all I see when she describes the lick I get even more interested… hungry.

All I can think of is this lick! Night and day, I thought about hitting it but whom could I take? This is a big jump from robbing hustlers and dope boys!

She goes on, "There's plenty of jewelry in that store and it's small, should be an easy task for you Pyro!" I shake my head, agreeing with her! My mind is racing! I want that money! All of it! And I'm going to go get it!

Chapter Twenty Five:
COUNT UP!

I couldn't go to sleep. I literally watched the clock switch number after number... clock ticking in my ear, I hear it... *Tick tock! Tick tock!* I'm ready, I want to go! Heart pounding, just thinking about the money in my hand! I jump up and start getting ready.

5am, I was up, laying my outfit out like it was the first day of school... black jogging pants, black hoody, joker mask, zip ties, rubber gloves... Everything I see laid out in front of me. I get dressed and pack the Nike duffel bag I will be carrying... Murph wakes up and I tell him to get ready... he gets dressed and calls the driver!

Waiting for the driver, we drink a bottle we didn't finish from the previous night. Passing the bottle back and forth, the driver pulls up... "It's go time," I say. We load up the duffel bags and ride out... on the way to the lick, we are meeting up with D's people! D is the person I included who was SUPPOSED to plug us in with the gun connect... this is the first sign when I should have said fuck it and called it off! But we are already in route and turning around is dead! I'm hungry and I want this money! We pull up to the complex and meet the connect!

We jump in their car and they immediately question us... what y'all bout do? Why y'all need us? I let them talk! I listen! After a few minutes of what seems to me like interrogating to me, I cut it short... We gotta go so if y'all gonna come through then let's get to it if not we can leave.... they look at me and look at each other... Murph nudges me like I shouldn't have said what I said... but I was ready to go! And they were slowing us up! The driver popped the trunk and brought a big duffel bag into the car, handed it to his dude and he unzips it...

Pain So Deep

I'm waiting on the guns that were promised to us... the guns my dude said he could get us GUARANTEED! A Baby 9! And two .40 cals was the order! This is NOT the guns they brought! I'm furious! They brought RIFLES! Three fucking RIFLES! I look at them and say, "We bout hit a lick and you want us to run down with shotguns and rifles? In broad day, huh?" Annoyed and frustrated, I get out of the car and head back to our car... mind racing, what do we do? Think! Think! We are already out here, literally 10 minutes away from the lick... time is ticking... stomach hot from the liquor and frustration! We all get in the car! We yell at D... the fuck was that bro? You plugged us with those weak-ass niggas ain't even have what we needed now what? He looks dumb and confused.

"Drive!"

"Where to?" she says.

"Just go to that Walmart so I can think..."

Who brings money with them on a lick when they about to go get some money! Nobody! With no money, Murph and I walk into Walmart. I tell him, "We have to make something shake, bro!"

He says, "I know, bro, I need this!" We walk to the sports section! The guns are locked! Think! If we could just get one or two of these guns, we can make this happen still! Fuck, there is no way to get the guns, we would literally have to strong-arm the workers once they opened the lock case! Think! I look around... last resort! I look at Murph and he looks at me knowing exactly what I'm about to say he walks over to the pellet guns with me... look for the realest one you can see... then take it! You snatch one and I'll grab the other! Bet he says! We look around check our surroundings and make our move... has to be quick! Has to be precise! I grab my gun and leave down another isle! Murph follows the lead, going down a different isle we move quick and aggressively! My gun is huge this has to be the biggest pellet gun I've ever seen in my life, as soon as I've seen it, I knew it was the one perfect for the job!

I twist the plastic in two separate directions with force and I hear the plastic snap! Not lookin' at the package only, keeping my head up, making sure my coast is clear, I use my hands to do the work! I feel the plastic and metal gun! I scratch my hand sliding it through the small opening I have… *Ouch*, I tell myself, feeling my hand scratched I'm almost there… got it! I hear Murph in the next isle and I know he is handling business… I tuck the gun on my waist and speed walk to the entrance… a few seconds, I see Murph walking down the backside of another isle. He sees me and we are on our way! "Wait, stop…you!"

At this exact moment, I do not look back and I do not know who they were talking to but I do know my stomach did flips and tied in a knot… my walking slowed at first, trying to not make a scene or get lost from the person, I speed my walking up again. Almost there… we reach the front door and take off in full sprint! Murph used to run track and was fast as fuck, another reason is that I was OK with him on this lick! I knew physically, he could handle it! We fly to the car… adrenaline pumping, I feel the gun slide down my leg just as I get to car. "DRIVE! Drive now! Get out of here!" She hits the gas and gets us out of there Head down, we laugh as we make it out! Close call, a little too close!

Now we are ready! We don't have the guns we wanted, and I'm pissed! Take all the stickers off your guns! Take all the plastic parts off too! Make them look official they just need to be scared I tell them! We put our gloves on and zip tie the hoody sleeves around the gloves! Just to be safe. I thought I knew it all! Dumbass!

We approach the store… adrenaline pumping… mind racing… I LOVE IT! I get excited! I'm ready! My mind goes black and I only think about what I want! $$$$

All in my head! I'll do whatever for that money right now! And whoever in my way is going to be sad today! WHOEVER! I look at them and we all say it together BE SAFE AND GET HOME.

We pull our masks down, I slowly feel the heat from the liquor, and my adrenaline mix… my whole body is warm and numb! Ready for whatever! I need mine! The Heath Ledger joker mask over my head, I can only imagine how insane I looked! Crooked smile streamed across my mask… I feel so… calm, but so grimy and disrespectful… another demon comes out of me, it takes over me! I snap! I'm on go!

Up the side of the building, we head towards the lick moving up the side of the building in unison like we are an army unit! Three of us! Murph in front, I'm middle and D is in the back! Broad daylight three teenagers 75 degrees masked up we only see one thing… our target!

We come to the front. The jewelry store is in the middle of two storefronts. A check cash and go spot which we pass first and a cell phone store on opposite side… the jewelry store sits directly in the middle of these two businesses.

We turn left following each other, crouching, heart smacking my chest! I feel my stomach tightening every step of the way… I get angrier. Why am I angry? Fuck it, who cares they about to feel my pain.

Pass the check spot… I see a few people inside… as we continue walking, I lock eyes with a female inside. Time freezes… slow motion as I'm walking, I stare her in her eyes! We lock-in! Staring at each other! Why? Snap out of it… I continue walking as we walk up on the door… Murph turns around and looks at me… I turn my head to my right just enough to see D and I look at Murph and give him a head nod! GREEN LIGHT! (Mind you, there is only supposed to be three workers! Two woman and an old man!) We rush to the store… Masks on, I remember it clear as day.

Duffel bag strapped across my body… 150 pounds, I stood as if I were 6'5, 250- solid. I was comfortable here in this setting! I stood there and observed everything! Even my crew! My stomach turns as we enter, and I look at what I'm seeing.

Three workers! Four customers… and when you thought shit was ugly, it got worse… a fucking electrician was inside, working on the alarm system, the day we decided to hit this bitch! Coincidence or a sign! Doesn't matter at this time, it's on the floor, I'm going for what I came for and I'm not leaving till I got it! I stand at the front of this jewelry store with Murph in front of me, D holds the door down! Nobody is moving! The customers are in shock! They have never been in this situation and I see red! I smack the counter and tell everyone, "GET THE FUCK ON THE GROUND!" Murph smacks a shelf of jewelry off the counter… Everyone drops in unison…. I almost laugh inside half drunk and half excited at how sweet we got it!

I grab the lady next to me and I tell her take me to the cash register… She walks me to the cash register and as we are walking past, I see the electrician… he is in a sitting upward fetal position, holding his ankles tight to his body… I kneel down and get close to him… not saying anything… just letting him feel my presence I point the gun at his head… I feel his body tremble… I have kids I hear him say! I tune back in… Why is he here? FUCK! Why are ALL THESE FUCKING PEOPLE HERE? There's was supposed to be three People an easy sweep! Now look we got a fucking class to take care of! Fuck it, we're here now.

Customers lying face down I walk to the register… I see Murph handling business and grabbing jewelry in my mind I'm hoping please, "Grab Gold." I know I can turn the gold into cash easy! I hope he gets it all, I think! Just as I'm thinking that a woman walks into the store, she stops and sees what is going on! Shocked and froze, we stare at each other and she turns around and walks out the store… JUST LIKE THAT! Like it was nothing, like I wasn't going to pull her ass back in there and lay her down too! I yelled to D, "MAN, GET HER ASS BACK IN HERE AND LOCK THE DOOR!"

I'm shocked at how he managed to even let her get out in the first place, but he yanks her in and locks the door! Flips the sign and turns around! Watching the streets and door, he regains focus! I walk to the counter shocked at what is going on… I unzip the bag and tell the woman fill it! She does nervous as the gun I pointed at her face I feel her body trembling! She drops bills, "I NEED IT ALL, BITCH, PICK IT UP!" She does what I say, she fills the bag with everything in the drawer… I lift the cash register drawer up and see the big bills… I look at her and she shrugs! I snatch all the bills making sure none have ink packs… as I'm tucking the money in the duffel bag I see a door closing out the corner of my eye… something wasn't right…

Instinct kicked in for me and it paid off literally! I kick the door open and see the man! He is old! But he is also at least 6'6, towering over me. I snatch him by the shirt and point the gun to his neck with the opposite hand!

There was a STORE POLICY on NOT hitting the "distress button" until after robbers are gone… this was a KEY DETAIL I was given when first getting told about the lick! This was the MAIN REASON why I set this lick up!

I snatch him down to my level, where is the master register? I ask him in an aggressive tone! He knows I'm serious, he's scared, he wants no trouble! He points… "Over there!" he says. I look and see what he is pointing at! I immediately say, "Open it!" He spins the handle! Mind racing! Heart beating a mile a minute… thinking quickly… I watch him spin the handle to the vault, it slowly cracks open! I push him to sit in a chair he does and puts his hands up!

I sling the duffel bang in front of me… looking inside this safe, I see four shelves… quick glancing, I see plastic bags, envelopes, and miscellaneous jewelry… and a metal box! The "Master Register" carries no less than $20,000 dollars in it! Also, another key detail I thought about plenty of nights…

I hit plenty of licks! Some petty! Some worth it! Some I'll never talk about! Some I'll tell you in person! It's simple this was my life! Facts! Day by day, I lived for the thrill of pointing a .40 at someone and seeing them lock up. Freezing in time! Stuck! Scared! And then TAKING everything they owned gave me a high! I LOVED it! Growing up, we all hit licks but none like this... this lick would set me on top of my class! We get out of here my name gonna ring for this I think to myself! Young and reckless, I'm about to learn life at a different angle... A different view... one most haven't seen or haven't been able to talk about... just know everything I am about to tell you is FACTS! And everything I am about to tell you, I have personally seen with my two eyes... I won't lie to you or mislead you! I'm writing this to guide you down a different route! I took the HARD WAY.

I pull the metal box out of the safe... heart pounding my chest as I look down at this metal box. *Thump! Thump! Thump!* Heart pounding, is this really it? Was it that easy? I open the box... my eyes grow in size and I immediately get excited... Eight slots wide, money fills the box, I'm in shock, is all this real? Did I really just get what I came for? Mind racing, I hope this isn't a dream. I hope this money isn't fake or ink packed. I flip through the money, they start small! stacks of 1's...5's... 10's...20's...50's...100's

I've never seen this much money in person! I'm only 19 at the time! Thousands of dollars have to be in this box but I count over ten off first glance... I read the slips...

I slam the metal box shut and slide the box in my bag... I'm ready to go! I got what I wanted and I know nobody got more than me so we need to leave now! Two minutes in, I look down at my watch... right on time... on our way out Murph is telling a lady to open the door and it's obvious she is giving him the run around and bullshitting him... I hear him, "Where is the key to the back door!"

Her: "I don't have access to that key..."

I instantly get furious and run to the back door... viewing the door, I see multiple locks... deadbolts and chain locks I unlock all the locks I physically can... the bottom lock is the lock I need a key for... I look at the woman and she sees my mask and immediately points! I see the woman who said she didn't have access whole body shut down... I grab the key, smack the woman who lied, and I unlock the door... I swing the metal door open, we rush our one by one... there's a gate as we knew there would be. I time it up and size it up taking a step back I go for it, a second attempt is not an option.

I hit it in one jump, duffel bag and all I head to the car, D goes next slips a little but catches himself and Murph clears it next... "Let's goo!" I mumble through my mask! Holding the door open, I push them in and we take off, laying down, the only person visibly being seen is the driver... all three of us laying down breathing hard in this car... we did it! We hit that bitch! Chest pumping! I'm happy! I caught my high! I LOVED it! We take our escape route and we get to the last light! I hear it... She says oh shit... the emergency lights come on the streetlights and I see it! *Flash! Flash!* Fuck! They got the plates... we have to dump this car... ASAP! At this moment, I know the store hit their button and the police are now in route.

On the freeway, we got rid of our gloves, zip ties! Got off the freeway and took some side streets and got rid of hoody's... now we feel safe! We all look at each other! Big smiles! I turn the music up and we celebrate! We pulled it off! LICK MONEY FREE MONEY, NEVER SPEND YOUR OWN MONEY... my motto was being screamed the whole way home... we decide we are going to split up and meet later... mad at D I plan to chalk him! But I let him slide and bless him... we pull up to drop him off, I say, "OK, we all are going to meet up later and split money and go shopping." He says, "That's cool, but let me get mine now so I don't have to wait!

Thinking, I say, "Fuck it," and give him a couple bundles of money, I read the slips, and my eyes are glued to the stacks I am giving away... easily four thousand if not more... he is satisfied and daps us up and leaves...

Murph: "We shoulda chalked him, bruhh!"

Me: "I know, but fuck it, we good now!"

Chapter Twenty Six:
CASH OUT!

We drive back to Painesville... the driver asks where we are going. I say, "Give me a minute..." I make a couple calls and arrange for us to go to spot I was living before I got kicked out! Only one person home and he is upstairs using the bathroom... he said we could stay, until that night when his girl came home... I said we wouldn't need that long... we walk down stairs and immediately get to it... I crack the cash box back open and separate all the bills... 50's over here 20's over there... 100's over here... 10's and 5's over there! The money looked fake, there was so much of it... Murph broke down what he got as well... disappointed; I see he didn't take ANY GOLD! I asked him, "Bro, why didn't you get gold, you know how we finesse with the gold!" I shake my head and we count the money...

Separating the money was insane; I had never counted this high... 15,000... 20,000... $25,000! Bitch, we up I threw 10 in the sky! Laughing as it hit the ceiling and rained down! We gave the driver like a thousand and some jewelry... wish I woulda kept my thousand dollars she folded in the long run! The other dude, I put in on the lick ain't gettin shit else... he didn't even come through on his part... I know I blessed him tho when he got dropped off I cashed him out and I wish I wouldn't have... he folded in the long run too... But that's later on, right now, we about to ball out like we use to this type money! All my niggas gonna eat! I ball, they ball!

At this time, one of the people staying in the house is selling weed and I buy it all... "How much you got left?"
Him: "Couple zips!"

Me: "Here's $400, roll that up till it's gone…" I can feel myself starting to become arrogant with the money boosting my ego! He looks confused as I hand him the money. I look at him and he finally realizes what is going on! Immediately, he starts rolling up! Murph and I run up stairs and slide two $100 bills under the door and run back down stairs… he comes down stairs with money in hand and says… "What's this?"

I reply smart, "Looks like money to me!" He laughs and says y'all tryna be funny… I look at Murph and he looks at me… I up my wad of cash… ain't nothing about this money funny! The two brothers' eyes damn bear pop out their heads, shocked at what I'm holding in my hand… over $10,000 me and Murph each had… it was our lick and he needed it, that's why he called me so me and him took the biggest cut! Plus, everyone else fucked up on their end!

Money doesn't change people, it brings out what not having money was hiding. For me, once I got that money, things CHANGED! I became different! Aggressive to some, arrogant to others, but to me, I was LIVING! And nobody was taking that away…

I got plenty money… I got plenty money! The plies song played in the background…

Sam walks in the bedroom I'm in and I shut the door, looking confused, she says, "What's going on, something is different!" I sit on the bed next to her and tell her everything is going to be good and to just not ask questions… she hates when I do this because she feels out of the loop! I pull the money out and I see her big, colorful eyes grow… she looks at me, I look at her, and she smiles… she says, "Idk, where you got this money from? But I hope you are safe!" I leave it at that and say, "We good now, I need you to count some of this up for me…"

She NEVER saw this much money! I let her count five thousand and separate it from the remaining money, now I have spending money and money I want to put up or invest! I was never a dummy! I always knew it takes money to make money! And you need multiple streams of income if you want to live a certain way! And I wanted that lifestyle... She counts the money and I ask her is it all there! She says, "Yep," and I counted it three times... I say, "Good shit," kiss her on the forehead and leave the room...

Murph did ONE GREAT thing when we were in that jewelry store! He snatched a black box, to him, the black box just carried little envelopes in it... on the way out of the jewelry store, he saw a box on the counter and grabbed it! We got back to the house later on and was sorting everything out when it happened...

> Murph: "I got all this silver jewelry, I shoulda grabbed gold..."
> Me: Looking at him, shaking my head... "I say don't even start."

I open the box and he says, "That's just envelopes, bro, idk why I even grabbed that dumb ass box..." Me thinking why would there be a box with empty envelopes in it? I start pulling the envelopes out, one by one... there are numbers written out by dimensions on the front... each one a different number and size! I feel around the envelope trying to figure out what the numbers mean I turn the little envelope over and open it...

What I see next blows my mind and I immediately feel my heart pound... did I just see what I think I've seen! A diamond! A small diamond had popped out of the envelope when I opened it up! Murph, sitting across from me, still playing with his money, says, "What it is!"
I say, "BRO...its diamonds! He jumps up! Get the fuck out of here!" First, I count the envelopes... if there is a diamond in every envelope, I want to know how many diamonds we have. The box is slim and about a foot long. 55 envelopes fit tightly inside of this box! *Do we really have 55 diamonds?*

I take each envelope one by one... taking my time! Nobody interrupting my focus! diamond after diamond! I hear them clash together as I drop them in the sandwich baggie... *clink, clink... clink, clink...* diamond after diamond after diamond! I'm in shock! Mind racing... I thought the money was the lick! THESE diamondS are the Lick! The $25,000 cash was all love! But these diamonds will set us up for life! This another level of robbery! I LOVED it! The thrill of this lick was lick no other... was it the rush from doing it in broad day? The rush from seeing those people's faces as I ran through the store with THEIR MONEY? The thrill of getting away? Or was it the HUNGER I HAD? The drive the ambition I had for this hustle? Imagine if I would have put this much energy and ambition into sports! I could only imagine.

Smoking wasn't getting me high, it was numbing my pain and clouding my thought process! Everyone deals with their pain and demons differently... me, I just smoke and bottle that shit up! Hoping I never explode or hurt someone... smoking was my way of thinking to myself and talking to myself... self-talks happened all the time in my head! I barely talked! I shut down socially outside of my core group of people I was with at this time! If you weren't one of them and we weren't talking about some money, then I wasn't talking!

Flashing back to the robbery, I replay us coming in... The lady looks me in my eyes... all she can see is my eyes! Mask covering my skin, she looks into my soul, as I get ready to snatch hers! Get the fuck on the ground! I snatch her to the floor! Kneeling down at my feet, I have her by her collar holding her as I look around the room... I see Murph grabbing shit, D is watching the door... pacing he is nervous... customers face down on the floor not moving a muscle... electrician in the corner in fetal position face in knees... I snatch her up... I hit the weed harder as I get deeper into my head.

Stomach hot as she fills my bag... I watch all the bills fall into my duffel bag, inside my head I'm saying keep going! 20's,50's,100's... the bills keep falling from her hand I can tell she doesn't want to give it up, but she has no choice I'm not letting up... and she knows it! Fear pours as I watch her fumble the money onto the floor.

"BITCH PICK THAT SHIT UP, I NEED IT ALL!"

Shaking as I yell at her, she picks every bill off the floor and places it in my duffel bag... I CLEARED that drawer but I wasn't satisfied that's wasn't my MISSION! That was extras... my MISSION was that $20,000 in that lock box!

Someone walks in the room and we start smoking together now... they talk but I don't listen I'm zoned out! Pocket full of money and he doesn't even know how I got it! I looked up to this person at one time... hurt my soul to know he turned snake on his own little brother! Damn, why? I was the one making sure we ate! I would ride or die for this person and I haven't said his name because he gets no recognition... none of them snakes do! I tap back into my head... flashing back to me looking into the safe...

Shocked at the different items in this safe, heart pounding... where is it? There it is... poking out like a sore thumb... it's cold I feel it heavy in my hands as I remove it from the shelf, I look over at the worker. He looks like he has seen a ghost! Looking up at my joker mask, fear written all over his face... I LOVE IT! The fear is what drives me; the fear is what pushes me! I tilt my head, making him nervous he puts his head down and hands up! I open the box...

Under this mask, I wear the biggest smile and nobody can see it! We did it! I did it! All this money! Eyes glowing as I look down on each row holding bills stacked to capacity! At that moment, I knew shit was about to change... did I really think this lick would be lick a regular lick? This lick is high risk, but so worth it... slamming the box down, I put it in the duffel bag and now we need to leave... now!

Everyone is in the room now! Me, Murph, Sam, and the two people that I was living with, they are brothers! They ask what happened or how we came up… at this time, so pumped from what happened and so comfortable with everyone in the room, we run the play down to them! One of the brothers says, "Damn, why y'all ain't take me!" The other brother says, "That's the lick you been had set up?"

I say, "Yes!" We show what we came away with and they are mind blown… "What the fuck? How much is that? Was it easy?" Everyone talking, I pull out the bag of diamonds and I put them in Sam's hand! At this moment, I know for a FACT no one she has ever been with has ever let her count five thousand dollars!

But handing her a bag of diamonds changed her whole outlook on me! Her eyes locked on the bag when I pulled them out! I poured them in her hand… seems like she melted with every diamond that hit her hand… she was in LOVE! Diamonds really are a girl's best friend! Mouth open, she says, "These are yours too!" I say, "Yes," and I give her one… big step for a girl you only been talking to for a couple months… I didn't care it was free money so in my eyes I was never losing! She takes me by the hand, and we go to the room.

Sam is white but she was aggressive when I wanted her to be and I loved that! Lights off, she never even let me turn them on… pushing me toward the bed I know what she is on… I smile!

Tearing the room up, we have sex! Loud, drunk sex as we've been smoking and drinking all day… All you hear is raw skin-to-skin and moaning! I know her body so well! Even for only a couple months, we are in unison and on the same page! She moans louder! Smacking her ass as we speed up… headboard smacking off the wall… *Smack!* her ass has my hand print on it… biting my lip, I dig deeper… she moans louder as she screams… IM ABOUT TO CUM… we both finish and I lay down, naked and breathing heavily, I light the weed…

Relaxing and feeling myself, I turn the music on as we lay there…. money wasn't a problem! We good now… she laid her head on my chest, as we lay there, heavy breath… She asks me… was it worth it? I look at her… I laugh and say, "Yeah!" She looks me in my eyes and asks if I will be OK or am I in trouble! I tell her to relax, everything will be OK… we go to sleep.

Chapter Twenty Seven:

Party Bus

Next day, we wake up and the vibes are different! Murph left the night before, so he called me… "What up bro… Shit, you already know we bout kick it… get dressed, let's hit the mall," I can hear the excitement in his voice! I say bet and hang the phone up… I tell Sam to get dressed and tell everybody we going to mall. Murph comes and we head out to the mall… Beachwood Mall! He arrives with his ride and we hop in…

A blue sun fire is the car we are in, muffler hanging and loud we pull up to the mall… Valet park this bitch! I yell! Everyone laughs but I'm dead serious… they ask if I'm foreal and I say yea! We got money, why not? She pulls into the valet parking. The valet looks at us like we are crazy, I get out of the car and see the cars around us… Corvettes, Benzes, and Audi's line the valet parking lot and then you see us hopping out of a beat down SUNFIRE! Arrogant is an understatement as to how I'm acting with this money! I move so freely so nonchalantly…

Walking into the mall, Murph and I are the only two with money! Everyone else is along for the ride. We go to the true religion store, it's 2011 at this time, true religion jeans are a big deal… the hottest jeans at the time! Walking through the store, I grab a pair of black jeans… $300, a black true religion skullcap… $100 and a black true religion scarf… $150! Nobody left that store empty handed! One of the brothers asks me can he get a pair of jeans… I told him get what you want bro, he tossed his pants on the counter… paying for these clothes felt so weird to me… I had $4,400 in $100 bills! There was so much money in my one pocket I felt like the cashier thought it was fake… how many 19-year-olds back then had 10 thousand dollars spending money? Not a lot…

The polo store is next, I tore that store up! Everything I wanted, I got from the polo store inside of the Beachwood mall! Boxers, a robe, pajama sets, socks, book bags... I had it all and I cashed out AGAIN on one of the brothers... He started to ask me if he could get something... I cut him off short... bro if you want it just put it on the counter I got you! Growing up, I was NEVER SELFISH! Always making sure my people were straight, I would give my last if they needed it... The love was never the same on the other end.

Me and Murph Split up and seemed to have a friendly competition going... We both had our hands full with bags; everyone had bags in their hands. Murph paid a girl we were with, to hold his bags while he shopped! I thought she was going to laugh at him; it shocked me when she said OK! I see him coming out of a store and he shows me a pair of shoes he got... they were fire! I asked him where he got them from and he wouldn't tell me... laughing, he said, "Gotta find the store yourself..." I laughed and said, "Bet!"

Later on, we meet up and I show him a pair of red and black Griffey's with the red Nike swoosh and red air bubble... straight fire! His eyes doubled in size when it was my turn to show my shoes! Before he even started to ask, I cut him short, don't even think about it I laugh and walk off... still standing there he says you gonna do me like that! I say catch up and we split again... the next time we meet, we compare who has been spending more... he asks how much you spent so far I bet I spent more than you, young and not thinking about how much I spent I tell him... I spent $2,600 he says, "Damn, you got me, I spent $2,300!" I tell him I think it's a good idea that we leave before we spend it all and be sick the next day!

Before leaving, we grab some jewelry; I buy a pair of screw back earrings, two small bracelets, a ring, and a rosary! I loved rosaries at this time in my life, I wasn't catholic I just liked how they looked! Murph bought two rings, two bracelets, and a chain… We spend another $500, on top of what we already spent on clothes… Now it's time to go!

Getting into the car was a task the trunk was filled with bags, inside of the car was jammed pack with bags, I remember looking in the car and barely seeing anyone! Bags everywhere! We spent a lot of money on clothing we would only end up wearing once if that!

We go back to Painesville and now at this time they let me move back in… I wonder why! Of course, it's because I had money now…

We wake up the next day and it's getting closer to the weekend, which is Murph's birthday! He is about to turn 21 and life has never been this sweet for us!

"Bro, I'm getting a party bus for my birthday, what you tryna do?"

He tells me as we sit there and I smoke… "I'm on it, what's up, how much is it?"

He says, "It's $1,700," and then asks me, "What I got on it?"

I hit the blunt hard… inhale…. exhale, giving him a moment to realize what he just said, I look at him and say, "I got whatever you don't got"

He says, "Bet," and gets on the phone to make the arrangements…

It's Thursday and we are throwing a party at Mike's house… "Invite everyone," he says, "Let's get this bitch going…" Music to my ears, I get on Facebook and invite everyone I know… people who don't even party stop by… music, liquor, beer pong, girls dancing, weed smoke, pills, it's a banger!

Freshest in the party Murph and I stick out like a sore thumb, but fuck it, we are living life right now… I leave the party to go get some more weed and meet my cousin!

"What up, cuz," he daps me up and we go into his room. "What you got going on tonight he asks?" I tell him about the party and tell him it's lit! He says he's gonna follow me after we done... he gives me the weed I give him the money and before I walk out I see it...

It's beautiful... sitting there calling my name it seemed like! Clip laying next to it, fully loaded! He sees me looking at it and says, "You like that?" I say, "Yea, that bitch hard!" He goes on to tell me I can buy it and it was only shot once... I ask how much and he shoots me a player price... I immediately go in my pocket and peel off what he asks no questions... it's free money so I spend it freely! I put the gun on my waist and head to the car! We drive to the party! Since I left, the party had grew in numbers... it's loud as hell! I can hear the music as I walk up to the door! Girls laughing and guys rapping the lyrics to the song, I listen as I walk up to the door... I walk inside and I'm shocked at how many people are inside! More females than males, I'm satisfied! Time to kick it!

Gun on my waistline I walk inside the party... my Spanish homie, Choco yells my name and I don't see him, but I hear my name being called... "Pyro... Pyro... over here," still I don't see anyone, then I see it! He holds a Corona up in the air and I walk over, we smack our Coronas together,
cheering and drink.... Sam comes over and grabs my hand to go dance... For a white girl, Sam is strapped and she knows how to move her body! Hands all over her as we dance, I start to feel my gun slide down my pant leg... I stop the dance whisper in her ear give me a minute and I step outside and fix myself. Laughing at what just happened, I take a minute and go back inside the party... Party still going and jumping, I start taking out small bills and throwing them in the sky... drunk and not caring about the money, I'm in the moment! I go down stairs to put my gun away... I wrap it in my true religion scarf and place it in a box; I'll come back after the party to come get it!

The party is loud as hell and I can't wait to get back up there, walking up the steps with Corona in my hand; I open the door...

Cops! They are here! Why didn't anyone say anything? Why was the party still going when they were inside? Why didn't they shut the music off? As I walk out the basement door a cop sees me… I try to walk back down stairs… "Hey you, stop!"

There's nowhere to run! Fuck! Knowing I have weed in my pocket, I start to think… is this it? Do they know about the lick?

At 19 years old, I received a underage consumption charge, a possession of marijuana charge for the quarter of weed I had on me, and a disorderly conduct for giving them a hard time…

Walking through the party, shaking my head, everyone staring at me… cuffed and sick to my stomach! Heart pounding, sweating, I hear people say, "He didn't do shit! Let him go! Fuck the police!" I laugh and keep walking… we get to the car and the officer knows my uncle and dad but not in the good way! He tries to compare me to them and goes on about how he hasn't seen them in so long but now he runs into their son and nephew! I shake my head, who gives a fuck!

Sitting in the back of a cop car AGAIN! It's tight in here, it stinks! Hot and humid, I lean my head against the window as I watch the red and blue lights hit off the houses. Mike comes out going off, "That's my brother, he didn't do shit, y'all trippin'," I hear him say! Picking my head off the window, I see what is going on! They put Mike in the car with me… in shock, I look at him like, what are you doing! He says, "Fuck that, we goin' together!" Asking me questions in the back seat, I ignore most of them and give short answers with attitude to the rest of the questions… Mike tells me to calm down! He doesn't understand that I think at this time I'm going down for good!

We ride to the station and they book us in. I had $5,000 dollars on me at the party, I watched as they counted my money out, dollar by dollar! The officer says, "Well, you got enough money here to bond a couple people out."

I say, "Get my brother and me out of there," and he does… In the holding cell, I wasn't sure if Mike thought I was going to leave him hanging or what, but the liquor was wearing off and I wanted to go ASAP!

Sam and Mike's girl come get us and we go back to the house! The whole time, I'm thinking to myself if I'm just so glad the police didn't find my gun! What if I would have never put it away and came back upstairs with it on me? I would have been FUCKED! Not only would I have caught that gun charge, but I also would still be facing the robbery charges… Dodged a bullet.

I walk in the house and go straight to where I put my gun… ITS GONE! What the fuck? I put it right here! Who the fuck saw me? Did the cops get it? Why is my true religion scarf still here but my gun gone? Confused and frustrated, I tell Sam let's go and we leave…

Chapter Twenty Eight:
SNAKES

Prior to the party, I rented out a hotel for a week! I didn't want to have to keep asking people to stay over and dude's girl was unreliable. One minute, it's OK, as long as I give her some money and the next minute, it's she can't let me stay... so I did my own thing! The hotel had everything I needed! Two beds, shower, stove, refrigerator, and a TV. I was good! Nobody to tell me I can't come in here or I can't stay! Nobody telling me what time to be home or what time I can leave! My way!

We leave Mike's house and go back to the room! Shopping bags everywhere, I clean the room up so I can go to sleep I'm exhausted and just want sleep...

We have court on November 17th and then I can get my $600 back that I paid to bond us out! I can use that money back...

November 14th, 2011... Murphs birthday was yesterday and we turn it up! But we just kicked it light because today we get the party bus and really kick it!

Me and Murph pay for the limo and get all the details, we got the party bus for eight hours! They pick us up at Harry Buffalos and then we ride to Cleveland from there! We run the details down to everyone who will be on the party bus... Bottles and bottles of liquor filled the buses min fridge and coolers, white liquor and dark Liquor bottles passing around left to right! Weed smoke fills the air of the bus! No tobacco, just weed! I love it! More females than males. As usual, we meet at Harry Buffaloes.

Stopping at Harry Buffaloes, we buy a couple more bottles before we head out to Cleveland... we load up the bus and get on our way...

Sam was very upset this night! I wouldn't let her go on the bus along with another girl who was with her. I told her we would be out and about and didn't want them getting in trouble. They weren't trying to hear that! I was just trying to be slick. But she listened and stayed home... She cussed me out and pulled off in her charger! I couldn't do nothing but get on the bus she was mad, and I understood why! I get on the bus and we ride out.

I bought a specific outfit for this night! Orange and grey Miami dolphin snapback, white & green windbreaker Gucci jacket, stone washed true religion jeans, and a pair of orange and grey Griffey's with the orange Nike swoosh and orange air bubble! Fly as fuck I'm feeling myself! Earrings in, bracelets on, I'm ready! I hit the weed and take a shot of patron! At 19, it looks like I'm in a movie scene... on the party bus surrounded by people, we had two strippers on the bus and it went crazy! Money flying in the air... ass-smacking, strippers on the poles, strippers giving lap dances... bottles going around! Weed being passed back n forth! I look over and one of my dudes is passing out pills I laugh and hit the bottle... it goes down and damn near comes right back up! I feel the heat hit my stomach. At that moment, I knew I was gonna be fucked up!

The driver takes us to downtown Cleveland. We pull up to a strip club and I have no ID I up my money and try to pay him to get in! He says, "I can't bro!" Upset, I get back on the party bus and drink and smoke. There are other people on the bus who either didn't want to go in or couldn't get in. I tell the driver to take me and my friend to get something to eat! We go up the street and get something to eat while everyone else is partying up! I pay we pick them back up and go to a club!

Walking in the club, I see a couple people I know from Painesville... everyone else is staring at us! Why they staring so hard? In Cleveland, there is always tension, I don't know if it's my skin tone or the way I dress but I definitely feel the vibes and am on my guard. First person plays crazy we tearing this bitch up! I tell myself, *we go to the stage where the girls are dancing*. We get a couple dances and then go back to the main floor. Drunk and hyped, I sing the song; it's Waka Flocka - Grove Street Party!

Clapping my hands, my ring hits the floor... *Clink, Cljnk, Clink...* it's dark but I find it! Can't lose this, I just bought it! The night goes on and as we leave, I can feel the tension rise! A fight breaks out on the floor... I knew it! Being in jail raises your awareness... Being in jail made me understand when shit wasn't right, when my gut tells me something is wrong, that's what it is and that's why I listen to my gut now! We get back on the bus and ride back to the city... On the way back, we turn up again, drink, and smoke.... One of my dudes is head down throwing up and we can't do anything but laugh it was one of those nights! We had a great night, definitely a night to remember!

Chapter Twenty Nine:
GOOD COP, BAD COP

November 15, 2011... I wake up to someone crying, talking in Spanish... Sleep still in my eyes still half-drunk from the night before, I wipe my eyes and try to understand what is going on... He hangs up the phone and tells me what his brother says...

He said, "They on to y'all bro, the cops came to the house last night, and asked him questions in relation to a robbery!" Said he knew nothing of it! His girl was trippin' and said she didn't want us back... I understood why but I'm coming to get my diamonds and clothes! His brother is scared and doesn't know what to do, I tell him to don't panic and tell his brother keep his story we will be to pick him up in a little bit!

Later that day, in the evening, we picked him up and were smoking. As he gets in car, I can see he has been crying, why the fuck is he crying he acting like he going to jail? Confused but feeling bad, I ask him what all they said and what all was said back? I want to know it all... I need the details; he goes on to explain... "Bro, they know! I don't know how they know but they know! They got y'all pictures and was asking us where y'all were, they know how y'all got there and back... he keeps going but that part keeps playing in my head, time freezes and my heart immediately hits my feet and shoots back up! They got her! Fuck! I told her to report that fucking car stolen! Now look! One out of four is locked up and the female driver at that! Now I KNOW she will tell if she gets the chance... everything just changed!

He goes on to say that he doesn't feel safe and wants to leave. I give him $400 and tell him to just take a little trip to NY till this blows over! He thanks me and gets out of the car... Now that's good, I feel better! I didn't want him to go down for nothing I just wanted him to STAND SOLID.... He didn't!

Phone ringing... he answers, I hear his mom going crazy on the phone... Talking fast in Spanish! I grew up with these two dudes so I know them and their mom very well... Especially when they got in trouble, I could tell in her tone she was not happy... what happened now? They got him? I hear him ask his mom... my heart pounds faster and faster, please don't tell me what I think he is about to tell me! He hangs up and drops his head. It's too much crying goin' on lately! He looks at me tears streaming his face... "They got him, bro!" Fuck, they got my brother! We gotta bond him out! Mind racing, I tell him I got him and his bond will get paid... I try to assure him his brother will be OK and he knows I'm not gonna bullshit them... I give his brother $500 to bond him out, not realizing what charges he had I just gave him the money and me and Sam left...

Fuck, they onto us! I feel like I'm in a room and the walls are closing in on me! Whom can I trust? Who told already? That's two people they snatched up who know details specific details about this case! Confused, angry, scared, emotions all hit me at once... What were his charges, I gave him $500 to bond out and $400 the night before so he shoulda been able to bond out himself something doesn't feel right... Something is off and my gut is telling me, he TOLD!

I call his brother who I gave the money to. He answers his phone, "What's poppin'!" His NY accent strong!

I say, "I'm chillin', had a couple questions for you."

He said, "What's good? I get straight to it... What were your brother's charges?"

He pauses... then goes on to say he had a F1 Aggravated Robbery, and Receiving Stolen property!

Did my ears just hear what I think they did? Emotions flooding my body, I'm enraged! I know personally that YOU DONT GET A CHEAP BOND WITH A FELONY 1! He's a fucking RAT! My gut never lets me down and I KNOW from personal experience that if you have a high felony your bond is gonna be high as well.. I went to Juvi and had Felony 2's and 3's and my bond was $20,000! So how was his a higher felony and a WAY CHEAPER BOND! I'm sick to my stomach at the thought of what is going down right now... I BLESSED him, bought him clothes, gave him money to leave and he does me like this? Why? Why not tell them he doesn't know anything they can't put it on him? I hang up the phone, sick at what I just heard...

In my head and zoned out I think to myself, *Do they know where I'm at? Who told what? At this time, I know they both told something,g but I just hope it wasn't anything involving me directly...* but was I WRONG! Wrong about them being able to handle pressure of police! Wrong about them being solid! And mad at myself I blessed these people and they still turned their backs on me... I'm confused? I scramble and tell Sam I need to go grab my clothes from the "spot" this is where I was staying at, I just want my clothes and diamonds then I won't be there anymore.

Pulling up to the house, I tell Sam to keep the car running, I'll be in and out. She does! I run in and see the house is torn apart! What the fuck? Who has been here? I look around the room shocked at what I see... Laundry baskets flipped, clothes scattered on the floor! Drawers flipped inside out! Couch cushions tossed around the room...

We got RAIDED! Fuck, where are my diamonds I had them in a small jewelry box and that box is gone! My heart breaks at the sight! Nobody knew that box was even here much less what was in it! I run upstairs and talk to the girl who owned the spot... What the fuck happened to my room? She looks at me and with a straight face, says that the police came and searched the house! My ears hurt from what I just heard; did they show you the warrant?

She looks at me and looks confused... she repeat what I said as if she was asking a question, a warrant? What is that? Fuck, I'm fucked bro... I shake my head and tell her its permission to search a house it's illegal to do so without one! Unless you gave them permission to enter the house? Her head drops! I want to literally throw this girl out this window! How can you be so stupid? Why would she let them in? How could she let them in here I keep asking myself... sprinting I go grab some clothes and run to the car! Let's go now I tell Sam and she knows something isn't right! We go back to the hotel so I could think... damn, I'm fucked, I know I am! There's no way they don't know I was involved by this time... two different people getting jammed up and them searching the house was NOT GOOD... Shit just got bad and quick.

Now I'm scrambling trying to make sure I watch my own back because the people I thought would watch my back, stabbed me in it!

I have been spending money freely and with helping everyone else out I just need to get away... Far away! It feels like everyone knows now, I get random weird looks from people. Other people's vibes are off and I feel stuck! Nowhere to go! Trapped! Chest feeling heavy, I need to get out of here! Packing all my clothes, jewelry, and miscellaneous items, I load Sam's car trunk to capacity. I had a few spare things that needed to be sold.

My guy, Matty, was one of the most solid people I know, God rest his soul! Anytime I needed him, he was there for me without question... He never took shit for granted and always wanted the best for me... This was one person I can honestly say was about his money! When money was on the line, you could count Matty in!

I called him (the last time I physically saw or talked to him before he was murdered).

He picks up his phone, "What's up, Pyro?"

"Shit chillin', bro, what's up with you?"

He answers, "Not shit, riding round the city..."

I tell him I need him and he asks where I'm at and says he's on his way... He pulls up to Mike's house an notices something isn't right... he can see it in my face something is wrong! I'm pacing in the back yard trying to figure everything out, but if feels like everyone is out to get me... he tells me to chill and run down what the problem is... older than me, he gave me advice and I took it! "You have to protect you now bro! Get out of here, nothing good is going to come from this but sooner or later you have to face your demon," he says meaning the judge... he goes on to tell me if they already have others, then they got me! "Not trying to sound like I'm against you, Pyro, but they already told so now it's your move! You can run or stay here and let them get you? You have to make a decision," he says.

I tell him I just have a few things to get rid of and I ask him if he is interested in anything I got! There's one item I have that he is in love with! He's been wanting me to sell it to him for weeks now! But I love it too! She's beautiful! Pearl-white handle, long nose Ridgeline .357... It's sick! As soon as I pulled it out, Matty immediately said, "I want that WHENEVER YOU DECIDE TO GET RID OF IT YOU CALL ME BRO OKAY?"

And that's why I called him, he always kept his word and so did I! Rest up Matty, we love you down here bro! He buys that and a few other things I'm selling I let him pick from, at this time, I'm just trying to get as much shit sold so I don't have to take anything or leave anything behind I'm about to leave Ohio...

Pressure and tension is building, I can feel it in the air... Sitting in the living room of Mike's house, I remember hearing cop sirens... they had me peeking out the blinds every couple minutes... the sounds kept sounding like they were getting louder and louder! Finally, I had to go outside, I felt like I had a panic attack. Something wasn't right I did not like this feeling. I felt boxed in inside the house; outside seemed like a better option! Standing outside, I hear the sirens again... Closer...

Louder, my head constantly looking to see if they were on to me and my hideout… I couldn't get caught! Looking at the house, I see a friend of Mike's girlfriend on the phone but looking out at me! My heart feels like it's about to explode! Was she calling in on me? Did she know too? *Go with your gut*, I tell myself, and I do, I call Sam and tell her to come and get me ASAP!

She knows I'm serious and she knows about everything. She picks me up and we go back to the hotel room. Everyone gone, it's just her and me, alone in the room, I feel content! I feel safe! We lay down, as I need to calm my nerves and relax! She asks me what's going to happen and if everything will be OK? I tell her I will be fine I just need her to stay solid and trust me! We go to sleep. Waking up I felt like we needed to get out of the room for a while since we would most likely be staying the night one more night! Leaving out of the hotel room, I see some workers peeking around a corner as I am shutting my room… *What the fuck*, I tell myself as they try to hide around the corner… something is suspicious but I don't know what, it is all I know is NOW I REALLY FEEL LIKE THEY ONTO ME!

Do they know I'm here? Nahh they wouldn't tell the police EXACTLY where to find me… I walk down the hall and wait at the stairs… I give it 5/10 minutes and then I pop out like they did me, except this time they are at my door about to go inside! "What the fuck are y'all doing?" They stutter and can't look me in my eyes… I repeat myself… "UM HELLO WHY ARE YALL IN MY ROOM OR ABOUT TO GO IN MY ROOM?" The person who was in charge spoke first! "Were you smoking in here?" she says. Totally avoiding my question, I tell her, "No!" She says, "Well, it smells like someone did and if that's true, you won't get your deposit back!"

"That still doesn't answer my question, why y'all are in my room!" They walk away not saying anything, all three looking suspicious I go in my room and slam the door! What the fuck is going on man I have to get out of here! I pack a few things I had left in the room and put them in a bag and leave… looking back over my shoulder, paranoia kicking in, I feel my heart rate increase and my body instantly gets hot! I need to get picked up and get the fuck out of this state! If I can get out of this state, I will be good, but how? I leave the hotel walking and make a couple calls… they were in our room bro! Idk why but they was nosey as fuck talking about who was smoking… never answered my question… meet me at ruby Tuesdays bro I'm walking! Ruby Tuesdays was a five-minute walk from the hotel I was renting…

Murph Sam and one of my dudes meet me at Ruby Tuesday's and they know I'm not feeling what is going on, Murph asks me if I'm OK ,I say, "No!" "They onto us, bro!" he says, "You tweaking, bro, just relax, we good…" he doesn't know what I know! Doesn't know that I know two people been caught already and one of them I bonded out! How is he so calm knowing they raided our spot and found our biggest part of the lick! I know he's hurt about that… that was a big move for us.

After figuring out we had diamonds, and how many we had to get rid of them and fast! But how? And to who? We obviously couldn't walk into a pawnshop with 60 loose diamonds, asking what we could get for them! I don't know anyone who will buy them piece-by-piece or even in bulk! I've never even seen this many diamonds! Murph had a connection in New York, who we would have taken the diamonds to and he was going to buy them all in bulk at a nice price… Very nice price, if you ask me! Especially, since it was free money! This would have put us ahead another $25,000! I was sick to my stomach like I never been before, when I found out they got the diamonds! Because I knew we had them sold and ready to go…

We order food and talk quietly! "We need to get the fuck out of Ohio, bro, before we get jammed!" "They onto us, you have to listen to me!" Murph says, "I know, bro, we will just get to this weekend and everything will be good!" I hear him talking but he's not listening to me, I want to leave now... Today like pack our shit and leave! We all finish eating, pay, and leave... we split up! I got in the car with Sam and we head to Greg's house...

Walking outside, he gives me dap and we walk in the house. He can tell something is wrong if anybody knows me, it's him! I grew up with him since I can remember this is one person I can count on! We go to the basement and leave the girls upstairs to talk!

"Bro I got some serious shit going on!" What you mean he asks? I mean that I hit a big lick bro and shit went south quick... it's only been 5 days at this time since we hit the lick! How much he asks immediately! I tell him $25,000 his eyes widen, and his mouth opens, you serious bro? And you ain't take me he laughs! I don't laugh! He sees I'm serious and I need someone to help me out! Stone face I look at him and he says what do you want to do bro? I tell him I need a place to crash tonight! He says OK and goes up to talk to his girl making sure it's OK!

"Bro, we got some bad news..."

Fuck, I can't take ANYMORE BAD NEWS! He says his girlfriend overheard us and doesn't think it will be safe if we stay the night. And she doesn't want the police kicking her door in, she has a daughter, he says... I look at him and tell him I understand! I say I can stay one more night at the hotel... we smoke one last blunt and me and Sam head to the room!

Prior to this, I had Sam turn all the room keys in except the one I had on me.... NOBODY ELSE HAD A KEYCARD! Laying on the bed, I feel myself in a daze, spaced out, trying to get a grasp on what is going on. I just lay there, staring a hole into the ceiling! Trapped! I feel trapped and it feels like every hour these walls in this room close in on me more and more...

*I smoke myself into a Kush coma! Half-asleep and half-awake,
it happens...*

Chapter Thirty:

COUNTY

3:00 in the morning, November 16th, 2011
I'll never forget this day, it happened clear as can be!

The phone rings… The phone hasn't rang since I've been here, half-asleep and half-lit from the weed I smoked, I pick up the phone… no answer! Not thinking nothing of it, I go back to sleep. These past couple of days just seems like everyone is closing in on me… the night was quiet until I heard keys jiggling and a card go into my door! I know I turned all the keycards in! There was a push and I realized I put the latch over the door to make sure it was secure before I went to bed… I heard a push and the door smack against the latch, I popped up, to my dismay, there is another push, and the door comes off the hinges!

My heart dropped to my feet, at this moment, I know it is over… there is nowhere to go! The window is too narrow to jump out! And we are on the 3rd floor! I'm stuck!

For a brief moment, it felt like the time stopped! Everything was slow motion for a split second! My palms instantly started sweating and heart began pounding faster and faster… it felt like an elephant was sitting on my chest! Fuck, I'm caught! Nowhere to go! It's over! I'm about to lose my freedom and I won't see it again for I don't know how long!

The feeling of defeat covered my body! I went from being on top of the world, spending someone else's money, and living life, to the bottom! All the way at the bottom! Jail is hell! Jail is pain! Jail has no age limits! They accept whoever fucks up! And that's was me at this time!

I would NEVER wish jail on anyone!

What happened next was a strike of lightning that would change my life completely! On the other side of this door is a unit of people put together to take me to jail at any means necessary. And then it happens... The flashlights beaming in my eyes, I can't see shit, only flashlights and riot gear! Guns out ready to shoot if I make the wrong move! I lay there, stiff and shocked at what is happening... this is it!

I remember cops yelling, "Get on the ground, don't fucking Move!" Another cop flips the empty bed over, "Where are the guns?" he asks. Confused, I tell him I have no guns and he says, "We already got information that you do, so when you ready to stop lying, let us know, you will have plenty of time to think about it..." They handcuff me and Sam... She is balling her little eyes out and I feel bad. She wasn't a troublemaker and had never even been in trouble up to this point! Seeing her cuffed and crying made me even more upset! Jaws clenching, tight! Biting down on my teeth, I can't stop thinking about how they got here? *How did they know? Was it the driver? Or was it the brother I bonded out?* Questions, I need answers...

I mouth the words to Sam, "It's OK," looking back, I know she had to be thinking I was crazy! There were cops everywhere, Mayfield Heights police unit joined forces with Painesville police unit! Everyone looking at me, staring... They walk me out of the hotel room and it hits me! I won't be home for a long-ass time! Damn, I fucked up, what is my mom going to say? Her heart is going to break when she hears what happened! I hate doing this shit to my family. This was the walk of shame by far!

Walking out of the room and down the hall to the elevator, me and four cops in the elevator, they are in serious business mode... head down, I stare into space. People are looking at me in disgust as they see me handcuffed and police escorting me. You would have thought I killed someone, how deep they came to get me! We get to the cop car and they put me inside... this is a undercover car, unmarked, I lean my head against the window well at least I don't have to worry about the police coming to get me, they already got me! A weight is lifted off my shoulders! The pressure of dodging the police and being on the run was building up! A part of me was glad this shit was over, now we can get this shit over with! One of the longest car rides of my life, I'll never forget riding on the freeway, hands cuffed behind my back, my wrist have to be bleeding by now these cuffs are digging in my skin! *Take the pain*, I tell myself, *You put yourself here and they don't care! Even if you say something, they don't care! It's their world now, I'm just a part of it!* They take me to Mayfield Heights police station...

They pull in the sally port and take me out of the back of the car.. Walking into this building I know nothing of, the only thing I know is its jail and there's a process to this jail shit! Their rules, their world! They book me into the jail, it stinks... Piss hits my nose as soon as I get to my cell... Single man cells is what they had at this jail! Which I was OK with, I just want to sleep, I'm exhausted, and I don't care I just want to sleep the day away... don't want to talk to ANYONE! Just sleep!

Knock! Knock! Knock! "Breakfast!" In a dead sleep, I hear someone talking! I pull the blanket from over my head and see a cop with a cart, I sit up and he sets my food on the table in hallway not caring if I took the tray or not he walks away... stale cereal, a milk, a piece of bread, and an orange... that's breakfast! Breakfast is served at 7:00 in morning then you don't eat lunch until 1:00, and then dinner is served early, which was the killer part because you had to wait to eat until the following morning at seven! Talking about hunger pains! I eat the orange, I try the cereal, it's terrible, it's either I have NO APPETITE OR THIS FOOD IS JUST TERRIBLE... I hate jail! I gotta make this my last time; this shit is killing me mentally!

Trying to sleep the hunger pains away, I doze off again... Sleeping on this plastic mat has my back fucked up! A thin plastic mat with barely any material on the inside... tossing and turning It takes me a while to get comfortable. Finally, I fall asleep... Dreaming, I'm running the last few weeks back in my head! Some of the most fun I had in my life! But it wasn't worth what I'm about to go through....

I hear someone calling my name but I'm not sure if it's in my dream or if it's in reality! My rack moves and I jump up... The guard jumps back thinking I'm going to spazz out... I look up at him, wipe my eyes and he says, "Get up, they want to see you!"

Who are they? I know it's not my family, so whom could it be? I think to myself.

They walk me out of the room and down the hall; walking down the hall, I see the other rooms walking past and there's nobody here! I'm the only one locked up here, Mayfield Heights holding jail was a dead zone, they must not do crime out here I tell myself! We get on the elevator; two cops escort me, as I'm cuffed and shackled. Finally, we get to where we are going. Legs hurting from the shackles digging in my skin... every step, I could feel the teeth dig deeper into my skin... *Take the pain*, I tell myself, nobody cares about the cuffs being too tight! And even if I said something to them, they would laugh and say I shouldn't be in jail... that is right but damn! Fuck it, we here now!

Walking in the room, I see two detectives sitting at the table with folders and papers! Looking like I've seen a ghost, they tell me to sit down, I sit and the cops who escorted me walk out the room! "You obviously know why you are here!" I shrug my shoulders; they say, "OK, I see. We are going to do this the hard way!" They lay out pictures... A picture of everyone who was involved in the robbery! And they had extra pictures of people who weren't involved but who knew about the lick! Trying to keep a straight face, without giving away that I knew these people...

I look down at the pictures and say I don't know them! They say I'm lying, and someone already gave them information that's why I'm sitting where I'm sitting! I say I still don't know these people... they ask me a few questions, "Where were you on November 10th?"
Me: "With my girlfriend."

"Short and direct! Be more specific!" I shrug my shoulders. "You're not making this any easier on yourself by playing like you don't know what's going on!" Still, I play dumb like I don't know what's going on… The detective points at a picture, who is this? Points to another picture, who is this? How the fuck do they know all of this? Fuck, they know everything I look at the pictures they have spread across the table… my picture, Murphs picture, the other two people we brought with us on this lick… the brother I bonded out, and the last picture made me furious… Mike's girlfriends picture! Whom the fuck told on her! She was the last person supposed to be getting in trouble for this! She was the last person I was expecting to see a picture of! Fucking rats! I can't believe what I'm seeing!

I tell them I don't know what they are talking about, he smacks the table! "You aren't going home! So you might want to start talking, everyone else is!" They try the good cop, bad cop scenario, but they notice it's slow and not working… this wasn't my first time being questioned, inside my head, I'm laughing when they do the good cop, bad cop scenario! Goofy-ass cops think I'm dumb… still sitting there, mad as fuck on the inside, stone cold stare on the outside… I CANNOT let these people know I know what they are talking about, I don't give a FUCK what they got, I ain't telling on MYSELF AND I DAMN, SURE AINT TELLING ON NOBODY ELSE…

"So where are your guns, Mr. Sheffey?"

"What guns?" I ask with attitude… he picks up a statement and reads, "Mr. Sheffey recently bought a .357, a .40, and a .22!" My heart instantly takes off! Bitch made motherfuckers! How the fuck they gonna tell this extra-ass shit! Furious, I instantly feel hot! Skin crawling! I know he told he's the only one who knew all this info! I can't believe this detective just read that! Still playing dumb, I shake my head and the other detective says, "Nice tats!" I got my wrist tatted before I got locked up, my mother's name with a halo and clouds in one wrist and my grandmothers name a halo and clouds on the opposite wrist! People always asked why I got that tatted on my wrist… and I tell them…

Without my mother, I wouldn't be here! And my mother wouldn't be here without her mother! If someone were to cut my wrist, I would bleed to death! This symbolizes that without one of them I wouldn't be here and this life would be dead! I'm blessed to have these strong females on my side!

The detective notices my tattoo peeling and sees the dead skin… I say, "Yea, it's old."

He says, "Try again, we have here someone saying you got tatted before y'all went out! Do you want to try again?"

"Actually, I do…"

The detective says, "Well… Go on!"

I look them in their eyes and tell them…

I'll wait for my lawyer!

Shocked at what I just said, they sit back and take a deep breath… the one detective stands up and grabs his papers and pictures up you can tell he is upset that he can't ask me anymore questions! OF COURSE I DONT HAVE A LAWYER! But I know once I say, get my lawyer, they can't ask me nothing else! I can see it on their face the frustration, the anger! "Good luck with prison," the detective says as he walks out… the second detective shakes his head and walks out as well! Sitting there, my mind is racing. Heart pounding! Fuck! I wanna yell and take my frustrations out! A cop comes in and tells me let's go, time to go back to my cell! We get back on the elevator! The cop heard what happened in the interrogation room and asked me did I really have a lawyer… I looked at him and said, "I'm on my way back to my cell, aint I?"

He laughed and pressed the floor button… we get off the elevator and I head back to my cell!

I just want to lay down and think! Really think! Whom does weak-ass shit like this? Which man can't take his own charge? How do you throw someone you call your brother to the police like this? So mad, I could cry, I suck it up and bury that pain! I'm here now! Man up! I roll over and close my eyes! Clinching my teeth, I feel like my jaw is gonna snap! I fall asleep, hoping it's a dream… it's not… *Chow!* Lunch is here! Wake up get your food, the guard says! I get up, wash my face and eat! Well, try to eat! The hardest thing to do is go from eating what you want, when you want to eat food you can't digest… this food looks like some shit humans are not supposed to be consuming! Forcing myself to eat, I feel the pain in my stomach! I need to get something on my stomach, the pain is unbearable! Stomach growling, I scarf the food down! Without tasting it, I inhale the food and I drink a lot of water! I drank so much water… the sink in the bathroom has a faucet built inside. So the same place you shit and piss in is the same place you drink water from!

I FUCKING HATE IT HERE…

Chapter Thirty One:
6 Years no Tears

The next day, the guard comes and gets me, tells me I'm gonna be going to CLEVELAND CUYAHOGA COUNT JAIL! I know nothing about this place but I'm about to learn it real well!

The dressing out process was long and tedious! Fingerprints, question after question. Where were you born? How tall are you? Social? Last name? Mother's name? Fathers name? Emergency contact? Tattoo check! Are you in any gangs? How many tattoos do you have?

At this time, I was into getting tattoos, I love the feeling of that needle hitting my skin! Therapy! After the first 15 minutes, the tat goes numb and I zone out! The pain doesn't bother me, this is how I cope with pain! I don't know how many tattoos I have, I don't keep track; this is the dumbest question ever I tell myself! Who counts their tattoos?

He tells me to go into the cell that is open as he gets paperwork ready! I see him bring out an orange jumpsuit, a T-shirt and a pair of orange crocs (nurses shoes) he tossed the clothes to me and says, "Get dressed!" I strip naked and get my new uniform on, he tells me to come out and takes my pictures... turn left, turn right, look here in 3, 2, 1, *snap!* My eyes burn from the flash! We finish and I go back in the cell for what seems like an hour... waiting on the van to pull up, I'm anxious and nervous! Where am I going? What will it be like? Are the movies I've seen about jail and prison accurate? The van pulls up and I get in, there are a few other people riding with us they picked up first! There are five or six people on the van already... I sit down and we leave... I remember people talking about their cases as we ride! Another long ride, we go pick up a few people then we head to the jail...

Pulling into Cleveland Count Jail was something different! We pull down into this basement parking garage… I see multiple vans! *How many people have been brought here today?* I think to myself… we get off the van and walk through a body scanner and metal detector! There's a room off to the side, where people were waiting to go upstairs. They give everyone a bracelet, plastic blue wristbands which have a small picture of us. They also have our "inmate number" on them, as well as our birthdate! Calling last names, we come out into the hallway… stand on the yellow line, taking more mug shots and pictures, we finish up and get on the elevator to go upstairs…

Walking into intake, I didn't know what to expect, I've never been into any county for a long time before this time. I went to the county before this but I bonded out and that was the county in my city! I'm out of bounds right now, this isn't my city, and I'm not from their city! So to them I'm free game! I hope that's not what they thought… They show me where I'm going to be sleeping and I get my rack ready, putting my sheets and pillow together, all while-looking around, making sure no one tries no dumb shit! I've seen too many prison movies and honestly, I'm ready to turn! First chance I get in taking it there, I hope nobody try me like I'm sweet! As I finish my bed, I hear the guard yell, "CHOW! CHOW! Line up and get your food, let's go!" I watch as people line up and I follow suit.

A older guy is talking to some younger guys and says, "Y'all better eat while y'all can, cuz y'all young dudes going to 3 in 3 out." Confused as to what he is talking about, one of them says, "What's that…" he laughs and says, "Y'all young dudes don't know how to act, y'all steal and fight for no reason…" so they put y'all on lockdown! Only half the unit can be out at a time! Top range gets morning and bottom range gets night! Then the next day they switch, and bottom range gets morning and too range gets night! Fuck! I'm about to be put in the pod that's going to be lockdown most of the day! And I have to be around broke ass scavengers! This is going to be interesting…

They keep everyone on the intake pod for a week and then we all go to different pods!

Intake was an open range meaning there were bunks everywhere and there were no cells! Everything was visible no doors on showers or toilet area... Privacy is out of the window here! Degrading is in full effect... My first time showering, I kept my back to the wall... I've seen to many movies and I am not going out like that! Nothing but orange shower shoes on I feel the water hit my skin! Fuck this shit, cold! I jump to the side of shower without getting out of shower... I didn't let it heat up enough, a lesson I learned from the first day and used until I left! I shower quick, hit all the key spots, and get out! One thing I know is you don't take a shower like you on the street in here!

On my way back to my rack, I hear an older guy walking around saying, "PUSSY POCKET FOR SALE," commissary or phone cards... "PUSSY POCKET FOR SALE," commissary an phone cards... what the fuck was he talking about... I walked to my bed, still trying to think of what he was selling... Pussy pocket? Finally, I asked my bunkee... He says, "It's a jail, pussy! What the fuck is y'all talking about I say! How you got a fake pussy in jail?" he laughs hysterically at me and I am looking at him with a straight face... he explains what it is and how you make it... he tells me that people got ALOT OF TIME TO DO! Some people are NOT EVER GOIN HOME! I would rather them fuck a fake pussy then fuck around with guys! From that day on, I knew jail was gonna be a LONG ROAD FOR ME...

The next morning, we leave intake and go to our pods... My pod is 5b! The young dudes 18-28 are on this pod! I'm 19 at the time! In a jail, I know NOTHING about, in a jail where I know nobody! I have to stand my ground whenever the time comes! Walking up to my pod, they have to buzz me in and open the doors that are controlled by guards in a booth! In this booth, the guards have access to all doors in and out of pods! You can't get in or out of these pods without them opening the door. Everything is ran electronically! They open my pod door and my heart stops! Dead silence! I walk in the pod and everyone is staring at me! Why are they all staring? Confused, I ask the guard where my room is, so I can get it together! He tells me and I go in to fix my room up! As I walk in the guard shuts my door behind me! Confused and nervous, not knowing what is going on, I ask why he locked me in my room!

He says it's not my ranges time to be out on the pod, my range comes out after dinner! "Three in and three out," he says! They call it three in and three out because after meals, it's every three hours, the ranges switch being out on the pod! Breakfast is 6/7 in the morning, lunch is 11, dinner is at four! If you didn't have commissary or go to the store, than you would starve inside of that jail! Commissary for those who don't know is where you buy your food! Food you can't get obviously off the chow cart… so kool aid, candy, cookies, chips, phone cards, meat to go in your food… etc! Commissary is once a week or every other week! This is why we are in lockdown so much! People stealing commissary and fighting over commissary! On commissary day, they call each person to the cart one by one! This way, there is no distractions and no stealing! There was a limit on the food you bought and hygiene didn't count against that…

I remember walking in the pod and seeing people on the top range just staring me down like they were trying to look through me. Like they were trying to stare into my soul! I looked them in their eyes and kept on my way!

Fear is what they lived off in this county jail! Show a slight sign of weakness and your dead meat, meaning they are going to take a look at you and see if you will stand up for yourself! This opportunity NEVER CAME FOR ME! I did five months in this county and NEVER got in one fight! I, to this day, don't know how this happened! I was going to the store and spending money so it wasn't like I was broke or didn't have shit! I was just laid back and nobody ever gave me any problems…But I was a Ot dude, I wasn't from here and some people didn't like it but I didn't care I was doing my time and not trying to make friends!

I walk out of my room and see there is one TV and three phones on each floor, metal tables take up most of the pod and that is where you see people playing cards and gambling! Today, there is a poker game going on… Football is on TV as it is around thanksgiving time! I over hear the people at the poker table! "Bro, go get my fucking money… I'm not playing with you, I need it all. I know you got it, you just went strong to the store! If you don't go get my money, we gotta work flat-out!" Tension in the air something is about to go down… I just paid you everything but .50 cent you acting like a bitch right now! You really want some work over .50 cent? The winner of the poker game points to the room and says meet me there I'm done talking… as he is walking to his room the other follows… as this is my first fight, I'm about to witness on this pod I fall back and watch! Stepping a few steps back allows me to see everything! Then it happens!

Both in the room, they pull the door close but not shut; if you get caught in another person's cell, you go on lockdown! This is from people stealing and fighting so much! Then you hear it! The rack hits the wall! Shoes squeak on the floor… rack smacking the wall again you hear it! Flesh hitting off flesh, people move closer without giving it away… Where did the guard go I know you're asking? He was in the control booth talking to other guards! As he walks in, he notices people standing by the door! Looking in, he sees what is going on and slams the door shut! Doesn't go in and help! Shuts the door lets them fight and calls,

"Men in Black." This is like the swat team of the county jail! Ruthless and aggressive, they play no games and it's them against you! And they ride hard for theirs! Plenty of people have gotten the wrong end of the stick messing with this team!

The two people fighting stop for a second to see who shut the door. They see it's the guard and tell him to open the door! He says, "No, y'all are going to the hole!" They bang on the door and he doesn't budge… mad that they got caught, the two start fighting again… they fight for what seems like 10 minutes and I turn my head and see six guards dressed in all black! Moving fast and as a unit, you can tell they have been doing this for a long time! They rush the room and separate the two! Blood scattered throughout the room, they both come out bloody! Gladiator School! Fight or get beat on! Those were the rules!

Thanksgiving, we were on lockdown for two fights and two peoples rooms getting hit! Meaning they got their commissary taken! The men in black come back! This time they come with what looks like paintball guns! Except, these guns have little rubber bullets, they also have cans of maze that look crazy I've never seen maze come in a size like this! Why did they come like this? What was different about today? They shut the pod down! Listen the fuck up! They begin talking… We are only coming in here once the next time we come this pod will get everything y'all think y'all can handle! I promise you guys won't last!

You see these guys one of the men in black in charge says as he points to the guards! They get paid to do exactly what we love… Fucking y'all up! "Don't threaten us with a good time," the guard says… he goes on to say that they are not CO's… they are a tactical unit built to fuck disobedient and disrespectful people like us up all day every day! They lock us down for two days! With the holidays here, this hurt because we couldn't get on the phones! This is our only daily communication with our loved ones…

Mail is backed up! So now, tension is building because people need to call home! Talking to your loved ones means so much inside! Can really keep you sane in there…

Our mail gets slid under the door. But on this day, they slide something else under my door… confused, I pick up what he slides under. I can't believe what I am looking at! My Indictment! Why are there so many charges? What do I do? This is a fucking packet of papers! I need a lawyer and fast! How can they charge me with all these charges there has to be a misprint or something I try to think of everything… I sit on my rack, head in my hands, I feel defeated! At this moment, I felt drained and felt like my world was over! I can't cry... not in here! I refuse to let them see me weak or vulnerable! *Blame yourself,* I tell myself!

My court date is getting close! They provide me with a paid attorney... I hear knocking on my cell door as I am laying down staring at the ceiling! "Attorney visit," the guard says! I walk out of pod and go to visit booth! A shirt, black man in a suit with glasses on is waiting on me! I sit down and pick up the phone! He introduces himself and I do the same! He runs it down to me... "I'm not gonna sit here and waste your time and I need you to not waste mine! I'm gonna look out for you but I need you to be real with me when I ask you a question!" I agree, shake my head and he continues... "It's looking bad for you! Not what I wanted to fucking hear right now!" He tells me to start I have one of the four horseman! What is that I ask him? He breaks it down and tells me everyone told! Except my codefendant, who was on the run, still! Someone even took a lie detector test! My mind is blown!

Out of all the years, I had been locked up or in trouble, I never in my life heard of someone taking a lie detector test! Whom the fuck did it? I ask him who it was, and he says he can't say personally but there is a motion I can file to get the statements! I tell him I want them ASAP! He looks at me and tries to explain that it might not be a safe idea because if they get in the wrong hands these people could get hurt! I tell him I don't care and to file the motion. I ask him how long it will take, and he says he will have them for me on next lawyer visit... they told everything! My attorney comes back in two weeks just before my court date! I walk in anxious to get my hands on these statements; I want to know who told what! I want to know EVERYTHING THEY SAID!

He shows me the Manila envelope and tells me to please be careful that he had seen this go wrong before! I'm not trying to hear any of that I'm all in now! Fuck these rats! I end the meeting with my attorney and can't wait to get back to my cell and read everything!

I tear open the top of the Manila envelope! I pull the paperwork out and see everyone who told! Three people told! Two people involved and the brother I blessed! I'm sick to my stomach as I see some of the shit they say! Some of the shit wasn't even true they just were scared so they made it sound bad! Two of the guys who told CRIED during their interrogation! I read in the motion! One took a LIE DETECTOR TEST! And everyone blamed me! Said I made them do it! I slam the papers down furious! Fuck! I want to yell at the top of my lungs, I want to punch a hole through these bricks in my cell! Heated! Skin Boiling!

Judge Kathleen Sutula! Ferocious, Aggressive, cold blooded… all terms people use to describe THE JUDGE THEY ASSIGNED to me! Of course, I get one of the four worst judges in this County! My fucking luck!

Chapter Thirty Two:

DISRESPECTFUL AND DISGUSTING

My court date has arrived and I'm nervous as fuck! Not knowing what to expect, I copped out to a Felony 1 aggravated Robbery, two Kidnap charges. and a gun specification! My attorney says that before I copped out and he turned the plea in, he would get me as close to four years as possible… if I get four years, I can file for a judicial after 18 months! Trying to hope for the best but putting the worst in the back of my mind, I try to focus! I personally am thinking at this time that I will get eight years! My dad thinks I will get 10!

I'm lost! I don't know what to think… Sitting in the holding cell outside of the courtroom, there is someone in court before me… I DO NOT WANT MY JUDGE MAD WHEN I GO IN! I need her to be calm and clear minded! Of course, it didn't work that way for me! My fucking luck!

He pisses her off so bad, she takes an intermission after his case is closed! I'm sick to my stomach! My attorney comes in and shakes his head! Why the fuck is he shaking his head for, this is not what I want to see! Clinching my jaws, nervous he looks at me and says, "She's not happy." I put my head down and he says, "Hey! Pick your head up and have faith, we got this!" I hear him but I feel the opposite! She comes back and is now ready for me to enter! They take me out of the room and shackle my hands and feet! Two cops in front and my attorney next to me we walk into the courtroom! Already in the courtroom is the driver… standing right in front of me as I walk in my stomach turns! The nerve they have putting this rat next to me! I see my family! Tears streaming down their faces!

Damn, that shit hits deep down in my soul! Seeing my mom and grandma cry always made me feel some type of way! Heart pounding and jaws clenched I feel the cuffs digging in my skin as I stand there waiting for my punishment! They stand me and my codefendant side by side with my attorney standing in the middle… the judge talks to her and tell her that she will be serving six to nine Months in Marysville (women's pris-on) and house arrest! My mind is racing, blood boiling! Waiting on her to finish telling her the rest of her sentence, she stops! Looks over at me and says, "And now to you, Mr. Sheffey, is there anything you want to say before I sentence you…"

I look back at my family and then I clear what feels like a frog in my throat, I begin to speak! Telling the courts and the judge that I was sorry for hurting my family first and foremost… then going on to let her know I made a mistake and using key words to try to persuade her that I'm not a bad kid, just made a BAD DECISION… she listens to me and then speaks… "We have a few people who would like to speak before I sentence you!" Looking around the room, I see a female step up to speak! I know her! She was inside the store when we robbed it! She is crying and goes on to say how scared she is in life right now! How she can't look at teens wearing hoodies without having flashbacks… how she will never be the same anymore! She says I'm traumatized! I can't go back to work there she says! They took a part of me that I would never get back… Heart pounding, I personally feel like the judge is hearing her pain and I'm about to get dealt with… she finishes her speech and goes to sit back down… The next person comes up and I have NEVER seen this person before in my life! Who was this person? Why were they dressed to the T like this? They had to hold some kind of high rank somewhere how he was dressed… He walked up to the podium and addresses the judge.

"Hello, your honor, I am the OWNER of all HOWARDS JEWEL-RY STORES IN THE CUYAHOGA COUNTY!" My heart hits my feet and lays there... Fuck! The owner? I know he has some shit to say... He goes on to tell the judge how he has never been robbed in all his time owning the chain of jewelry stores, "I had to put a security guard in each one of my stores to guarantee my customers will be safe in our stores. Your honor, what they did was wrong, and a lot of people got hurt directly and indirectly (Ripple Effect), some of my workers had to go on paid leave! Some quit and I will never see them again! Your honor, I ASK THAT MR. SHEFFEY RECEIVE HIS FULL MAX TIME! He deserves the time to sit down and change!" He acted like he was just a shot caller! He wanted me to get the full 17 years! For a robbery? He is out of his mind! I pray I don't get this time!

He looks at me and I look at him giving eye contact he knows I mean business I didn't look away until he finished his speech!

The judge turns to me and asks me about my family! She says I have a strong family behind me! I start to fight the tears as I feel my family staring at me, I can feel their stares burning into my back! She goes on to say that I need to take this time to think of what you want to do in life! "The community doesn't need you on the streets right now, Mr. Sheffey; I sentence you to...six years in prison to be served, starting at Lorain Correctional Institute.... Following your release, you will be out on parole for up to five years max!" The judge looks at me and tells me she has faith that I can turn this around! "I know a lot of bad people and you aren't one, Mr. Sheffey! I deal with different types of people all the time. I know when someone has potential and when one is lost... You graduated high school! Played sports growing up! Something changed you, tho, and that is what you will have to dig deep inside of yourself and find it! And then you will become a man! A successful man!"

I listened to her and I took everything she said into consideration... She asks me do I understand and I tell her yes! They escort me out as I look to my family! I give them a head nod to let them know I am OK! Everyone looks like they've seen a ghost! Their faces were so pale! Tears streaming down their faces... Eyes blood-shot red from wiping the tears away! Damn, I hurt them BAD THIS TIME! I'll NEVER forget this day and how I hurt them! *How could I be so selfish? So disrespectful? How could I not see what I was doing to my family?*

They take me back to the holding cell... Still in shock, I feel numb to the pain! Numb to the feeling of what just happened and what could have happened! I literally don't feel anything... it's doesn't hit me until I get back to my cell... I walk into the pod and by this time, I have been here for a while, so I made myself comfortable talking to a few people, but outside of those few people I kept to myself! Walking in something heavy hits me! Like a ton of bricks all, my emotions hit me at once! What they give you one of my dudes ask, "Six," I tell him shaking my head. He daps me up and tells me keep my head up... this is important because later on he gets sentenced and his sentence makes mine look like a week! It's sad how they throw football numbers at young people on the first time they made a bad decision! He was 23 and they gave him 24 years! Was it that serious? Did he deserve to get 24 years? What about his daughter? Questions ran through my head when he came back balling his eyes out!

Walking into my cell, I remember it all hitting me as I sat down! My bunkee left the cell, he knew I needed alone time! I respected it! Furious at what just happened and how it all played out I sat there blank-faced! Heart racing! Mind going crazy! Six to nine months, are they fucking crazy? She is a fucking rat! How did she only get six to nine months... In the back of my mind, I feel blessed tho... six years compared to 17 is a huge deal, I would still be doing my time to this day! But six years! I won't see freedom for six whole years! Fuck, I done, fucked up this time... Everyone I talk to says keep my head up and stay busy and the time will fly, I hate when they say that shit! Six years ain't gonna fucking fly by! Whom are they trying to fool! All the older dudes I talked to who been to prison ran it down to me... "Stay to yourself and mind your business," one person says! That's easy I already do that... another says, "Don't fuck with gangs, they are going to have you somewhere looking silly!

I take that note! "Don't share your food with anyone! And NEVER LET SOMEONE PLAY YOU LIKE A BITCH! Or CALL YOU A BITCH!" I took everything they said and made sure I stood on those things!

After court, I called my mom and talked to everyone! Everyone who was in the courtroom was in my mom's car and on speakerphone! I could hear the sniffles and tears being cried out, shit broke me! Trying not to cry on the phone, I turn, so my back is facing everyone...

"I love y'all and I'm sorry," I tell them. "I mean it, I really love you guys. Y'all are my world and my backbone, I just want y'all to know this..." My mom could hear the pain in my voice! We hang up and I call my dad! Getting my phone calls out the way because after today I'm going to be very anti for a little while most likely, until I go to prison... My dad picks up and says he heard I got six years. I say yea and he says I'm going to be good! "Son, do you believe in faith?"

I say, "yes." He tells me to read the book of Job in the Bible and tells me to call him back after I do. My father was different when it came to religion! He studied and practiced certain things on the behalf of Muslim and he still read parts of the Bible and knew what he could relate to and what he didn't! I read the Bible and studied the book of Job, when I called him back, the first thing he asked was did I read the book of Job? I said yes and ran down what I took from the book and how I could relate to it... phone calls were only 20 minutes, and that 20-minute phone call was probably one of the most interesting calls I made before I went to prison!

He taught me so much just through a phone call! This man truly is something special! He did six years, so he knew what it was going to teach me and show me. He goes on to tell me that prison is a battlefield, "People are going to test you, and people are going to try you. It's your choice to let it ride or stand on your two feet like a man and handle it!" Tells me he loves me and is always gonna be there for me… "I'm not gonna hold your hand or baby you, but I'm your father and I love you son!" He tells me before he gives me the best advice and most critical piece of advice he can give…

"Son, I want you to listen to me and listen close…you're going to witness some deep shit in them prison walls and I want you to mentally prepare yourself for that! STAY AWAY FROM THE THREE G's!" Confused, I listen as he pauses, "gays, gangs, and gambling."

"Listen to me son, I won't steer you wrong if you stay away from these three things I just told you, then your time will be more productive and a lot smoother… when you add those three things into your bid, then time slows up and time gets crazy, you go from six years to 15 years real quick if you're not paying attention… a lot of older cats are gonna try to manipulate you! That's what they do inside they prey on the young, and they prey on those who are blind to these things! That's why I'm preparing you now! Listen to me and I promise everything will work for you…"

I tell my dad I love him and tell him to tell my brothers and sisters and Maureen I love them and will talk to them soon! The phone call ends and I go to my cell!

The day before I ride out to prison, there is a big fight! It's one on one but the reason for the fight was DISGUSTING AND SOMETHING I'VE NEVER SEEN OR HEARD OF…

Commissary was the day before and we all went and cashed out! We knew I was riding out this week, so we bought enough commissary to make breaks and cakes for the week!

A break is jail term for a meal! These meals vary depending on who is cooking or what items y'all have… The base of the break is either noodles from the food we get on our trays or rice we get on our trays… the county doesn't sell rice and noodles so we have to get it how we live… "Everyone save y'all rice," my neighbor says! He comes to my door and asks what I got to throw in, I put my bunkee in, he didn't have any money, so he was eating when I ate I couldn't eat in front of him I never been that type of guy! Any bunkee I ever had my whole time being locked up I looked out for if they needed it…

Beef sticks, rice, cheese crackers, shabang chips, honeybun, hot fries, squeeze cheese… Ingredients we used for this specific break… I know it sounds terrible! Mix it all together and it's a way better meal than what they serve us on our best meal! That chow cart will starve you and the people passing food out on the cart only look out for their homies or if you pay them! Anything else you get the bare minimum food…

Chopping the beef stick down and breaking all the crackers down, my neighbor preps the rice and breaks down the honey buns… everything has to go under our door so we put the breaks in a chip bag and slide it under.. Once our doors shut, there is no coming back out so we use the "porters" (cleaning crews) to move things to different cells for us… We finally get everything together and eat… I skipped chow so I could eat this because I knew I would be more full from this meal than the food they brought us for dinner…

Earlier on that day, we all were swapping commissary and eating on the pod! We had all been here on the same pod for 4/5 months! Everyone knows each other for the most part! Then I hear someone say, "Bro, what the fuck is this?" We all turn, and we see two people who were at the table opening a bag of chips all the way up, they move the chips around and there it is…

Foul as fuck! I shake my head and watch, as I know what's about to happen… "Bro, why are these chips wet?" he says, he snatches the chip bag and splits it open and chips scatter on the table… we look and see most of the chips are wet and not only wet but sticky wet! He jacked off in this chip bag and handed the chips to this man to eat! Not thinking anything of it, he eats the chips only to taste another man's cum! I cannot believe what the fuck just happened! He hits him so hard that his head smacks the table behind him… the person who ate the chips is furious and we understand! He beats him for what seems like forever… bloody. The guard finally steps in and shuts it down! This is the reason I ate by myself for so long!

"Spider! Ima call you Spider my dude," from 30th says!

"Why you gonna call me that?" I ask laughing.

He says, "Because tats on your elbow and because how quiet you are! This name traveled from the Cleveland County all the way down to Marion, where I was in prison! The people who were in the county with me and had to go to prison ended up going to the prison I was at and that's how people in prison started calling me Spider!

The morning before I leave, I give my bunkee and my neighbor the rest of my opened commissary! "You can't take anything open with you," the guard says… we make a County Cake!

Two honey buns, box of brownies, Twix, Snickers, Oreo cookies, and Nutter Butter Cookies! I smash the honey buns flat, showing my bunkee how to make this cake is something he been asking me to do… I toss him the candy bars and tell him to break them down to small pieces, smoothing the brownies out until they are paper-thin; this is the layer that goes over the top of the cake to wrap the cake in! Smashing the Nutter Butter cookies in a cup, I add water and it turns to peanut butter! I do the same thing with the Oreos! Now I have a chocolate topping and a peanut butter topping! Honey buns are the top and bottom layer of the cake! In the middle, the candy bars are placed! Broken and mixed, the Twix and Snickers are perfect for this cake! Next, the peanut butter topping! Then the top, honey bun goes on! Sprinkling the remainder of candy bars on top the Oreo chocolate topping goes on top! Finally, the brownie wrap! The brownie gets flattened and stretched out so it is able to fit over the entire cake. This is one of the key parts, especially if you are going for a good-looking cake! Nobody wants a sloppy built cake! Finally, it is done!

Pain So Deep

A compact cake, full of sugar, we save our milk from breakfast and store them in our toilet! Keeping them cold and only removing them from the toilet when we have to use the bathroom they are the key factor to this meal! You cannot finish this cake in one sitting! It's so rich and so fulfilling you have to set it down or break bread with someone! My bunkee thanks me for dropping the game on him and I say, "No problem, bro!" We dap each other up and I pack the rest of my things as the guard tells me I am about to ride out! Making my rounds to the couple people I was kicking it tough with I get their "inmate numbers" so I can write them, we tell each other to keep our heads up and I leave… just like that off to prison I go!

Walking down the hall, we stop at several different pods to gather others who are riding out to prison! We are going to Lorain Correctional Institute! This is intake! This is where you get classified and find out which prison you will be going to… I'm by far the youngest person in this room!

Cop out sandwiches are by far the worst meal I ever experienced in jail! "We are grown men, how are y'all feeding us bologna sandwiches with no water," someone asks the guard!
"Drink from the sink," the guard says… They call us into the hallway, one by one, to search our property and make sure we aren't taking any contraband! One Bible, 10 pictures, legal mail, 20 envelopes, writing material, and your mail are the only thing you can take with you from this jail! Your other pictures will be destroyed if they aren't mailed out or picked up! I lost a lot of pictures but I had plenty of time to get those and more back… finally, after sitting and waiting for them to check everyone's property, they tell us to line up two by two!

Walking into the basement, where we came in at, I notice multiple sheriffs vans, they handcuff us and shackle us! There are 10 people on my van and of course, I'm the youngest! No one even close to my age, everyone else is in their late twenties or early thirties! We ride for what seems like two hours to Lorain, finally we approach the prison, and the view is something you never forget if you've been in this situation… open fields! Miles of cut down trees and dry land. One of the guys says they started this so no one can escape! It used to be easy to try to make a run with the trees being up but now they can gun you down if you get that far… I think to myself, *Nobody gonna make it tryna run in an open field when the guards are in towers with rifles!*

Barbwire-fenced line the outside of the prison! Double fenced! No way, anyone is escaping to myself; I think it's physically impossible! We pull up to the entrance and one of the guys must have seen the confusion and frustration on my face as I try to make out what I am seeing… "You gonna be good, young," it's not like the movies! Trust me, this my 3rd time here… that doesn't mean shit to me, that only means to me that you like it here or you just dumb as hell to keep coming back here I think to myself! I look at him and nod. Another person chimes in, "Stay to yourself and don't take no shit, you'll be fine…how much time you got?" they ask. I tell them six years and everyone turns around and looks at me! "What the fuck did you do young that's a fat-ass minute to be sitting in here for! I'm only doing 18 months I never done more than two years…" I look out the window, starting to feel my stomach tighten at the thought of six years… I want to throw up right where I am sitting! We pull into the prison and we get off the van. Walking into the prison, they put us all in one room…

The other vans pull up and they put them in the same room! There's 20 grown-ass men, all in late 20's and up! And here I am, fresh 20 with six years to do! Baby face! No facial hair, No deep voice! Young and innocent looking!

A guard comes in and tells everyone to follow him… we walk into a room that has a Chinese guard in it! The way down to Lorain, people were talking about how this guard was an asshole! How he got a thrill from degrading inmates! He's so small how is he so tough! A badge and some power give these guards the big head! They feel like they can talk to you and treat you however because you are locked up!

"Strip naked... ass naked... NOW! Line up feet on the yellow line and faced the wall! I don't want to see any of your ugly ass faces turning around! I want to see the back of your heads!"

"Squat!" I said, "Squat!" He walks in the middle of us, we all are lined up ass naked against a wall, surrounding him! Spread your checks and cough! What the fuck did he just say! He repeated himself with aggression the second time! "Spread your fucking ass cheeks! Let's see who had the biggest man purse! My heart is pierced by the disrespect and arrogance of this guard! What type of man likes this type of job? Why anyone hasn't beat this motherfucker up yet? Cough he says! Louder! He laughs and says it again... I HATE IT HERE!

"Turn around and face me!" Everyone does! Not use to being naked in front of just men, I grab my dick and cover it up! In my head, I'm thinking, *These people fishy last thing I want them doing is staring at my junk!* "Mouth sweep," he says! "Use both pinkies and spread your lips," the same hands we used to spread our asses are the same hands they want us putting in our mouth to do a mouth sweep, disgusting! "Fucking foul! Lift your tongue!" He walks in the circle and checks everyone to make sure no one is hiding contraband! He walks up to each person individually! His skinny five-foot frame could easily be tossed around and beat up in here but this is their world! We just live in it now! I smell beer and cigarettes on his clothes and breath...

We get dressed and go back into the room we first were in before stripping out... haircuts were MANDATORY when I went to prison! There was no skipping out; you had to cut your hair even if you had dreads or braids! I had a head full of hair and they cut my shit against the grain! No styles, there was no taper fades or bald fades it was SIMPLE! Low without being bald no line up! "Torture," I say. "How are you going to cut my hair and NOT at least line me up?"

"We see medical and take our official prison picture! This is the picture that is on the website when you look up a person's prison number online!" I looked crazy as hell! They had us in orange jumpsuits and before we left to go to our specific pods they made us dress out again, this was one of the most awkward and embarrassing moments in my stay here at Lorain! I'm the last person to get my clothes to dress out, I walk into the room to dress out, and everyone is staring at me! 20 men just staring!

They are all dressed out obviously comfortable being naked in front of each other they look at me and say, "You gotta get changed, young! You can't wear that orange on the compound!" I think to myself, *I'm not changing in front of y'all, what the fuck type shit y'all on?* I scan the room, looking for an empty corner or something anything I can change behind! I refuse to get naked AGAIN in front of everyone staring at me, they got me fucked up! Finally, I see a laundry cart and I go behind it and get undressed! Not caring what anyone has to say, I'm not feeling this prison life already! I like women… I LOVE WOMEN! Nothing makes me wanna get naked in front of a group of people… men at that! We dress out and they take us to our pods…

I'm on 4A, which is my intake pod. I spend two weeks on this pod! I never had one bunkee while on the intake pod. You didn't leave your cell unless you had a reason… nurse, church, school, recreation, and chow hall were only reasons you could leave and those were only done at certain times on certain days! There were multiple housing units, this compound looked huge to me! There were at least six housing units outside of intake! 23-1 once you were back in your dorm! Not having a bunkee wasn't a bad thing for me I wasn't trying to make friends but after a while I wanted someone to talk to I was tired of rapping old songs and talking to myself… it was starting to get to me.

Chow was served and you had 15 minutes before the guards made you get up and dump your trays, finished or not! Sitting side-by-side, people I knew nothing of, I watch as one person snatches something off a person's tray! They didn't do anything; I'm shocked at how smooth it went... why did he let him do that? I'm right handed but from this day on I learned to start eatin' with my left hand so my dominant hand would be free if someone tried to play me sweet like they just did that man.. Chow is over!

This table dumps your trays and line up! Next table! We clear the chow hall as I see the next pod lining up to enter for their turn! As we are walking outside the dude who got his food taken punches on the thief without questions or talking... they hit the grass tussling and throwing punches! The wind is blowing crazy and the guard runs up and sprays his pepper spray! It hits the wind and smacks me right in the mouth! My mouth immediately goes numb! Fuck, I feel my lips tingling... the guards break it up and cuff them up and take them to the hole! Walking back to the pod I see someone I know I say what's up! We talk for a minute and he tells me we will catch up... he starts walking away when I hear someone say, "Ay bro, ol boy looking for you," he responds... it's not hard to find me plus I keep that HAWK on me! What did he mean? A HAWK? I don't get it at the time but later I find out exactly what he meant.

The next day it's our pods turn to go to rec! Walking to the Yard I listen to people, talk and they seem so comfortable. How? They really like it here! They OK with being in here? I HATE IT HERE!

This is my first time on a prison yard so I don't know what to expect... there's a huge track made of dirt, four basketball courts, two handball walls, two softball fields, and a section of pull up bars! Inside there is a workout area, two basketball courts, and a bathrooms, this is also where you can get your haircut! Not a cut like when you first get to intake! This spot you can pay someone to actually take their time and give you the cut you want! I still didn't get a cut because one I didn't have commissary yet and two I didn't know any of the barbers or how their cuts looked! I'm very picky with my haircuts so I'll wait until I can find my barber! I was in Lorain "intake" for two weeks then they moved me to the next unit over which was 4b

I got a bunkee and he was cool overall but I still kept an eye on EVERYONE! There were a couple people I became cool with, just from playing basketball and being on the same pod! One of my dudes had the weed and surprised me when he popped up and asked if I wanted to buy some… "Hell yea, bro, I been tryna smoke since I got here… How much it's goin' for?" He tells me eight a limb (a single joint) or two for $15… I think to myself oh yea it's goin'! I go to my room at this time I had a little bit of commissary I go get $8 in commissary! Coffee costs $3.00, so I bought two of those… A bag of chips was $1.50, so I bought him one of those and two soups… Soups costs .25 cents a piece! He shows me the weed before he accepts the money, which I respected because he could have easily, took the money and left… Looking at the weed, I look back at him, waiting to see him smile or say I'm just fucking with you! I ask him if he thinks I'm a bitch? Why you tryna play me like a fiend bro? He says what you talking about bro?

Now he laughs and says I forgot you just got here from the streets! This how it is in here bro, you not gonna be smoking no grams in here unless you drop that cash and that's pointless! I guarantee you get high from this! I can't believe what I am looking at! Literally the shit people were saying when they came home from prison was true… I never believed them when they would describe how small the joints were but how high you got from them until I experienced it myself… Smoking in prison was something different! I'll never forget it! From the amount to the process of rolling it up! It was unique and showed me that people in prison are talented as fuck!

He tells me he will roll it and show me the ropes… taking a paper towel, he uses coffee and water and wets the paper towel with the two… damp, he places the paper towel in the microwave and in intervals of 10 second he keeps pulling it out checking on it and then repeating process..

Finally, the shell is ready! My mind is blown as he hands it to me! Feels like a Swisher Sweet! He then rolls this little-ass amount of weed up inside the paper towel... and tells me to grab my bottle of honey... As I walk to my cell I think what the fuck he need honey for? Better be a good reason I don't share my Honey that shit $3.00 for a little ass jar! I laugh as I think to myself... He puts his finger out and drips two drops on his finger, spreading the honey on they limb he covers it completely! Almost drenching it in honey! We let it sit during shift change and when they let us back out we smoke in his room! Fan in the window and a prison made incent burns! One person stands at the door spraying "smell good" and the other person smokes blowing the weed out of the window or into the fan, which then blows it outside!

Before we started smoking, I told myself there was no way I was gonna get high off of this little amount of weed, I was just smoking big blunts! Being sober for eight to six months threw me off; I hit that limb two times and inhaled deep... I needed this session! I needed to relax! Almost coughing a lung up, I quickly cover my mouth and pass the limb! We go back and forth a couple rotations and the limb is finally gone... the honey caused the "shell" to burn slower than average! I go back to my cell when the guards shut us down for the night! I get the munchies and at one in the morning, I tear through my commissary! Candy, Chips... cookies! Laying in my rack I remember laying on the top rack and looking at the ceiling, thinking! A lot of deep thinking...

At night, they pass out classification papers! These papers tell you what prison you will be shipped out to! Mine slid under my door and I was hoping it was going to say Lake Erie because it's close to home! Instead, they send me three hours away from home to Marion Correction Institute! I remember asking my bunkee where Marion was, I never heard of it until now! He tells me that spot is the best spot to get your mind right and make some business moves at! The next day, they let us out I hear people talking about BELMONT! They called Belmont "Gladiator

School" meaning off the bus, you gotta fight for yours or it's getting took and it's gonna keep getting took! One thing you can't do is fold and let someone take from you, then you become prey and ANYONE will try you... A few people were scared to death to go to Belmont... "I'm gonna try to get re-classed I can't go to Belmont, they gonna eat me alive," I hear someone say as I do pushups! Another says, "Damn, I'm going to Belmont too, I gotta go talk to the case manager!" *Damn, they really don't want to go... is it that bad?* I think to myself...

At this point, I don't know what to expect from prison! I'm learning daily, what to do, how to move, what certain things mean... I'm a walking sponge, just listening and observing! Paying attention to everyone and every move they make... keeping to myself is my GOLDEN RULE! Never let anyone get too close I don't care how "cool" or tight we get.

The cooking has changed, and I don't know what I'm going to do... I'm not hip to this type of cooking or any of the terms they are using to describe things... "Bro, you tryna eat?" my dude I smoked with earlier asks.

"Yeah, I say what do I need? You know I can't cook but I'll help bro..." he laughs and says, "Ima have to get you hip to a few things! He goes on to tell me to bring chips, a summer dog (jail term for sausage), a bag of rice, and whatever condiments I got I can bring. I bring everything I got to throw in on the break and my bowl. We go into the "day room" another jail term for where they keep people playing cards, watching TV etc.

There are two microwaves and two small wooden tables used for cooking. Break these down like these he tosses me two soups (Ramen Noodles)... smacking them on the table and smashing the noodles together, they turn into a rice form, "Add them with the rice," he tells me, we mix the two together and add Sazon and the seasoning packs that come with the Ramen Noodles, we just busted down. He says now we cook the soups and rice! As he is explaining to me how to make a break he cuts down the summer dog, small pieces as he cuts away… piece after piece, he placed the meat inside of a bowl. "Frying" the soups, we remove them from the microwave then place them back in… one-minute intervals… the rice and soups start to burn and when you add hot water and continue the process your rice and noodles come out tasting like something you never had before, I was in shock when it tasted the way it tasted I didn't think it was going to taste right! I was use to cooking soups in the microwave at home, adding water and cooking them for six minutes, then draining the water! THIS IS SOME NEXT LEVEL SHIT! *Who made this shit up? Whoever did was smart as fuck*!

He places the bowl with the cut-up summer dog in the microwave, but before he does, he adds barbecue sauce and honey, giving it a glaze and sweet taste he heats the meat up for two and a half minutes… mix this with the rice bro, showing me step-by-step how to make a break my mind is going crazy taking mental notes… He grabs the bag of chips, opens the top, and smashes the chips with his hands… I hear all the chips crunching in his hands, confused, I look at him and he says just watch! He grabs the cup of hot water and pours a little inside… then grabs the squeeze cheese and adds a few squirts into the bag… he mixes everything up, squishing and smashing the chips, they turn into potatoes! He pulls them out of the bag and dumps them into a bowl! Places them in microwave for a minute and a half, he does this twice and then places them back in chip back! He places the bag on the table and with his hands he smooths the potatoes out making sure it's flat and even… Watching, I can't do anything but look in shock. I'VE NEVER SEEN OR HEARD of anything like this! I have ALOT TO LEARN!

Finally, he cuts the chip bag open and I see one big sheet of potatoes flattened out! He takes a knife and cuts the potatoes up into small squares about 15 squares…

Placing our two eating bowls side-by-side, he gets ready to prepare the bowls… Barbecue sauce, ranch, squeeze cheese, and honey are the condiments we have to work with. He adds the soups/rice/summer mix into our bowls first making sure both bowls are even! Next, he takes the potatoes and places them on top of the rice and meat mix he then takes the condiments and adds them in a diagonal design on top of the potatoes! Criss-crossing the different condiments... ranch from left to right, barbecue the opposite way, squeeze cheese following and honey after that! He then takes the last of the rice/meat mix and adds it on top of the potatoes and condiments he just put down. Making a second layer, he repeats the process! The final layer is done and he goes into his bag and brings out some seasonings he had... Mrs. Dash and Sazon, along with a lemon pepper seasoning he got from a food box (I'll explain this term later on).

He puts the condiments on and then sprinkles the seasoning over top of the bowls! My mouth is watering! I haven't ate anything that looks this good in a long-ass time! Chow hall food is processed garbage... They feed us two mini hotdogs for lunch like that will fill us up or hold us over... I HATE IT HERE! He tells me, "There it is!" I smile and dap him up... I make a jug of Kool aid and we sit and eat! I take my first bite... not knowing what to expect! I taste the combination of different flavors all hitting my taste buds at once! The rice and noodles are fried perfectly, not too chewy and not too solid they blend with the summer sausage perfectly! The potatoes are cheesy and fluffy! Condiments add all the flavor! Without condiments, it's a "struggle meal," meaning you are down bad so you don't have condiments or the break material so you eat what you have... I've done the "STRUGGLE MEAL" plenty of nights that shit made me appreciate money and my hustle 10x more!

He asks if it's good and my face is in the bowl scarfing... he tells me chill this ain't the chow hall! I stop and laugh, mouth full of food I say bro this shit hit! He daps me up and says now you got the blueprint! He goes on to tell me you can't eat with everyone, people aren't clean, and some people don't care they just throw food together and don't take their time! Plus, you don't want any leaches around you, now you know how to cook you don't gotta ask anyone to cook for you because that's how these mother fuckers try to finesse you…

I respected bro because he didn't know me! Wasn't like we were cool outside on the streets he wasn't from my city, he fucked with me because I stayed to myself and he was on the same shit… I wanted to make my own way, stay in my own lane, and go THE FUCK HOME! We hooped together, mostly against each other, because the competitor in us wouldn't allow us to be teammates, which I liked, I need someone to push my talent on the court! He had been there for going on eight months, waiting to ride out to Lebanon (a prison in southern Ohio).

We walked the yard and he gave me the game on a lot of shit! Some shit I would have probably had to learn the hard way once I got to Marion… I was glad I ran into someone who wasn't on trash who was solid like me! He never asked me for nothing! He genuinely wanted to give me the game knowing I had a stretch ahead of me…

Chapter Thirty Three:
MARION CORRECTIONAL INSTITUTION

"Sheffey, pack your shit, you ride out in the morning..." Half asleep, I hear the guard yell through door! Packing everything up, I give my bunkee the opened commissary I have because it can't go with me! I tell him to make sure my dude gets a few items and he says he will... He gives me a few envelopes to take with me in return for some of the food. The guard comes and lets me out of my cell... walking to the compound, I carry my metal box that contains everything I own! Yes, everything you own has to fit in this box because wherever you move in prison you have to be able to pack it up and move right then and there! Pictures, mail, commissary, everything had to fit and if it couldn't, then you had to send it home or trash it! Walking into the building, they walk me into a room with 21 others... we all are going to Marion!

I see orange jumpsuits again; they make us dress out again... I HATE IT HERE! ... Squat, cough! What the fuck, ima take from one prison to another prison, they trippin' I think to myself. This shit weak as fuck, not being able to do anything but get it over with, we all get dressed and they handcuff and shackle us. This time they shackle us together! Connected by a small chain from our waist we stand 2x2 this is how we sit on the "Blue Bird," the bus they drive you prison on! Imagine being shackled! Hands at your waist handcuffed to a chain around your waist! But it gets worse.... Now your shackled and chained up with another man! Shoulders touching side by side we sit on this hot musty-ass bus! Riding for three hours! This is the longest ride of my life! My ass is numb from sitting on this hard plastic bus seat!

The person I'm shackled to stinks and is asleep. I keep nudging him when he tries to fall asleep on me! I HATE IT HERE! Finally, we approach Marion! I see it from a far, barbed wire fences, two fences! Passing the yard, I see people walking, playing basketball, and working out! I scan the yard quickly! We pull in, they pull us off the bus, and we walk into a building… The guards are standing with the warden and a couple other high rank officers… they un-cuff us and unshackle us… "Follow me," the Warden says… We follow to quartermaster! (Place in prison where you go to get your prison uniforms and clothing). This is connected to the laundry room! At 20 years old, baby-faced, I had to have looked like a lost soul! Young, with a lot of time to mature and grow! We get our clothes and we change into our "blues" (prison uniform), everyone walking past, staring at us! I hear people meeting people they know! "What's up bro, how you been? Haven't seen you in years, how long you got?'

This is usually how conversations start in the joint. When I first got down to Marion, I didn't know anyone! There was no one from my city down here! And if they were then they were old heads that were old enough to be my dad! At 20 years old, I'm lost in a world I know nothing about! This isn't the streets and there's a big difference on how you move in here and how you move on the street! Confrontation is direct in prison! No sneak dissing you come correct and you stand on that shit! On the streets, people twitter beef and talk shit over the internet all day without being dealt with! For your first month or two, you have to go to an orientation pod, which was three dorm! This is the door they place the people fresh off the "Blue Bird" in… this pod helps you get use to the prison movement and after a certain amount of time, they class you out and you go into a new pod which will be your pod you stay on unless you go to the hole or you can't take the pressure and they make you kite off the block! Kiting off the block means, they pressed you for money or your food and INSTEAD OF FIGHTING FOR YOURS; you tell the guards you need to be moved to a different unit!

I learned a lot on this pod! I had a little bit of help when I was in Lorain, just from my dude explaining a few things to me! I kept what he said in the back of my mind at all times!

Chapter Thirty Four:

LIFE INSIDE

Walking into the pod, I remember just seeing bunk bed after bunk bed! 350 people jammed in one room! What the fuck is this? Mind racing! People staring at me! I can only go from what I've seen in movies, and what people have told me from their experiences... You can literally reach out and touch the next "rack" (another term for bunk beds)... so close, no privacy no personal space! 16 pods in this prison... 2,500 people... and another 500-600 out at Marion's Camp! Marion's Camp is where you go when your level gets dropped! Staying out of trouble and being involved in programs allows you to have less restrictions and more freedom! Out at the camp, you basically have free movement once "count" clears... "Count" is when you stand at your rack while the guards walk around making sure everyone is alive and accounted for! This started because someone died and the guards didn't know because at that time you didn't have to stand and count! They then changed the name to "Standing Count," this takes place at 4:30 EVERYDAY, NO MATTER WHAT! Annoying as hell! But this is their world and we put ourselves here, so we have to roll with it...

They place me on the top rack and I have an old bunkee, he's 35 years older than me... the craziest part is that I was putting my clothes away and getting my bed together when I see his I.D! Brian was his name... His birthday, January 8th, why is this important you're probably asking yourself? That's my birthday!

January 8th, 1992! I never met someone outside of my cousin who had my birthday! And definitely haven't met anyone in prison with my birthday, but what was the chance that my first bunkee in this prison had the exact birthday as me just 35 years older, he was a cool older cat and was really into god and spirituality! We talked about god a few times and he told me all the time I'm too humble and I didn't belong there. He use to tell me take my six years and learn from it so I'm not 40 years old, looking back like I should have listened! "Get an education and workout," he tells me! I take notes! I'm a walking sponge; I listen to the older humble cats' young dudes just wasting time and think everything is a joke! I'm tryna leave with a career and a lot of tattoos I joke with him... he tells me I can definitely get both of those I just need to be careful.

Later that night, my neighbor tells me it's Friday, so it's a late night, meaning the guards do a count at 9:00 then again at 11:00 and after 11:00 you can get on the phones and chill until 2:30! Normally after the 9:00 count, you have to lockdown or be at your bunk area... Late nights, when your regular guard wasn't working, meant it was gonna get wild! There was a lot going on and I just sat on my rack and watched everything! I didn't want to move until I knew what was what! This was a different movement than Lorain! I had to keep my head on a swivel, I couldn't get caught lacking and I damn sure wasn't about to be the trending topic! 8:00 rolled around and I could tell the energy had shifted! It was getting turnt every hour that passed by... my neighbor tells me after count he got something for me... confused as to what he is talking about, that's all I think about during count! They clear count and turn the lights out and I smell a strong odor! He hands me an orange juice bottle 16 oz., I ask him what it is and he says it's

"Jungle Juice" (Prison term for Hooch).

Hooch is prison wine! The smallest amount got me lit! It snuck up on me... I haven't felt this good in a minute! Still aware of my surrounding I pay attention to everything going on around me... They have music playing in the day room, people drinking foxy (jail term for an energy drink)... I ask my bunkee what a Foxy is? He goes on to explain how it is made... My neighbor over hears us talking about it and asks if I wanna make one? I say, "Fuck it, let's do it!" I ask him what I need and he tells me to bring coffee, Kool aid and a pop, and he will show me how to make one! Learning new things daily is something that never went old; I was always learning and paying attention! Even the wrong shit I wasn't supposed to see or know about I knew about and kept it to myself!

"Bring me your water jug, lil bro," my neighbor says... he opens the Kool aid, Kool aid comes in a pouch, and cost $1.50. He pours half the bag in my jug and the rest in his jug. He starts breaking down candy, jolly ranchers, and fireballs! Smashing them into little pieces, I watch and learn! Taking notes, he adds a little bit of water into a plastic cup and adds the cans covering the top he lets the candy melt into the hit water he has in the cup! Turning it into liquid and a syrup form, next he adds coffee to both of our jugs he add two spoons into my jug and three and a half spoons in his, I ask him why so much in his? He says, "I like mine strong! You might not like the strong coffee taste, so you use less coffee..."

I take that piece of information and store it with the rest of the notes I have been mentally taking down... using the pop, he adds it to the coffee and Kool aid mix! This breaks the two mixes down and it fizzes up, "Let that sit until the fizz goes down," he says, as the fizz goes down he grabs his jug tells me to grab mine and we go to the ice machine, each pod has their own ice machine! We fill the juggs up with ice and add the liquid candy that got melted down, pouring that over top of the ice... This is crazy, there is no way this can taste good but I said the same thing about the break and that shit knocked my socks off! He looks at me and says I got one more thing to set it off... He goes to his rack and comes back with a MONSTER ENERGY DRINK!

Thinking to myself how the fuck did you gets that in prison! Not asking because one thing you don't do is ask another man where he got something from.... He pours the can into both our jugs and tosses the can in the trash... we let them sit for five minutes, then shake them up! There you go lil bro now you got the game on how to make foxy!

The exact reason I kicked it with mostly older cats is that they gave you free game! They didn't expect anything in return except for you to stay focused and use what they teach you! 80 percent of the people I kicked it with were older than me and had wisdom! The other 20 percent were badass lil young cats, gang banging, stealing, fighting... doing the most! But I understood they were young minded and wanted to live their prison life to the fullest so I let them do them and when it was time to link we NEVER crossed my lane with theirs... meaning they did their dirt on their time and left me out of it! We were on the same page they knew I wasn't into the fuck shit!

The night got late and the Hooch started hitting people differently... Some people got too lit and passed out, others turned up and drank more, me... I noticed I was getting too lit and took my ass to my rack and sat down, my bunkee had extra headphones so he let me plug up and he was old school, so he passed out early leaving the TV for me to watch! "The Block" was a TV station that played all rap and r&b songs... they took this station out later on! Music kept me sane in prison! I could easily zone out and block people out! I could easily reminisce about being on the streets and having fun, missing my family I would sometimes get inside of my head and think about them... looking over my pictures trying to remember my family was hard as hell! I missed them so much and there was nothing I could do to see them!

I've only seen my family ONCE out of my whole stay in prison! It was my fault though... I didn't blame them for not coming my mother had four more kids she had to raise! What type of man would I be to tell her come see me 3 hours away when she had 4 other kids looking up to her for guidance and direction! I was never cut like that to be selfish! I'm here now! I need to man up and handle what's on my plate! That's what ran through my head constantly.... ONE DAY CLOSER!

Music playing, I close my eyes! The food and Foxy has my stomach rumbling... I go to the bathroom and try to get myself right... There is no privacy! What is privacy anymore... The guards watch you get naked and squat in front of them... the showers are wide open with four water spouts on each side, toilets lined next to each other with no stalls or dividers... NO PRIVACY! But that's what happens when you put yourself in jail, you can't blame anyone but yourself! I take my spare shower shoes these are what we used to sit on the toilet! Instead of putting toilet paper down and making a birds nest we put the shower shoes down and sit on them, this was a way of not sitting your ass on a toilet where people piss...

20 years old I can only go off experience and what I've seen in movies! I remember all the jail movies and what happened! I tell myself I won't be a victim! I'll die in here before they play me like that ... that was my mentality from the jump! Shut that shit down from the jump, my dad's phone call plays repeatedly in my head... Never let anyone play you like a bitch or take anything from you! I stood on that shit and it worked for me!

I'm the only one in this bathroom! Nobody else, just me! I think for a second I get a little privacy as I think to myself and try to get my stomach together... Then it happens...

Two people bust in the bathroom, I immediately pull my pants up as I stand up to get ready to fight! Mind racing a million thoughts a second! Fighting is the only option in this position there is no talking!

One white guy and one black guy walk in... Both grown, middle to late 30s, then there's me 160 pounds, skin and bones, baby face... I'm ready to take it wherever it has to go I can't go out like that... Then they turn and face each other and "NY" the black guy starts talking to the white guy... "So I'm a nigger huh, you get that hooch in you and forget who you're talking to... ima show you a nigger!" I pull my pants all the way up now not even wiping my ass! I'll be damn if I bend over and wipe my ass during this moment that shit can wait idk what's about to happen but I'm in the middle of a serious situation!

Both of them have been drinking and now one of them has to get dealt with... They both put their hands up to fight, NY obviously comfortable in this situation connects first... Flesh to Flesh, he hits him. Smack, Smack, two jabs and the white hit stumbles back, NY pushes him into the corner of the bathroom up against the urinal!

The white guy tries to cover up but it's not working, NY furious throws a combination of punches, and to my surprise he is landing them... ALL OF THEM! Flurries, you can tell this isn't his first fight in prison! The last punch he throws is an uppercut and connects smoothly! My mind still racing I'm up close in personal on my first night in prison! *Is someone going to jump in and help this guy or are they going to just let them get the fair fight!*

The white guys head bounces up and hits the wall from the uppercut, they grab each other up, and NY slams what seems like the life out of this man! I heard his head hit the concrete floor... *Smack!* I thought for sure the fight was over... Standing over top of him now NY proceeds to punch him repeatedly... if I could say NY missed a punch it was very few, all his hits were accurate and on point! Smacking his fist off this man's flesh, I watch as he pounds away... talking to him NY repeats himself... I got your nigger right here! Bitch! Bitch! Smack, Smack the force is shocking but what happens next blows my mind; I'VE NEVER SEEN THIS HAPPEN IN PERSON!

He connects on a mean jab right down the pipe and I hear the white guy say... "OK, OK, I'm done!" NY says "nah bitch you done when I say it's over"! He then connects with a thunderous punch I hear it! This was one of the hardest hits of the fight! The white guy goes out cold! Laying there not moving! I think for a split second he might be dead and I might gotta run up out of here so I don't get in trouble for this dead body!

But then NY hits him again and wakes him back up! Trying to do everything in his power to get him to stop NY hits, him two more times, then kicks him in the face on the way out... How were they able to fight for so long? It seemed like they fought forever! But how did they get it off when the C.O's desk is stationed right by the bathroom, I know it was loud in there... All you heard was Flesh smacking Flesh, Sneakers squeaking on the floor and NY talking to his victim as he made his point!

Immediately, he walks out of the bathroom and I watch as the white guy slowly gets off the ground and cleans himself up... wondering if he felt embarrassed, I stand there and watch, still drunk he limps out of the bathroom! In my mind, I'm thinking, *Damn, shit just got real quick!* Crazy how people can go from having fun to fighting in a split second! After they leave, I get myself together and get up out of the bathroom as quick as possible... I get back on my rack and don't say anything, NEVER SPEAK ON WHAT YOU SEE! A motto I stood on... in prison you mind your business and keep your mouth closed if not that shit then becomes your problem and now you find yourself in a fucked up position... so many times I've seen shit I couldn't speak on, even when asked what happened I said I didn't know or wasn't paying attention! This was something I learned from day one!

After that fight, me and NY became close, he knew I was solid and could have easily told on them if I was built like that... but I kept my mouth closed and they never got caught for that fight! He came to me later on and told me I was a solid young dude for that and from that day on, we had a mutual respect for each other! Later on, he would always joke around saying... "Remember when I fucked that dude up for calling me a nigger"... I would always laugh and say, "Yeah, I remember!"

Later that night tension was still high on the pod! There were many gangs on this pod! Bloods, crips, gd's, Aryan brothers, Felons, Latin Kings... Every gang I've seen in movies or on the shows I watched about prison was here! The bloods were trying to recruit me from jump! I have a red start tattoo on my chest and that's a green light for them, they im-mediately asked me where I was from and if I was Piru! I said no and told them where I was from! Their next question... You wanna get put down? Meaning did I want to join their gang! Only one way in and out of a gang in prison! You get jumped in and you get jumped out! I'll be like damn, if

I let three people jump me just to take orders from someone… that's not my style at all… I simply told them no I'm good! They were shocked; I was 20 years old with no gang behind me or no city behind me! My city was irrelevant down here, Cleveland and Columbus had the compound on lock at this time!

Gangs didn't read to me because I always felt like they were just taking orders and being sent on missions! There was no structure! There was no loyalty! And they weren't organized enough to even be making money moves! Not only that I'm 20 years old if I haven't joined a gang by now I will never join one and that's what I stood on! My whole six years, I never joined a gang! Everyone I knew or associated with was in a gang outside of the few older cats I kicked it with! I knew so many people in gangs and associated with them I ended up getting a gang tag! But these were people I grew with in prison! People I ate with and played basketball with! I wasn't going to stop kicking it with them because they were in a gang! That just meant to me that when it was time for them to get with their gang I went one way and they went another!

Racks moving I hear the bed scrape the concrete and make a loud screeching sound! Sneakers squeaking! Then I see it! Two bloods fighting each other! I'm confused for a second! Why are they fighting each other if they are in the same gang? Rico was a laid-back dude always laughing and cracking jokes, until you flipped his switch! Then it was on the floor he was all in! Another member who always would tell me, "Come on home! You got the tats you might as well become a blood!" They were drunk off the hooch just like the first fight I've seen… Everyone saw this fight, they fought twice… at the rack, they were fighting over bed space!

Rico told the other guy to stop moving his bed over, he said he knew he moved his bed because he marked it on the floor where his bed was before and now it's not on the spot he had marked! "This my 2nd time saying this!" I'm not gonna say it again… The other guy got up and walked up on Rico and that was that! Rico hit him twice and body slammed him…

Get your bitch ass in this bathroom so we can really work! Rico started heading towards the bathroom passing my rack I can feel the tension! I can see the other guy slowly following behind Rico... All you hear is sneakers squeaking on the floor! And flesh against flesh! Then you hear the loudspeaker saying "Signal 3, 3 dorm"...

Whenever a fight happened, the guards would hit their button, on their walkie talkies, this would send a message to the front desk, and they would relay the message over the loud speaker... Signal 3 meant a fight and then they would add the dorm number or letter, depending on where the fight was... the loudspeaker saying signal 3 would let any free guards know that a guard needed help controlling their pod! They called this the "Man-down button." When I first got to Marion. That's all you heard every 30 minutes, it felt like...

Fighting in the bathroom for a minute next, you see guards rush in and turn the lights on! Everyone on your racks they yell! Removing them from the bathroom the first person is Rico... two guards have him cuffed up and he is limping... idk how he messed his leg up, but he ended up needing crutches... the next guy comes out and is leaking blood! Shirt ripped he looks bad! It's obvious who won the fight! 15 Days in the hole "O block!" That's what you got as punishment if caught fighting!

My first night was one I would never forget! All this happened so quickly, it was crazy to see how quickly things could escalate... and prison hooch had everyone fucked up like it was Patron or Hennessy!

Chapter Thirty Five:
O'BLOCK

April 2011 was when I got to Marion, that summer was crazy! 2011 and 2012 were probably the worst years being in this prison... After 2012, they started riding people out to other prisons... whole gangs where getting rode out... if you had a gang tag you were riding out... this was their way of cleaning the prison up! My first summer, I didn't play basketball or take working out serious! I had six years to do the fuck I look like working out my whole six years I'm 20 years old at the time.. I wanted to kick it! Get drunk, smoke weed and get tatted! And that's EXACTLY what I did!

Two things I promised myself I would do is to get an education or degree of some type and get a lot more tats... Before I went to prison, I had tattoos but nowhere near, what I had when I walked out those prison gates in 2017! I was getting tatted every other week until they sent me out to the camp in 2014... Chino was my very first tat man! He slept next to me and once I figured out, he was shooting tats it was over with... Commissary was what we used to pay for the tats... he would make a list of what he wanted from the store to add up to how much the tat would cost... If the tat costs $25, he made a store list for $25 and when I went to the store, he got his money! Good business or no business was and still is my motto! Some of the most creative and talented people are in prison and I don't care what anyone says! Some of the best tattoo work I've ever seen in my life was on the inside! Some of the best athletes I've ever seen in person was inside those prison walls! The creativity blew my mind every time...

Making a tat gun, I sat and watched this man take a CD player and break it down to make a tattoo motor! Taking a guitar string, sharpening it on a fan, and using it for a tattoo needle! Cut a pen down and rubber band it to the motor, sliding the guitar string through the pen and attaching it to the motor and plugging the adapter to the motor, we now have a fully functioning tattoo gun! My mind is blown as I watch Chino prep the gun and my design; we used parchment paper from the chow hall and clear deodorant to set the design on my skin! The deodorant rubbed against the paper made the ink from the design stick to my skin so he could do the outline! Brilliant if you ask me! Creative as hell!

Chino was a Latin King and also tried to recruit me after weeks of getting to know each other he said I was different I moved different then the other young dudes my age! I declined of course and he respected that even more… If you ever want to join an organization fuck with the kings, he told me! We take care of ours, and we are loyal to those who are loyal to us! He wasn't lying tho, and I respected it! The Latin's were the ONLY GANG I've personally seen from experience who weren't out to get their race from the jump!

If you crossed, the Latin's then you were ass out you never could get their loyalty again! I stayed on their good side! It's sad because I watched and observed everything… Blacks stole from each other daily! If you had something they wanted, they would try to take it! If you were in a better position than them, they hated it and wanted to either fight you or take what you had… Latins were the total opposite! They wanted their people to be in position! They gave their people shoes and food if they didn't have any! Rarely did I see a Latin steal! Blacks, I've seen it with my own eyes, gang members stealing from their own gang! You tell me where the LOYALTY is? Because I sure was, paying attention and I was damn sure knew there was NO LOYALTY in gangs! How can I put my life and freedom on the line for someone who will steal from me when I'm not looking!

Tattoos are cheap inside prison, they were also illegal, meaning if you got caught, you went to the hole and had to pay $150 for a HIV test in medical! So getting caught wasn't an option for me, NEVER GOT CAUGHT! We used a "6-5," meaning a lookout to let us know when the guard was coming, so we didn't get caught! Some guards didn't care, they just wanted to do their eight-hour shift and go home to their families! "As long as y'all not KILLING EACH OTHER OR FUCKING, I DONT CARE," one of our guards uses to say!

His shift was smooth, and we kicked it when he worked! A lot of guards had families to make it home to and that was their main goal! I respected those guards; the guards I didn't respect were the dick heads! The ones who made our lives hell because they could! The ones who would tear our racks up and make us put them back together for no reason! The ones who wouldn't let us get out to rec on time! And the ones who just talked to you crazy because they had a badge and some pepper spray! Those were the guards who I looked at differently, but those guards were all over there was a handful that let us have our way!

That tattoo needle hitting my skin was exactly what I needed! All the stress I had on my shoulders in that moment went away, zoning out I just relaxed and let the needle take my stress away! "Trip" was my tat man after Chino went to the hole! Trip was also a Latin King and was real laid back, always about his money and doing good business! He did a few of my tats and then they moved me to another dorm! Moving dorms was bullshit! I hated it! You had to pack all your shit up… Undo your sheets and blankets fold them, take them to your next dorm, and re-make your bed! Then you had to get use to another pod, different vibes! Each pod was different and needed time to get use to! I always was quiet and stayed to myself, only talked to people when they talked to me for the most part! I hated moving pods because I didn't trust people especially after seeing people steal from their own race or people, they said they would die for!

When I moved, I went to B dorm, which was a pod that was upstairs! Meaning I had to carry this heavy ass box up two flights of stairs then come back down to get my clothes and bedding! B dorm was sweet!

Wasn't too many fights but it's prison so of course shit happened! 300 men in one area, of course, people are going to disagree and fight! But I became cool with a handful of people and everyone on the block saw me as laid back and down to earth! My group I kicked it with was Twin, Poncho, and Damo! There were others I "associated" with, meaning we might have played cards or talked but we weren't "cool" or we didn't eat together! Poncho was my older cat he was late 40's but had a lot of game to give up and I soaked it all up! Twin was my age and I was locked up with his Brother in the county! His twin! Thus, the reason they are nicknamed Twin!

Damo was my dude I hooped with! We beefed on that court and he was nice with the basketball! Young and aggressive! But calm until you flipped his switch! We all ate together and saw eye to eye! Never once did we fall out about some simple shit or dumb shit! Whenever it was time to cook we all put in and did our part! We took turns cooking and cleaning, but we all brought food to the table and that's what I respected!

I didn't have the most money, but I had money when my people could send it in to me! I hated asking for money, so I rarely did it! I just always felt like this was supposed to be a punishment! How could it be a punishment if I was getting visits regularly or if my mom was putting money on my books every week! That's a vacation NOT A PUNISHMENT! I needed those hunger pains and that struggle to make me the SOLID MAN I am today! My father let me know from jump he wasn't sending money but every year on my birthday him and Maureen would send me a "Food Box."

A food box was something you could only get two times a year unless you had someone else order you one in their name. Many times, people who had money would find people who didn't use their two food boxes a year and would pay them to let them use their boxes. So if I didn't use my boxes, I could sell one and make money that way or I could give them a list of food box items in exchange for them using my extra boxes! Everything was a hustle in prison! If you had no Hustle, then you wouldn't eat or survive! Or you would be calling home begging for your peoples to send you money! Me... I didn't do the begging shit, if I didn't have it I went and got it! Or I went without!

Everything was going good money wise! My mom sent money when she could and I hustled when she couldn't! I knew how to cook by my second and third month in prison. I caught on early and if I didn't eat with the people I cooked with then I ate by myself! So the repetition turned me into a beast on the cook side! People started asking me to cook, either they paid me, or I got a bowl of whatever I cooked! Sometimes, I didn't need to use my food because I would just cook and get a bowl for payment! Another hustle I adopted early on! But one day something happened and it changed the whole COMPOUND! Everyone was affected!

When I first got to Marion, anyone could put money on your books! Didn't need to be on your visiting list they just needed your name and number! A lot of junkies were affected by this and were calling home to pay their people they owed money to! Just like the streets, people don't play about their money! Extortion was heavy in prison! I see it all first hand; I didn't understand how someone was willing to pay someone to "protect" them! Why not fight, win or lose, you keep your money and you're respected! I see so many people go to the store just to give away their commissary to their "protection", shit made me sick to my stomach to hear them call home and beg their people to send such and such money!

Their families sending hard earned money in to these dudes just so they can give it to someone else! Once again, WHATS NOT YOUR BUSINESS IS NOT YOUR BUSINESS... *Stay focused*, I told myself! The prison changed the money rules! You now had to be on someone's approved visitation list to send them money! No more sending money freely... This made it a lot harder for people to pay others, which in turn made people more aggressive when it came time to collect! People who couldn't pay either doubled up their payment on the next store day or "checked in"... Checking in meant they went to the guards and said they couldn't be on the compound anymore and they would then go to the hole and wait to ride out to another prison! This was also called a "PC" move... Protective Custody!

Drugs were all through the prison, anything you could get on the streets you could get in here... ANYTHING! You name it then it was in there... Tobacco was a high commodity in Marion! Flipping your money with tobacco was too easy! Two fingers worth of tobacco ran you 50 dollars! And sometimes more than that, depending if it was a drought or not! I know you're wondering what I mean by two fingers... Put your hand sideways in the air and hold two fingers out imaging that amount filled in a plastic baggie... That's $50 dollars! A pack of cigarettes on the street costs six dollars you do the math! Half of a pack would equal more than two fingers in a bag! They loved the tobacco, they were fiends for it! Sending how much too wherever you needed it to go! Weed was another high commodity! Depending on who you got it from or if it was a drought or not also depended, how much you would spend!

A basic limb was five to eight dollars, that's one joint! A $50 of weed was a 20 oz. pop cap filled! Some people finessed and sold a Chap Stick cap for $50! The hustle was wide open when I got down to Marion! Everyone had their hand in something! Loud sold differently! $100 a gram or $100 a pop cap as it was sold inside! Think about it! A gram on the streets is $10-15 at this time and people are finessing $10 into $100! That's just one gram!

I've literally seen people get rich off these two hustles alone! Hustling was necessary for some; not everyone had a support system. A lot of people burned their bridges before they went to prison and others just simply didn't give a fuck unless you were on the streets... OUTTA SIGHT, OUTTA MIND! Meaning when you were home, it was all love and people would be happy for you, but when you get locked away and you're not, physically, there they don't give a fuck! They don't check on you unless you reach out to them! They don't send you money even if you asked! Another reason I never asked people outside of my family! One thing I hated was someone saying they would do something for me then NEVER showing up! I would rather you keep it real and say you can't do it!

With the rules, changing things got crazy! Stealing was at an all-time high! And hustling was right behind it, if you weren't stealing you were hustling and if you weren't hustling you were broke! Simple!

Then they dropped another rule that really affected everyone probably more than the Money Rule changes! They swiped everyone's accounts! If you owed court cost and had money on your books at the time they took it ALL! Not taking half, ALL OF YOUR MONEY WAS GONE! Was this legal? How can they do this? Going to the store a lot of people started flipping out about this situation we were going through! I had literally just received money from my mom, I was sick to my stomach when the courts played me like this! I didn't understand what was going on and I received a letter in the mail the next day saying I owed $800 in court cost!

They just took $200... I'm not giving them $800 in court cost and doing six years fuck that they got me fucked up, and I have to be on PAROLE FOR five years when I get out! This can't be right! A lot of older dudes who been down a while were heavy into legal work! Some of these dudes were fighting appeals! Some knew loopholes to get your time reduced! And some were fighting for their life, not guilty or guilty that was their business but one thing I know for sure is someone can help me figure this out! I talked to my legal guy John and he gave me the run down on what the courts were doing! Yes it's legal, is it fair? Hell no... But you're in prison so we have to figure it out ourselves.

Another good dude dropping knowledge on me! He gave me two options! File a motion to give the courts $4 a month but I can receive outside money from my family or pay the $800! I replied I'm not giving them that money they got me fucked up! He says I agree, so I went and bought a copy card from commissary with my "STATE PAY." State Pay was $20 starting for me! $20 a month they gave you to buy hygiene and food! Imagine surviving off $20 a month! A grown as man trying to make it happen with $20! That's not even it tho, after I filed the motion I was only left with $15 remember they take $4 out of my state pay but now I can receive outside money! $15 a month I had to work with some months! Like I said, I hated asking people for money! Especially my mother who had four others to look after and help! I just always felt like deep down I couldn't ask like I wanted to! Of course, I wanted to eat every night and have a box full of food but I had to figure out how to do that without being a burden on my family! So I did! I made my way and Hustled Hard so I could survive!

I'll NEVER forget the first time I walked into the gym! There had to be at least 500 people packed into this gym room! Walking in, they had a game of basketball going on, half of the gym long ways they had two hoops so they were running full court! A ping pong table in the middle of the court separated the other side where they played basketball half court! Four sets of pull up bars lined along the wall! One set of bleachers for each basketball court! And a weight cage! I watched some of the most talented basketball players I've ever seen in person play basketball! The talent was pure! The full court was the better players and the smaller court was for the ones who couldn't get picked up or weren't as good! You had to show up and show out to get picked up! These games were intense! Arguing and shit talking was common, fouls and blood were common! Prison basketball at its finest! "Quit crying and play ball with your bitch ass," I hear one player say!

"Nigga, you fouling like fuck, learn how to play D," the other player says as they go at it on the court! My heart was pounding and I wasn't even in the game, I could just feel the energy! I could feel the tension! The weight cage had a nice amount of machines... weight benches, pulley machines, and curl machines... pretty much all the standard gym machines! They only let 20 people in at a time and you had to place your prison I.D in a bucket that would be collected by the guards on your way in. They did this so they could keep track of how many times a week you went in the cage, you were only allowed to go in the cage three days a week! This specific day, I wanted to venture around and I went inside the cage! Minding my own business not talking to anyone, I started looking around the cage and jumping on different machines! Just testing my strength and seeing how much I could lift, I go to the pulley machine and work on my arms! Not serious I keep moving the weight and look at myself in the mirror that faces me as I lift the weight! They have music playing on a loud speaker! But something isn't right I hear a group of people talking but they sound different...

What the fuck I know I'm not trippin'... I look to my left and outside of the cage, I see it! A group of MEN, dressed with their shirts tucked inside out and wearing high shorts... Lips red, I'm confused and sick to my stomach at what I am seeing! This shit scarred me for life! Nobody wants to have a visual like that stuck in their head; nobody wants to remember that type of shit! Their voices hi-pitched and trying to talk like females, I immediately stop working out! At 20 years old, I had never experienced someone trying so hard to be a female! Being gay was around when I was on the street, but I could avoid it or it wasn't really in my face... but here it's everywhere! This is their home!

They are comfortable here and NOBODY says shit to them! If you fought someone gay and lost, you were the talk of the compound, and that would stay with you even when you went home people would say, "Hey, didn't you get your ass beat in the joint by a gay man!" Them talking and standing there wasn't even the worst part tho... they were trying to "twerk" to the music being played! I HATE IT HERE!

I rushed out of the cage and walked outside! I need air I need to get away! I'm stuck in here for six years around this shit EVERYDAY! What the fuck was going on, they had to be sick in the head to actually think they were females! Wearing red Kool aid on their lips as lipstick! I can't believe I've just seen that I tell myself as my mind races and I walk the yard alone! Clinching my jaws, I'm so mad, they didn't say or do anything to me specifically so why am I so mad? Why am I here? I need to get out of here... I HATE IT HERE!

Walking the yard was a daily thing for me, I needed the fresh air, and I needed to get away from everyone! Peace of mind was something I NEEDED! Something that was important for me to keep my sanity! This yard was big as hell, nothing like Lorain. One lap around the track was a mile! Everyone was on the yard, especially during the summer time! Walking the yard was TMZ, every day I've seen something new! Two big softball fields! Three full court basketball courts! Two Handball Courts! A full field used for soccer! Two separate sections used for working out on separate ends of the yard! Each workout section had multiple pull up bars! Each pull up bar had a dip bar and pushups section connected to them!

This was my favorite workout to do! I could work out by myself and not have to talk to anyone! Just in my zone! Gang fights happened all the time! The "backwall" was where it went down! Any gang initiation took place on the back wall; the back wall was the handball court... Getting into a gang meant you had to get jumped in... Two or three on one... you fight until the leader feels like it is enough! They didn't want any weak members, so this was their way of testing you! I watched plenty of these initiations take place! Cameras couldn't see these spots behind the back wall, it was a blind spot! So a lot of these fights and initiations didn't get caught! There was a patrol car that roamed around the prison to make sure no one threw any drugs or phones over the fence! If it were to happen and someone was to throw something over the fence, they would lock the yard down and search everyone until the contraband was found!

I walked the yard alone many days! I was used to being by myself, NO GANG! NO GROUP OF "friends" … of course, I had people I occasionally walked with if we worked out together or if they weren't handling gang business then we would link! Everyone I was in the Cleveland County with ended up coming down to Marion, and they all were in a gang! This is the reason I ended up getting a gang tag for being affiliated with gang members… but at 20 years old in an environment I knew NOBODY who did they think I would kick it with? Of course, in my free time I kicked it and played basketball with the people I knew! The guards would see me walking with them and automatically assumed I was associated with the gang!

You can sense the tension in the air! My heartbeat immediately starts pounding as I'm in the gym, I watch everything go down! I put my back against the closest wall, making sure no one can sneak behind me or sucker punch me! I've seen it happen too many times, someone in the middle of a gang fight gets knocked out for being in the way or mistaken for a rival gang member! Once the doors shut in the gym, they don't get opened until rec is over! 300 people in this little ass gym all split up into separate sections! Most people have no clue as to what is going on! I'm very aware of my surroundings, head on a swivel I watch everyone around me! I only trust myself because I know at the end of the day I got my back! This particular day Akron and Cleveland are butting heads! Some shit happened on the yard and it spilled over into the gym the following day! I'm up and close in this particular fight because I was sittin' with my Cleveland people! I had a few people from Akron I rocked with and they both know I'm neutral in this fight! They know when it comes to city beef and gang beef I don't mix in! I stay in my lane and let them handle what they need to handle! The energy is raw and tension is high! It gets almost dead silent! I zone in on what I see! The guards can sense it they stand up in their booth where they can see the whole gym! And then it happens…

They clash right there in the gym! No sneaking around, No going in the bathroom to settle this beef! Right on sight! Cleveland runs up on Akron and they get it cracking! Everyone is fighting at least 10 on 10. I counted! My back against the wall still watching over both shoulders I stand there and watch! People are getting jumped and running after other people in the gym! SIGNAL three RECREATION! SIGNAL three RECREATION! I hear the loud speaker go off! I hear the flesh-on-flesh contact! I see people getting slammed! Another guy is getting jumped on the bleachers and is doing his best to fight these three rivals off! His homie comes and hits one knocking him out cold! In my head, I think, *Damn, this shit is crazy*, exciting and I don't know why! I'm watching as everyone is scrambling as five guards come in and lock the doors behind them! Fuck, I already know what's coming next!

The guards run in and take out there pepper spray I immediately pull my shirt over my face and run to the nearest door that faces outside. There were three doors that had gates connected so air could come into the gym for ventilation! Black metal gates locked from inside and out, with another door outside that would remain open during rec periods! The smell of the pepper spray stung my nostrils! Chest immediately burning I can't help but cough, which is intensifying the smell and burn! The guards round up and cuff the people in the fight and lock the gym down! They had to review the cameras in the gym to make sure they got everyone involved and nobody was able to leave until then! Stuck in this gym filled with pepper spray, I can't help but cough and choke as the smell chokes me out! Standing by the door I catch a break others not so lucky, vomiting they can't take the smell and the pain is unbearable… they tap out and are rushed to medical! After they check cameras they line is up and do a hand check! This is where they go person by person to see if anyone had blood or cuts on their hands, this indicates that you obviously were fighting! An hour passes by and they finally clear us to go back to our pods! I just had to be in the gym when this popped off I think to myself…

B dorm was laid back, a lot of older dudes who didn't tolerate stealing! There was one person who if he found out you were disturbing the peace of fucking the vibe up on the pod would get you out of there just as quick as you got there! These older dudes moved different and they didn't care if you were younger or could whoop their ass, they would get back there with you, and after the loss, they would get you off the pod and moved to another pod! These older dudes had been on this same pod for years! All the guards know they and they built a bond from the years of being around each other...

Snitches and pedophiles had it the worst in prison! Which they should! Anyone who can touch a kid or child is sick in the head and needs to be dealt with! And they did, a lot of times they would do funny shit while they were asleep. Dumping ice-cold buckets of water on them and then smacking them with baby powder socks! Multiple people just blasting them as hard as they can with the powder socks! All you see is clouds of powder and the guy struggling to see what is going on in shock from the ice-cold water only to be blasted by multiple people with powder socks! Funniest shit I've probably seen! I had no RESPECT OR REMORSE for how these people got treated! Nothing worse than a pedophile or a snitch! Lowest people on the earth!

Extortion was heavy in this prison! I've seen ALOT of people get extorted! Multiple ways, it amazed me how slick these people were and how they would finesse someone into sending them money without getting in trouble for so long! FEAR is what these people lived off, they sensed a drop of fear in you, or your body language and that was that! People going to commissary only to give their food away to someone else! Why not just fight? Win or Loss you keep your respect and you're good! Putting someone under their "wing" was a term you heard a lot on this compound! This term meant someone was too scared to stand on their own two feet like a man so they run to a gang and PAY FOR PROTECTION! Once that gang had you then you would owe them money or drugs or whatever they wanted! They OWNED you after pulling a move like that! I saw often times, two gangs work together to extort someone! Making him pay twice so each gang still got paid!

This was gang's favorite move! It was easier than stealing or taking from someone! This was smooth and successful! Commissary was one thing but some gangs took it a step further and would make the person they put under their wing send money home! Money orders and Western Unions were the golden ticket! There was no stopping it and there was no faking it! The money had to be there or there were repercussions!

Chapter Thirty Six:
23-1

Smoking, drinking, and tattoos became a regular for me! I had six years to do so in my eyes I was going to kick it my first three and then handle business my last three! And that's what I did... Hooch was coming off every couple of days! This was another hustle I learned and stuck with! Hooch was made from letting orange juice, sugar, and fruit spoil! Once the orange juice and fruit mix the bacteria mixed with the sugar turns it into wine! Two bottles of this wine would put the biggest dude down! Took me one bottle to feel it and two bottles I would be having a great night! Five dollars a bottle for a quart jug, this hustle saved me many times! I hated asking for money so in my eyes I needed to have my hands in multiple lanes and multiple hustles and that's what I did! Sugar costs $1.85 and everything else we got from the "chow hall" aka, the cafeteria.

I had a plug in this kitchen so getting food or supplies was easy! Me and my older dude, Poncho, went in on this hustle and we split the money! Of course, there was risk and consequences if you got caught! We rotated holding the hooch in our locker boxes. I could have easily paid someone to hold it but then there's the risk of them getting caught and telling on me or wanting half of what I had going on and at that time, this was a no no! I needed all my money!

There was a close call one morning... I woke up to the smell of alcohol! I immediately jumped up and two of my bottles spilled over and busted open! The whole area I was living in smelled of alcohol! I smacked my dude Poncho's rack and woke him up ASAP! "Get up, help me, clean this shit up real quick bro..."

We both jump up I run and grab the mop bucket and some chemicals to clean my area! He grabs bleach he got from his laundry guy and sets up his smell good spray so when we are done we can spray our area with the air freshener... we had to be quick! Every 30 minutes to 45 minutes, the guard would make a round and walk through the pod to make sure everyone was OK or not doing anything illegal... count time in five minutes, I hear him say loudly as everyone heads back to their racks! Cleaning still, Poncho and I hurry up! Heart beating out my chest if they even smell a hint of hooch they are going to tear my area apart and find it... Then I lose money and I go to "O-Block" aka the hole...

We finish up and the guard starts count! Spraying the smell good, I hope he doesn't smell the hooch over the scent I keep spraying... he makes it to my side of the pod and stops...Dead in his tracks... Eyes glued to my TV, I don't budge... I just watch the TV feeling the guard's presence close to me he taps my rack and says hand me those spray bottles they need to be turned in before I can count! Fuck! Heart about jump through my throat I hand him the bottles quickly so he can leave... Close fucking call!

I wasn't so lucky a month later! October 2012 was a cold month! Not because of the weather but because of where I was headed...

I honestly feel like I got caught lacking... Became too comfortable with people around me and how I was moving! I was selling a lot of hooch and was just in the moment! Eating good, hustling became a habit for me! I was addicted to the process of making hooch and then getting rid of it! Every batch that came off sold out ASAP because it was fire ass hooch and people were scared to take a chance on making it so it was easier for them to just buy it with no consequences... this was how I ate tho and in my head, I'm already in prison what else could they do? Little did I know they had a spot just for me...

I had a batch of hooch cooking with my dude poncho, it was going to come off on Friday, and it was football season, so everyone was waiting! What's better than getting drunk and watching football! Shit, I do that in the real world! People placed their orders early and we let them know it was cash on delivery we weren't taking pre payments because one thing I learned is; once you take money from someone you owe them now! And I hated owing people money! Thursday night we checked it and made sure everything was going good and we were on track for the next day to pull it off! Poncho pulled out a cup so we could taste it to make sure it was legit and it was! As soon as it hit my stomach, I could feel the burn! I looked at him and he looked at me and I said yeah it's going tomorrow!

We closed the box up and gathered all the bottles we could find! Three gallons worth of hooch! Easy $60 from something we paid under $10 for... Profit is what I looked for I didn't care about people asking for deals or any of that because at the end of the day, this was how I ate and nobody else was putting food in my locker box! I put my headphones on and went to sleep listening to Jeezy Tm: 103, I loved this CD and it always got my mind thinking! Reminiscing about the streets, money, and girls, I finally pass out! Only to wake up to the worst feeling! Shakedown!

Guards everywhere! But only on my side of the pod! They know there is hooch in my area they just don't know which rack it is at! All I hear is walkie-talkies going off as I wake up! Wiping my eyes, I can't believe what is happening right now! My heart is on the floor right now, how did they know? Better yet, who told them? Someone had to have said something! There's no way this is a random shakedown! In disbelief, there's nothing I can do! I can't move the hooch there are guards tearing people's racks up in the front of me and a rack down! The only way is to walk it past them and there's no way I can do that! They come to my rack and pull my locker box out! They open it and I know it's over!

The guard looks at me and says this yours as he pulls out the three gallons of orange potent hooch! I look at poncho and he puts his head down! I say yeah it's mine and I stand up! Turn around and cuff up!

He tells the other guards they found it! And they walk me out of the pod in handcuffs! The walk of shame I called it! Head down, I couldn't do anything but shake my head as they take me to the hole…

Chapter Thirty Seven:
GANGLAND

Every Pod was called a dorm, if you were in a pod, it was open range, meaning there were no cells it was just an open dorm with racks everywhere! The pods with cells were called cellblocks! Meaning there was no racks out in the open there was all cells! Some people preferred cells over dorms because there was more privacy and you didn't have to deal with everyone... I personally grew to favor cellblocks over dorms, most likely from being in a cell for so long! Dorms were wide open; anyone could see what you were into. Anyone could see what you had! In a cellblock the only person you had to worry about was your bunkee, other than that you could keep your business to yourself! I learned a lot being in the cellblocks a lot helped me and a lot of shit scarred me for life! Not from anything happening to me personally more so what others were, doing around me... fucked me up mentally! Why did I witness the fucked up shit! Why me?

O Block was the hole! 23 hours in your cell and one hour of recreation! The guards rotated showering, one day the top range went then the next the bottom range went! There was no showering when you wanted to! There was no showering every day! I always been a clean person and my mother and father always taught me to keep up with my hygiene! So this bothered me, not being able to shower when I wanted to or needed to!

Walking up to the hole to see cages! Nothing but cages! Where they fuck, are they taking me! This visual is so raw and uncut it's insane... walking in there is a small holding cell with a separate door locked and has two people inside. This holding cell was one of the two cells they called "ice"... you got put on ice for small trouble, this was an adult timeout! You were only placed on ice for hours not days! Once they let you off ice then you would go back to you dorm or cell block! One shower downstairs and one shower up stairs! Both showers had metal bar doors so once you were locked in you couldn't get back out! 10-minute showers! Cell by cell they would handcuff you and escort you and your bunkee to the shower!

Guard's desk sat in the front of the hole across from the downstairs shower! A "control booth" was stationed in the front of the hole as well! The control booth is exactly what its name is… this booth controlled EVERYTHING! All doors opened manually with keys carried by the guards or electronically by the control booth! The guards would walkie-talkie time the booth and tell them open a door and a guard in the control booth would hit a button and that cell door would open… Two SUICIDAL rooms were located next to the control booth so they could watch them closely!

These suicide rooms they called "SUICIDE WATCH," meaning there was either a guard sitting outside your cell making sure you weren't doing anything to hurt yourself and they also had cameras watching to make sure when a guard wasn't there that they could monitor you so you couldn't kill yourself! They made people who went on suicide watch wear an outfit called a "turtle suit," they called this outfit turtle suit because how it made you look! It was green and a Velcro outfit! One size fits all! It looked like a green Velcro dress! I always wondered how people could do that! How could they want to just kill themselves. I didn't understand!

The next cell closest to the suicide watch room was the room they used to get drugs out of you! If you were caught in a visit, trying to smuggle drugs in they would place you in this room and monitor your shit! Yes, they would make you stay in this room and wait for you to use the bathroom and wouldn't allow your toilet to flush! As soon as you used the bathroom, they would take you out of the room and search through your shit to find the drugs! Sick! I HATE IT HERE!

65 cells in total! In 2012, this cellblock was packed! They were filled to capacity, people who got in trouble ended up having to wait sometimes because there was no room! Sometimes, they let people out early for less serious trouble! This freeing room up for those who needed to be put back there!

Open cell 23, I hear the guard walkie-talkie to the control booth! The heavy metal door slides open! It's loud in the hole! People banging on their doors! People rapping! People yelling through their doors to people they know in other cells! I walk in and toss my things on my rack. Only thing I had at this time was what they gave me upon entering O block! One towel, one wash cloth, one tooth brush, one hard plastic cup, one roll of toilet paper, and a generic bar of soap! The soap was only good for a weeks' worth of showering! We didn't shower every day, so once a week, we would have to ask for another bar of soap! A small skinny window is the only way you could see out of your cell and this was only so the guards could see into your cell! If it was up to them, they would just put cameras in your cells and watch you from the booth, but that would be invading privacy so they had to do rounds and make sure everyone was still alive! Fights happened all the time!

You have to think, 23 hours a day, you are in this tight room with someone you don't even know! Is this person homosexual? Are they a child molester? How can you have pictures of your family posted on your walls of this man you share a cell with is into little kids! If you put him in my cell, "Ima beat his ass..." I hear someone tell the guard! The guard was trying to put a known sex offender in someone's cell and they weren't going for it! The guard says there's nowhere else to put him if you touch him you will get more time and possibly an assault charge...

He locks them in the cell and walks away! Then I hear it... The metal rack smacking against the concrete wall, grunting, flesh-on-flesh contact! Help! Help! I hear the man screaming for the guards! Blood hits the window as the second offender gets what he deserves! Bitch! Bitch! I hear them in the next room getting busy! I told y'all don't put his bitch ass in my cell I hear him say! I hear the Signal 3 O Block go off on the loud speaker! Guards rushing to the cell, I hear the keys but can't see how many because my window is narrow! Only hearing everything! They slam him against the cell I hear it! "Cuff up!" they tell him! Separating the two of them, I finally see the sex offender, face busted open! I stare him in his eyes and he looks at me as I'm standing in my door looking through the window! Face bloody, lip and nose busted! And his eye had a huge gash in it! If I said, I felt bad I would be lying!

My bunkee was a cool dude! Honestly, now that I look back, I NEVER had a bad bunkee! I was always blessed to never have anyone who was homosexual in my cell or a snitch or child molester! I was always just blessed to be around solid people!

I want to clear the air before we move on! Don't take me talking down on homosexuality as degrading anyone, so if you are reading this book and are homosexual, that's OK! I just don't rock like that, so I speak how I feel on it! I'll always keep it real and uncut in this book! To each his own!

My bunkee was from Mansfield, Ohio! An ex-army dude who went AWOL… He was Spanish and real chill! Taught me a lot about the hole and how to do time! He had already been back in the hole for three weeks and had two weeks left! We kicked it and told good stories! He asked about my city and I told him, I asked about his city and he broke it down for me! He would always go to rec in the morning and I would sleep in! One thing I never was into was talking to people I didn't have to! I'm not wakin' up out of my sleep to go and sit in a cage and talk to people I honestly didn't give a fuck about. Obviously, when you are in a cell 23 hours a day, you get cool with your bunkee as long as they are official! I just never understood why people would go and sit in these rec cages for an hour just to talk!

The rec cages were close to the cells so if someone wanted to talk to you they would ask the guard to put them in a rec cage by your cell! And you would talk through your cell door and they would talk through the gate… Rec cages was also the place you went if you wanted to get something off your chest with someone! Say you had beef with someone and you were in cell five, but they were in cell 10! There's no physical way you can touch him because you're locked in a cell all day! You send a "kite," a jail term for a letter or note! There were three "Porters" on each shift! The term porter is used for someone who cleans, passes food out, and does whatever the guards ask him to do! Sounds fishy, I know, a lot of people accept this job because it's a HUSTLE!

Yeah you have to do what the guards ask you to do BUT… you are out of your cell the entire shift! Meaning you and two other people are the only ones out and about! High demand for this position, they made a lot of money just from taking something from one cell to another! A simple job as taking coffee from one cell to another would get the porter a couple "stamps." Envelopes! Coffee and Envelopes we the highest commodity outside of drugs and tobacco in the hole!

In the hole, you needed stamps to write your people so a lot of times you would hear people auctioning off their lunch or dinner trays for coffee or stamps! I got two stamps for dinner tray! Eating in the hole was scarce, unless you had money or something someone wanted! If you were cool with the porters, they could get you extra trays! Breakfast came at seven in the morning, lunch was at 11, and dinner was at five! After dinner, if you weren't full, then that was your fault! This wasn't like the compound where you could have commissary or eat when you wanted! You were in the hole as a punishment and that's exactly what they did, starved, and mentally fucked you up! There was always a hustle! Always a way to make money! Even in the hole, you could get your hands on commissary and sell that for food!

People I was on the pod with sent me commissary back to the hole! Jolly ranchers, coffee, and envelopes, and a Kool aid were the easiest things to snuggle! The coffee and envelopes I sold for extra trays and the jolly ranchers and Kool aid I kept for personal use! I loved my Kool aid had to have it! Kool aid and coffee and jolly ranchers also was the simple way to make a foxy, back in the hole you didn't have all the material to make a foxy but the basics would get the job done! Many nights, my bunkee and me stayed up and talked about the streets and our cases! If you couldn't talk about your case, then there was something fishy going on… either you were a RAT or you did some fuck shit to get in prison! Meaning you were a child molester or rapist, something along those lines.

He taught me how to make dominoes using cardboard boxes… We ripped cardboard up into little rectangular pieces and used a pen to draw the different domino combinations! This was our way of passing time! We played game after game and bet pushups, whoever lost had to do pushups! That wasn't a problem for either one of us we were both in shape!

Using the bathroom was the most awkward part about sharing a cell 23 hours out the day! There were no dividers or anything to separate the toilet from your living area! The toilet was literally right next to the rack you slept in! Piss could splash from the toilet and damn, near hit the bottom bunks sheets! To take a shit you had to hang a sheet over the bottom bunk or tell your bunkee you were about to take a shit and he would face the wall respecting what you said!

Everything came through a little slot in your cell door! Your mail! Your food! Your laundry! They played us like slaves and I felt that shit ever day! I use to depend on mail and pictures back there! That's the only thing that really kept me sane! I would look at pictures for hours just staring at them and thinking… Family pictures were the worst! I would feel so bad for how I did them! Why put them through this? They loved me and had my back every situation and it felt like I kept letting them down! Every time I said I would do right, I fell back into my old habits and old ways and would hurt them… A lot of people stopped writing me! A lot of people NEVER wrote me! This made my heart go cold! How could they play me like this? Like I wasn't busting my ass and risking it all for them to be happy and have memories… Fun-ass memories! Girls who started writing me fell off after just a few letters, but a part of me knew this would happen! Six years is a LONG ASS TIME! Not many females can ride six years and write letter after letter! I understood they had lives to live, so I was satisfied when I did receive a letter from them!

Pictures say 1,000 words and I finally understood that! I would read my letters but nothing was like those pictures! Nothing was like laying in my rack and reminiscing!

They gave me 60 days in the hole! 60 days straight… 23-1! No phone calls! No visits! No commissary! 60 days of being in the bottom of prison! Being in prison was one thing but then to be in the hole in prison was the worst of worst! I've been at the bottom and that's why I can honestly say that I made it through the struggle! I made it out and I'm here now! My bunkee went back to the compound after doing his last two weeks. He left me whatever he could and said he would see me when I got out! Before he left, he was telling me he was going to become a Latin King! And he did!

I had two other bunkees during my stay in the hole… My next bunkee was from the west side of Cleveland! Leebo was his name! One of the realest people I met in prison! To this day, we talk and check up on each other! My first day in the cell, we were quiet trying to feel each other out! Making sure our cases weren't fucked up, we told each other why we were in prison and told our stories! That was the icebreaker for each bunkee I had! Leebo ended up becoming my bunkee when I got out the hole as well! All I remember when first seeing him was this big ass fro! His hair was long as hell and mine was growing as well! We locked it and he gave me the game on prison! I soaked up all the game I could! He was a couple years older than me and was laid back and quiet just like me! He caught a dirty urine! Meaning he was smoking weed and when they did the random drug test, his piss came back dirty for marijuana! So he had to do 45 days!

I woke up one night randomly to use the bathroom! Standing there, pissing, I heard a weird noise! We had newspapers under our rack and I heard it shuffling around! I looked around the room and didn't see anything! Looking into the toilet, I pissed!

Then I see it... Fast as hell! I jumped on the rack and woke him up. He said, "What the fuck you doing, bro!"

I said, "Niggas, it's something in here, bro, wtf on the floor!" He started busting out laughing! I'm looking at him, confused as to why he laughing when I'm serious! I watch the door and I see two mice running out of the cell! I grabbed a spare sheet we had and stuffed the bottom of the door! "You got me fucked up," I said as I start laughing! I jumped like a little girl when I see them mice! This shit is dirty as hell how we got mice running around in and out of our rooms! He said they been coming in here you just now getting hip!

Even blocking the door their little spineless frames figured a way to get in our cell! I didn't understand it! I was mad as hell, I hate this dirty-ass shit! Looking out my window, I see the mice running in and out of rooms! Different rooms, you see them running out of! Scrambling looking for food! This shit can't be legal! This shit has to be against some type of sanitary rules!

In prison, I thought it would be a lot like the movies I've seen or TV shows I watched! It wasn't though... it was different! Being in the presence of everything was wild! To actually be inside of prison was crazy to me because it's like I once watched this shit now I have to live this shit! Washin' my boxers in the same sink, I brushed my teeth did something to me mentally! Scrubbing my boxers, I thought to myself like, *Damn, I'm really at the lowest point in my life!* Not seeing my family for YEARS broke me! But whom could I blame? Definitely not them!

This was my fault! This was my problem and now I had to fix it! Suck it up and take your punishment like a man! That was my mentality! Don't call home and ask for money! Figure out how to eat on your own! And if they want to look out and shoot you some money than that's OK but after a while I stopped asking feeling like I was being a burden! My mom was going to school for nursing and worked a job and took care of my four siblings! How the fuck could, I stress her out by askin' for money! That's weak as hell and that wasn't how I was cut so I did my time and made my money how I made it! Legal or illegal I made it! And I ate!

Leebo did his time and left just like my bunkee before him, it just seemed like everyone was getting out before me! I took the bottom rack after he left. First thing I did was carve "ONE DAY CLOSER" into the bottom of the rack I was looking up at! Laying there I thought to myself, *They can't keep me forever...* every day in, one day closer! Every day I'm closer to coming home and being free! This isn't life! This shit hurt me deep and I did it to myself but I gotta man up, learn, and grow! Always had a good head on my shoulders but prison... that made me! Made me the man I am today! Made me have the hustle I have today! I wouldn't take it back because I would be a little boy not a man.... I NEEDED prison! I know you're wondering what I'm talking about or saying I'm tripping but trust me I was wild as hell and out of control! The shit I've seen and woke up to daily made me open my eyes and want a different lifestyle! Life is too good and too short to be trying to hit licks and trap all day! I'm changing my ways and I'm going to be successful when I leave these COLD prison CELLS....

Getting close to my release from prison, I just remembered how cold it was! December 2012 was a cold winter! I could literally see my breath in my cell! The heaters in the vents worked when they wanted to! Not enough blankets in the cell, I felt my heart freezing! Pushups were my way of warming up! I hate prison I hate cellblocks, I hate keys jingling, I hate the sound of those gates or metal doors shutting and locking behind me! It replays in my head daily...

Like I said, the hole was dirty as hell! I never saw a place so ugly and cold! Loud at all times! Disrespectful was an understatement! Female guards had it bad! People calling them out their names degrading them! Masturbating on them whenever they came around I never understood it! That was so disturbing to me, creepy! This shit was sick! Getting off to a female who doesn't want you or asks you to stop is like verbal rape in my eyes! They don't care! Literally, I've seen it with my own eyes a female run away crying, hurt from a sick individual jacking off on them! I HATE IT HERE...

One of my last days in the hole was a revelation! There was some foul shit I had witnessed or heard back in the hole! This day was different! From the morning I could tell shit was gonna be wild! In your cells 23 hours a day, you get creative! A lot of times, people would flood their cells! Meaning they would clog the toilet! Clog the sink, and let the water run and keep flushing the toilet! This over flowing the toilet and making the water spill over and slowly flood your cell! This was done to get at the guards or to show disobedience! If someone didn't get what they wanted or simply were just upset that they were in the hole they flooded their cell! Water everywhere!

The top range was worse because if they flooded their cells the water would run out of their cell and spill down onto the bottom range! Slinging urine and shit also was a big level of disrespect I've seen go down! Especially with the porters. A lot of times when the porters wouldn't do what someone wanted or asked, they would get caught slipping! Styrofoam cups filled with shit and piss! They let it sit for the whole day! Sometimes multiple days! The smell was something fierce! A smell you never forget! Imagine scooping a cup of shit and piss from a porter potty! And then throwing it on someone! All of this is happening in one day! People laughing and banging on their cell doors! Loud as hell! There is no sleep! guards getting shit cups thrown on them was how some people laughed! You have to think we are in the hole!

People are riding out to other prisons so they have nothing to lose! Waiting 5 or six months back in the hole they let you sit! I did 60 days and was ready to go! I can only imagine 5 or six months! So they didn't care at all about anyone! Why would they! Savage! Their only thought was passing time and getting their time over with! So if throwing shit on someone made their day go by then that's what was going to happen! If jacking off on a female guard helped them, that's what it was!

The guards come to get me from my cell to shower! They handcuffed you before you left your cell to go to the shower. Then once you reached the shower, they un-cuffed you through a metal bar door! I remember my wrist indented from the handcuffs! Walking into the shower, I turn them on… ice cold I tell the guards and they say I have 10 minutes, I better figure it out! I FUCKING HATE IT HERE!

Getting undressed butt naked with my shower shoes, I go to step in the shower and I feel something squish under my shower shoes! They placed old used blankets down to stop the floor from getting wet and at the end of the day; they would pick those blankets up and place new ones down for the next day! I showered plenty of times to know how the blankets feel when I step on them! This felt different… something wasn't right! I flip the blanket back curious as to what I just stepped on! Sick to my stomach looking at what I just stepped on!

Someone took a shit in the shower and covered it with the blankets! Furious! Sick fucks! Whom does this weird-ass shit! "Five minutes!" the guard yells at me. Quickest shower I EVER took in my life! Pretty sure, I still had soap on me when I got back to my cell! I never experienced anything like this! Confused! Mad as hell I go back to my cell!

A couple more days, I lay down in my bed and look at the saying I wrote… "ONE DAY CLOSER" I cannot wait to get away from these weird ass people! Dirty ass people! No polish, no respect! I HATE IT HERE… Just laying there mind racing I think… And then I hear it! Someone screaming, "HELP He's trying to kill me."

I jump out of my bunk and go to my door! Looking out of my cell window, I see the guards running up to a cell above me! "Signal 3 O

Block! Signal three O Block," I hear the loud speaker go off! Keys jingling from the guards running! I watch as I see them pull an old white man out of this cell! Bloody and limping, they walk him to medical! What the fuck! Mind racing! A child molester was raped and tortured for days! Food trays got taken from him! Beat up and raped daily he finally had enough and spoke up! Sad, but this was how prison was! I only heard of a few rapes my whole time being locked up… It happened daily people just didn't speak up about it!

And to be honest, the prison was so homosexually built, meaning they embraced it so much. Raping someone wasn't a big thing! But as I said, it happened, it was just about if someone would speak up about it! I was cool with the porters on both 2nd and 3rd shift, so I found out easily what happened! It was important for me to be on the same page as the porters in case I ever needed something! This was something I learned early! Nobody said be BEST FRIENDS, but to get where you needed in prison, you needed people in position, people who help some kind of power you didn't have! And that was something I learned an always kept in my head!

Finally, it's my turn to get out of the hole! I felt like I was up all night anxious for them to knock on my door and say, "Pack it up," meaning I was getting out! You would think I was getting out of prison, how anxious I was to leave! Clothes packed up and all my sheets and blankets together! As soon as they crack this door, I'm out of here! An hour goes by and I fall asleep mad, I'm still up, I had to relax and understand their world, so even when I was supposed to be released, it would be when they got ready NOT ME! Waking up to a guard opening my cell door! He hands me a piece of paper and says let's go… I grab everything and I walk to the front of O BLOCK! I read the paper and it says J Block! This is a Cell Block on the compound. This would be my first time being in a cellblock on the compound and I knew things ran differently than how they ran in O BLOCK!

Walking out, I felt a huge relief as I leave the dungeon of cells! Felt like a slave pod! No respect for us! No care in the world how we survived! It was like once you were back there you were dead to the world! Especially if you didn't have mail or pictures coming in, that shit kept me sane!

With no mirrors to look in, I could only go off others reactions! At this time, I had my hair growing, obviously I wasn't getting a haircut in the hole, even tho they had barbers come once every two months. I began to let it grow and my shit was long, I could tell by the look on the sergeant's face when she walked past me! Your hair had to be braided or couldn't be longer than six inches when in an Afro! My hair was longer than six inches and she told me I was lucky I was just getting out of the hole or she would have "made me" cut it! I smiled and kept walking! I did this a lot when I didn't want to talk to someone or if they were trying to get a rise out of me! "Never let them see you sweat," I remember my older dude telling me!

Walking to the cellblock, I was moving to I had to first go to the "vault," which is a place where all of your belongings go when you go to the hole! So anything you owned was wrote on paper and packed up in your metal box you carried when you first came in! Some guards didn't care and threw away your items that you didn't have ownership over! Marion was a hot prison! Having two fans was mandatory, but was also illegal to the prison rules! So you had to finesse… Televisions sold for $200-$300 for a 17" flat screen!

Walking my property into the cellblock, I ask the guard where my room was, he pointed and I headed that way! 65 Cells in total! Different than the dorms that hold 250-350 people! These cells are different because they were only people who came from the hole! Anyone who was in O Block came here directly after! This was a program called 2B! Meaning one more fuck up and you were a level three security and would be riding out! Aka, going to another prison that held level three & four inmates! This pod had controlled movement! Meaning they lined you up and walked you to the chow hall at a time when no other pods would be in the hallway or chow hall! Right after count, they would walk us to chow. Then when we got done eating, they would clear count and feed the rest of the population! So again, if you had no money or hustle you were starving in here… that was just prison life!

Crip or Blood?

The cells were jam packed with gang members. Every gang on the compound had someone from their squad go to the hole and end up in "J block"! I won't lie to you and say I didn't because I did! Those sixty-nine days in the hole was serious. It was an entire new mental challenge. I wanted to kick it and drink, so when that hooch came around it was guaranteed that I was buying a few bottles. You better believe when that weed hit the compound I had me a stick or two!

I needed something to pass my time. The only thing that I wanted to do was get my time done and over with. After getting out of the hole, I began to move differently. I made sure to keep everyone out of my business and I kept a low profile.

"J block" taught me a lot. There was some shit that I needed to know, some shit that I wanted to know, and there were some things I wish I never heard or seen. I started off downstairs in cell 6, my bunkee was an older Muslim man. He was in his late fifties always worked on his legal work.

A lot of people were in to doing legal work and fighting cases. A lot of people were fighting for their life through doing legal work or trying to get an appeal and get back to court to get time knocked off their sentence. I couldn't do anything but respect their motivation and daily hunger to get back home.

I won't sit here and say that everyone that worked on their case got out or prison or beat their case, but a lot of people, mostly older people who were serious about it, were getting back to the courts and getting time knocked off. I saw it with my own eyes. A man waking up daily to work on his case, and everyday people would tell him he was crazy or wouldn't win. I've seen that same man knock *years* off his sentence and walk out those prison gates earlier than his first release date; All because he was hungry. Hungry to get back to *real life*. Not this routine ass shit hole they call prison.

My bunkee prayed five times a day and showed me a lot of the Islamic ways. Even though I didn't take those ways in, it was interesting to learn and hear him break his beliefs down. Muslims were some of them most clean and respectable people I met in prison.! They moved together and I respected that.

A younger kid stole from a Muslim guy in C dorm. That was a wild dorm. Constant fights and stealing *all the time.* If you had food and you weren't established in the block, it was guaranteed you were fighting! Fight for what's yours or get it taken, the rules were simple!

Well this time they stole from the wrong person. The Muslim man snapped and stabbed the kid for stealing from him! It's not the money or price of the item when someone steals from you, It's the principle behind it. You have to understand what I mean... Once you get something taken from you and don't stand for yourself or fight you are a TARGET! Then everyone thinks it's sweet and people will start to feel like they can have a piece of whatever you have.

A gang that the young kid was apart of was ready to jump the Muslim man and that was not flying with the Muslims in the dorm. See, the Muslims were often times looked as a gang. They ate together, they prayed together, and they worked out together. Everything was in unison! Fighting and standing up for each other was *mandatory* for these guys.

Every Muslim I had ties with or was cool with was always levelheaded, broke bread, and always stood on their respect and beliefs. Even when the guards got out of line and tried to play tough, they didn't back down. Growing up in this prison in this environment I knew nothing about was different for me. My eyes stayed open and my head was always on a swivel! Learning people and their body language and the tension in certain situations allowed me to get out of the way of a few close calls!

"J Block" was a jungle at nighttime! My whole time being locked up, 6 years in total this cell block was the worse block. It just seemed everyone had something they needed to get off their chest! And the easiest way to do that was stepping inside of a cell and handling it like a man. NO GUNS! Two hands and two feet. Getting in that room and sliding the door shut, and only one person leaves a winner!!

There was always so much going on in this block. You had to keep your head on a swivel and your eyes open. *Pay attention* I constantly repeated to myself. There were at least four tattoo artist on this block. Well, four *good* tattoo artists. There were a few others, but they weren't worth the time or money. I was always the type where I had to see some of their work before I sat down and let them tattoo me. Otherwise, there was no real way of seeing if they were as good as they said they were. Anyone can say they shoot tattoos, but only the real ones showed it.

A lot of the people I was in the hole with ended up coming to "J block". My bunkee, Leebo was there and he stuck to what he said. When we were in the hole, he used to always talk about fish spaghetti!! It sounded nasty when he would describe it and he knew how I felt from the look on my face as he told me. I remember him saying I'm going to show you bro, because I know it sounds nasty". Eventually fish spaghetti became one of my favorite things to eat! The combination was flawless. The meal lasted for two days easy and I never tasted a break like it before. There were two microwaves for 130 people. That's where we seen each other after I got out the hole.

I was downstairs and I was sitting on the laundry cart. They had big metal laundry carts they loaded up and pushed down to the laundry room. Laundry days rotated, so one day we washed whites and the next day was coloreds. Your laundry was put in a net bag and washed together!

Basically, the laundry people wash your clothes with whoever puts their clothes in that bin.

Some of the dirtiest people I have ever met was in prison! Not showering and not washing your clothes was the worst. That smell hit different and in tight spaces like prison it intensified the smell even more. I heard Leebo call my name but the first time I didn't know where it came from. I looked around and then I heard him say it again! This time I look up and he throws his hands in the air yelling "what's up"!

"What's up, bro?"! He waved for me to come up stairs!! He was sitting at one of the tables upstairs. "J block" was set up in a Circle. The guards needed to be able to walk two laps. One lap starting at cell 1 and ending at sell 31. Walking upstairs, the first cell was 32 and the guard would walk in the second circle ending at cell 65. Three times a day the guards made these "rounds" making sure everyone was accounted for! 4:00 everyone in the whole institution had to stand to let the guards know you were alive. This is called "standing count". If you were asleep then they woke you up! Even if you were using the bathroom, they didn't care! Be up and standing or go to the hole, the rules were simple! Fall in-line or fall out of line.

One thing about those cold prison cells was that they filled up quickly! It seemed like as years passed on, the age group kept getting younger and younger. There were eighteen-year-old guys getting off the bus with sixteen-year old kids. They'd have tears rolling down their faces, scared of the lifestyle they weren't ready to be a part of. A lot to learn they walked in the prison only to either be tortured or do the torturing.

There were multiple metal tables lined the inside of "J block". Four metal tables in total, one ice machine, one jpay machine, and 3 phones. There was one shower room downstairs and one upstairs. There was never any privacy, at any time someone could see through fiber glass. The guard's desk was downstairs by the door.

Leaving the hole and going back onto the main compound was definitely a transition. I went from not having to deal with or interact with people at all, to constantly dealing with people rather I wanted to or not. Hundreds of people lined the hallways. There were gang members throwing their sets up. You could hear the gang salutes in the hallways!! Everyone was either going somewhere or just trying to pass time.

Every race is in prison. Asians, Puerto Rican's, Haitian's, Mixed Cultures, El Salvador, Mexican, Black, White... I literally walked the prison halls in amazement. Because I'm from a small city a lot of people looked like aliens to me. There were only Hispanics, blacks, and whites in my hometown, so a lot of nationalities were new to me.

Everyone's body language was different and reading those body languages is what I lived off of. Energy! Vibes! Off the first conversation I can tell if we will be having another later on. If that vibe or energy is off, I'm cool and I will never lose sleep from not talking to another man. And I stood on that. I wasn't here to make friends or join a gang to "fit-in" and that's what it was! They respected that more than anything.

Leebo was probably one of the closest people I had on this block just because we had already been bunkees and learned how each other moved! So, we kicked it and talked shit up at the big table. That's what we called the upstairs table. This is the table that we broke bread on. The table that people gambled on, we hustled on. We talked shit and cracked jokes here. This table was a place where a lot of fights started! Big meals got cooked here! Big Foxies got poured here! This table became the block! The kick it spot!

Dominoes was a big game being played in prison. But there was one game people played more than dominoes, this game had the prison in a frenzy! CHESS! This mental game started with the OG's and went all the way down to the youngest in the prison. Everyone wanted to learn and be the best chess player. It was crazy how this game took over peoples mental. It really made people lock in and think. I saw some of the most dangerous people calm all the way down and focus on their game. *Why was this game so different than all the others?* Chess and Dominoes all day.

Either you were focused on a more serious game or you were playing the hood game, dominoes.

"25!" Leebo smacks the table with the domino and folds his arms across his chest. He leans forward and laughs as he says "I told you I was going to do two things when we were both out the hole! Whoop your ass in dominoes and show you that fish spaghetti." We both broke laughing! As we continued the game, I reminded him, "It still ain't sweet over here!' and we set up for another game so I could get my revenge! As we play dominoes, we also pay attention to the intense games of chess that are surrounding us. People standing around watching them play as they make moves and the people around them grows! Move after move, they go back and forth claiming territory and hostages. Last move... "check mate!" the older dude says! They showed respect for the game and gave each other a handshake and then the next person sits down to play.

"Rise n Fly" they called it. Meaning the loser gets up and winner stays until someone beats him. This also was a speed way of playing dominoes! Games went quick, and different players played by different rules, so everybody had to check that during beginning of the game.

Being in this block meant that you had sanctions meaning you had a specific outfit you had to wear to let other guards know you were on the 2B pod. Blue state pants with an orange stripe down both pant legs was the first sanction outfit Marion came with. This was a new rule and they were trying to figure it out as the prison became overpopulated quickly from all the young ride ins. There was always a way to maneuver and finesse the prison.

Wear two pairs of pants the first pair you put on would be regular state blues and the second pair would be the 2B pants! A lot of people did this and if you got caught you would go to the hole but if not then you had a full rec day meaning if you had a "non regular" guard or a guard who didn't know you by face you could get it off! The regulars wasn't going for that because they knew everyone by face if they didn't know you by name!!

A few guards were known for searches! Raypole was the worst!! If he hit your block there was for a reason, he was there to find whatever contraband he could find! And he did, every time!! Hooch! Weed! Tobacco! The places you would think he would never check he checked those spots and found what he was looking for! And let's be honest a lot of times people tipped him off as to what was going on or where to find the spots but he was comfortable tearing peoples shit up and looking for the illegal shit!!

Stratton was just a pure asshole! Things were his way or no way! Stuck up and cocky in his own way! He also use to terrorize blocks if people seen him coming it was for a reason! He was locking someone up or finding something illegal!! Raypole has two sons who also became guards which I'm pretty sure is against some type of rules but they got it off. Turned his sons into miniature versions of himself!! There were a lot of fucked up guards! But at the end of the day this is their world! We just live in it! 2B you couldn't get commissary only hygiene and put money on your phone account! They put a block on your commissary account until your sanction time was up! Another easy loophole we found! Trade someone hygiene for commissary! Find someone who was going to the store buying whatever hygiene you had or were able to buy and then give them a list of commissary you want and BOOM! Everyone wins! $100 LIMIT!!

For all you street hustlers who think y'all eating now... you can only spend $100 a store day!! That's NOT a lot of food when you actually start cooking and realized each break is costing you $5-10 easily!! Do the math! You can only go to the store maybe 2 times a month because you have to remember everyone in the prison receives STATE PAY! Some people only get a certain amount due to what they owe the state... child support, court cost etc.!

This isn't a place where you can spend what you want and prison definitely isn't a place for all that street flexing! I say this so that you hear me and understand me when I say that money flashing isn't impressing anyone! And if you go to prison there is no more money flashing! Be smart and Be successful it's easier than trying to fit in!!

When I got out of the hole the prison changed! Flipped! There were young dudes everywhere, some so small you had to ask how old they were! Dudes walking down the hallway looking like a middle schooler! With more time ahead of them then they have lived on this earth!! Shit is sad but it is reality! Gang Numbers went up and so did the level of violence! Extortion was heavy!

Plain as day! People getting their commissary bags taken from them right after they leave the store! As soon as they open that store door and close it behind them they were handing over there money! $100 worth of food! Head held down they can't tell because then it gets worse! Snitching is a no no especially in prison! Once labeled a snitch you can't be on the compound because everyone will try you! Tease you about being a snitch!! Or worse just simply beat your ass because you are a snitch and they don't want you in the pod anymore!

I never understood why they didn't just fight! Blew my mind the first time I seen someone just hand their big bag of commissary off to someone just because they threatened to fight them!! It was so smooth like not one word just a scared look and then the handing of the bag!! Signal 3 main hallway! Signal 3 main hallway!! I already knew what it was!! Commissary all over the hallway, blood leaking from the scared kids mouth and nose!! Sitting down knocked out I walked past as I seen him snoring!! There was no commissary bag, so it was obvious they took his food and knocked him out!! The guards shut the hallway down and medical cleaned the blood up! Looking at the cameras they eventually find out who is was but by then the food has been back to the block and divided up! They didn't care this shit was fun to them!

J BLOCK was a different vibe! People from other blocks would sneak into this block just to kick it! This block was going crazy! Hooch! Weed! Tattoos! Fights! It was my TMZ... I didn't need to be apart of anything just sit back and watch!! Tension rising in the pod you could sense it in the air!! Nobody was going for any bullshit! If you wanted to fight there was plenty of cells to step in and a lot of times it didn't even make it there! Fights broke out all the time in the pod or in the hallways some people just didn't care about going to the hole! Plenty of times I walked down those prison hallways and seen people get knocked out or seen gangs jumps someone. It's was a lifestyle in prison! This was a everyday living for them! We smoked and listened to music in the cells and it passed time!

Damo went to the hole and came to Jblock and we linked ASAP! Damo was my age and we played basketball and competed with almost everything! Friendly rivalry! Dominoes! Basketball... damn near everything we did we played against each other! He was a cool young dude and I fucked with him tough! He kept that chip on his shoulder and if it was time to go and get inside the cell he was first up!! Never backing down and always showing up he was with the shit! Tj was another young dude I met with and got cool with!! Tj was a savage! He just simply didn't care! Keeping him close was mandatory because he was solid and loyal! If he was on your side y'all were good! On your bad side that's another story!

He was so small! Couldn't have been no taller than 5 foot! So much energy and pain inside his body you could tell he came from the trenches! He was in a gang and made boss moves! They listened to him and did what he said! And if they didn't, they got whacked! It was simple! There were a couple people my age, young at that time who were really high ranked in the gangs!! Everyone else was a foot soldier! Doing missions and bringing money back to the gang they were pawns! ANOTHER reason I never wanted to join a gang!

How could I be a pawn? Seemed like I would belong to someone or something if I did that and that feeling was something that didn't sit right with me.

"Leebo what we cooking this weekend bro?" He said Fish Spaghetti you already know! What do I need bro? We sat down and broke the list down of commissary items we needed for the meal to be complete!

Spaghetti noodles, Mozzarella, Squeeze Cheese, Goya, Italian seasonings, Jack Mac "Mackerel Fish" , Salmon, and Tuna... Cream Cheese, Olive oil, A bag of chips and Our drinks for the famous FOXIES!!

It was summer 2014 and I still had 3 years still to do before I was home! At this time I was halfway through my time! Working out here and there just to keep my body in shape I told myself I wasn't really pressed in working out till my last year! At this time I just wanted to get this year over with and get to 2015. Because at that time I knew I would have 2 years left and the countdown could really begin!

So my whole time in Jblock I did what I wanted! Smoked in moderation only after they did the random piss test! I knew from doing time and paying attention they never did back to back drug test and at this time I had NEVER got called for a random drug test! So after they came around and did the drug test I would smoke! Knowing I was safe! Hooch was easy to get away with as long as you didn't get caught with it in your hand! They got creative with hiding the hooch! We started off hiding it in our boxes and that elevated to creating hiding spots to hide the hooch or other contraband!! The drop ceilings were clutch!! Being able to stash 5 gallons and better in a ceiling was sweet compared to only stashing 2-3 gallons in your box and putting yourself at risk to go to the hole!

With the new hiding spots there was no way to tell whose it was! So the only thing that would happen if it got knocked was you chalked it up and counted it as a Loss!! After a while the guards caught on and figured it out and we had to get more creative!! And we did!! It was always us against the guards, we had to outthink them and outsmart them! Being a step ahead of them was mandatory!!

The yard and gym was always packed and always had something going on! Walking to the gym and yard was like walking in downtown NY! Shoulder to shoulder with people you don't know or want to get to know! Hallways filled! Loud! People cracking jokes, people talking shit! People passing their homies in the hallways dapping them up and talking about meeting back up on the yard after chow! The yard and rec opened only before and after chow! Morning time they called rec and then chow, then once chow was over they would clear rec and call it again so people could go back and forth! Controlled movement! Lunch and dinner was the same routine!

Summer time we would stay on the yard all day because we weren't missing anything in the chow hall! They didn't feed us right! It was a waste of time! Feeding grown men the shit they fed us was not Right at all! I wish I could have taken a picture and showed you guys! Slop was a understatement! Some nights I went to bed hungry and full off of water! Some nights I skipped chow and would just make food from my commissary! Some people were blessed and didn't have to goto the chow hall! Others were down bad and asking for trays to stay full through the night! I was in the middle I hustled so if I ever thought the chow hall wasn't going to do anything for me I would cook! But there was times when I had no money! There was times when I HAD to go to the chow hall to eat because times were hard or my money didn't hit my books in time!

I look back and think about how hard it was and how real that struggle is in there! How did I make it out? How am I not out here wild as hell? I became a man out of that situation! I HAD to become a better man for MYSELF! This wasn't about my family or friends this was a test for me! To see how solid I could remain! To see if I would remain solid! And I did! All ten toes I stood on and I made it out the struggle!! I think about prison everyday, and it fucks me up but I'll never forget I was at the bottom!! Lowest place on earth outside of being dead!

Gang members always would try to give me dap and shake my hand into their gang handshake... I would just pull my hand back and laugh! They would laugh to because they knew that I wasn't going for that I would have been got into a gang my first year if that's what I was into or wanted to do!! I was here to grow and get my mind right! Nobody was gonna trick me out my spot and when I get home I'm coming for everything I deserve!! Those were my thoughts and I expressed those thoughts to other homies I had that were in gangs and they understood what I meant!

You might as well come on home BLEED! My blood Homie would always tell me! And I would say on 2017 I'll be home! He would laugh and say yea I know. See it wasn't about being tough or trying to fit in with me! I never been one to NEED someone's approval! I would rather walk my own walk and see how it ended up! My Crip homie Cam was cool as hell!! Laid back but a dog! Probably why we clicked so well! He was finishing up 8 years and came from a level 3 prison! He joked and he played poker! He was a barber! But one thing he wasn't big on was talking when it came time to fight he just wanted one thing and that was for you to get in the cell with him! We ate together and played basketball together always was a cool dude but one day we really locked in...

When I first got to Marion in 2012 they gave us a orientation of the prison and programs they had to offer! Marion was one of the best prisons as far as leaving with a education or degree! I loved that because I didn't ask to go to Marion I wanted to go to Lake Erie! T

here was a reason they sent me to Marion and now I know why! I was definitely leaving with a license or degree in something, wasting my time was not a option! The warden talked about the different programs Marion had to offer and went on to talk about welding and auto mechanic programs they had! All of that was cool but didn't really excite me! Then he went on to say they were building a barber school! As soon as I heard that he had my attention!

He went on to say that it would be a few years before it was built and up and running but it was going to be added to the prison! He said sign up sheets would be passed around and I signed! A few months before the barber school opened there was a sign up sheet in the block!! There was a bulletin board that kept the mail list and other odd papers attached to it! I was reading the mail list checking to see if I had anything when I seen it! Shocked I ran to the closest table and used their pen to sign my name!

I didn't know the requirements but I knew I needed to be apart of the barber program!! Not thinking anything of it I go back up to my cell!! At this time me and Leebo pay the clerk so we can switch our bunkees our and become bunkees with each other!

We already were bunkees in the hole so we knew how each other moved and had a mutual respect for each other!! Leebo being from Cleveland and already being on the compound for 6 months before he went to the hole had knew pretty much everyone! Standing on the top range looking down I leaned on the railing... looked like a movie view, why was I here so young though? And why wasn't it like they showed on the movies? I always said my dad went to prison ILL NEVER GO and they use to tell me ... never say never!

So that got to me a lot.... as I'm zoned out staring at the people playing cards and people cooking at the microwave! I see people waiting in line to use the phone for 15 minutes... seems like you wait longer in line than you get to actually talk on the phone!! Shit was a headache! And a lot of people got into it over phones.. some blocks had city phones I personally never been in a block where they said only Akron or only Cleveland can use this phone... BUT IT DEFINITELY WAS A THING!

Painesville was a small city I was the only person down there for a minute! People would ask me if I was from Lorain when they seen the "440" tattoo on my stomach!! I would say no in from painesville! One thing I told myself I would NEVER do is say I was from somewhere I wasn't! I would never say I'm from Cleveland because I'm not! I'm from PAINESVILLE.... OHIO!! and they knew that especially if I fucked with them they really know I'm official "not to brag but my name good" did my whole 6 clean no fights! no extortion plays put down on me!! No calling me to the back wall and not showing! Not none of that trash I seen on TV OR IN PERSON!! It Everyday was different, the routine was the same... wake up brush your teeth use the bathroom wash hands. Chill at the rack and watch tv till lunch or go workout or hoop! After lunch on the yard you either walking getting your mind right or you are into something whether it's working out, sports or gang activity you were doing something if you weren't walking the yard!

The summer of 2014 was the most aggressive and violent summer I had seen in prison my whole 6 years! Everything was gang related or involved a gang in some way shape or form! Everyone was on the yard during the summer, and if you weren't it was because you were either scared to leave your block or were a old person who didn't care for going outside! Why else would you be cooped up on a block with hundreds of men doing nothing... I wanted to get away! And the yard was my way of cutting people off and getting my peace of mind! Marion was close to civilization, meaning people drove past all the time! Females would drive past and flash the inmates screaming out their windows!! Inmates would throw their hands up trying to get them to stop or slow down! Summer time was the most active! There had to be at least 2,000 people on the yard playing baseball, basketball, working out! Kicking it with their homies! And of course every gang has their own section of the yard they meet up at!! GD's over here Bloods over there! Crips over here Felons over there! AB's "White supremacy Group"

Over here Latin Kings over there!! You could tell which gang was which if you paid attention or knew what you were looking for... Red obviously was blood, Blue was Crip! Latin King yellow, Gd's black felons didn't have a specific color and neither did the AB's... The "ab's" were easy to spot because they were a WHITE ONLY GANG! Felons you could tell because they moved different and had the compound on lock as far as numbers! Their numbers ranged from 18 and up! They had the most young people in a gang they just loved the idea of joining as soon as they got down there! Getting put down was fun to them! Going on missions was fun! Stealing and Fighting was fun to them! This is why they were one of the most dangerous gangs! A lot of people didn't like felons because they jumped people... a lot! There was no fair fight to them and that's what they stood on! If you played one of them you had to deal with the consequences meaning they didn't care who started the fight they would finish it....

In the gym everything is normal, unless you are like me and paying attention to EVERYTHING going on around me!! The bathroom in the gym is where people met to fight or get stuff off their chest!! On this day the gym was packed because it had been raining outside! Two gangs had problems and you could tell by the tension in the air! I focused in on what I was seeing! Body language tells it all! As they walk over to the bathroom they wait for the guards to make their round and then two step inside!! After a few minutes they walk out of the bathroom! One laughing and smiling and the other not so happy! Straightening his shirt that is ripped one of the gang members toss him a new shirt! They didn't care for the win or loss but they did care about the RESPECT! Respect is huge in prison because once you let someone disrespect you or your gang then nobody will fall in line and think you are a joke! And then I see it the bathroom is full of gang members some standing there arguing and others going in to fight!! Something wasn't right this wasn't normally how it played out! Normally they let the two people go in and work it out! Sometimes one gang picked a member from the opposite gang to fight! This time two went in and two more from the same gang ran in!! 3 on 1 there was no way he was making it out! In this bathroom it is one way in and one way out! Only way you make it out of there is if your a winner!! This was a bad day! They jumped him and beat him with a inch of his life! The guards Called the signal 3 because they seen people standing by the bathroom looking in and running back out they knew something wasn't right!! Lock the Gym down the guard says! Nobody in or Out!

Of course the fight had been over for a minute by the time the guards caught wind of what was happening!! I remember them putting him on the stretcher and watching his bloody body leave the gym! Head swollen! Eyes barely open! Blood gushing from his mouth and nose!! Shirt ripped!! My heart beat increased! I wasn't even in the fight but I felt like this was about to get worse!! And it did! As they were wheeling him out another brawl broke out!! Two gangs fighting in the gym! All you seen was people getting slammed and kicked in the face! I put my back on the closest wall making sure nobody could sneak me and knock me out I seen it too many times!! The smell of Pepper Spray hits my nostrils!! Fuck!! I run to the door gasping for air! Snot running out of my nose I feel my chest collapsing!! Getting tight I try to remember to calm down when breathing and it slowly works! They cuff the gang members and send them to the hole! Rules have changed as the violence got worse on the compound!

There is a no tolerance for fighting at this point a simple fight is a ride out! Which sucks because anyone can run up on you and start a fight just because they want to "check in"... checking in was a coward way to go out!! But I seen it happen many times! A crash out dummy! Someone willing to crash out just because they couldn't take the pressure of everyday living in prison! The crash out dummy was the worst type of person! They would crash at the weirdest times.. like when there are 3 guards walking by in the hallway they just randomly pick someone and start fighting! Or stand in front of the guard and take off punching on someone knowing your about to get caught! That was the oldest trick in the book! Checking in was popular!

Everyone involved in that fight and the fights before when they reviewed the camera Got taken to the hole and shipped out to another prison! Most likely a higher level prison. Young and wild with a lot of time to do they didn't care about riding out! They were living in the moment and not thinking about the future because the future was 20 years to them! They weren't seeing the streets for 20 years why should they get in school or care about anything else that was important for the time being!!

The yard was locked down for a week!! People who weren't involved still went to the hole under investigation, and if you had gang ties or a gang tag they questioned you.... next time we went on the yard A Cleveland riot popped off!! A block called 10-5 fought with another group and they shut the yard down!! Was a rainy day earlier on so it was gloomy later around 5 when the riot popped! I call it a riot not because it was a huge fight or some known fight nationwide...

I say that name because for this prison and how quiet it use to be the fight was a big difference from a small one on one fight or a quick scuffle!! This was several mini fights all over the yard happening at once!! Two sets getting to it!! Some people getting jumped some getting stomped out! Others dodging hits trying not to get hit! The guards don't know what to do the mission was simply ON SIGHT!! And both sets were with that shit!! Signal 3 on the yard! I hear the loud speaker above my head as I stand on the yard back against the steel gates fence!! No matter where I was I always tried to put my back to something to make sure nobody could sneak me or knock me out!!

This was something I adapted to after being in prison for so long!! You had to be able to adapt to your environment otherwise you would be taken advantage of! Sheep in a wolfs den!! In Lorain I seen multiple people get food taken off their tray right in front of me!! I am right handed I began eating left handed so I could swing my right hand if someone ever tried me!

This wasn't something I told myself daily to do! This was something I naturally adapted to! Something I taught myself to do without thinking! No one ever touched my food or played me crazy but just in case I had taught myself a valuable skill!!

This one day changed me and opened my eyes! This day I woke up furious!! Half sleep waking up I'm hearing moans! Multiple moans!! I wake up and instantly feel my heart beat increase! What the fuck! I'm not dreaming these dudes fucking next door!! I hear the moans and jump off the top rack!! I put my Timberland Pros on... the Knock off timbs! This is what they sold us for $80 a pair!! Something that cost $40 on the street!! Everything was a hustle and I respected it!! A new pair of timbs was like having Jordan's on the first day of school!! It was something they went crazy for!! Stealing these boots was a trophy in the joint! People got their boots taken daily!

There was a time someone got their boots taken an put a lock in the sock! This was a prison weapon invented and was serious! This weapon swung with the right force could put the biggest & strongest man down! I seen it with my own eyes! Jumbo lock in a tube sock a knot tied at the end! This weapon put people in medical and worse... Making it home to your loved ones was THE MISSION! I didn't care I wanted to see my brother play sports and I MISSED THAT! Wanted to see my little sister graduate high school and I MISSED THAT!! That shit cut me deep!

My mind racing pissed off I slam my cell door shut! It's 9 in the morning! Waiting down stairs I wait for the next rec call and I go out to the yard and walk!! Before they call rec to the yard I see two men leave the cell!! One white and one black! Our cells were connected and the vent we had that blew our air or heat out sent the moans into my cell!! I couldn't believe this shit! How bold were they!! To say fuck it and do this shit right now!! Furious they call rec and I'm the first person out the door!! I HATE IT HERE! I just need to let it all out one time!! I need to fight! Need to scream! Need to let these tears out!! I can't though! Never let them see you sweat!

Crying is out of the question! Man up! Bottle that shit up an deal with it on your own!! This the shit that fucked me up... Mental shit! I never faced a physical problem being locked up! It was weird because I fought mental fights and mental demons daily!!

Walking the yard, I try to gain my composure and just relax sitting at the table watching cars pass back and forth I think deep! Is this life! For a lot of people this is it! For a lot of people they will never see their families or loved ones again! For a lot of people they will never step a foot outside of these prison gates because they've made a dumb decision that cost them their life!! Cooking started to become a everyday thing for me!

I linked with the right people and we cooked and everyone who was eating brought something to the table! And if they were down bad then the others knew and helped out!! But I ate with solid people!! People who respected each other and respected what we brought to The table! It was easy to say you were a real one! The test comes when you have a real decision to make!

Finally me and Leebo get together and put all the commissary we have on the table and begin to prep for this meal!! This meal looked like a holiday dinner! People asking what the occasion was or why we were cooking so heavy!! We been plotting on this meal! Cheese first we cut everything up! Put the noodles in a bowl with seasoning and olive oil! 6 minute increments we put the water and noodles in the microwave!! Checking them and making sure they don't stick we separate the fish! Packs and Packs of Mackerel and Salmon and Tuna we mix all the fish and add Italian seasoning!! Making the potatoes from the bag of chips I crunch them all the way up!! Add water and Cheese I mush the mix together! Rolling the chips up I let them sit in a solid form!! Letting sit for 10-15 minutes!! I come back and flatten the chip bag out! Making a flat layer of potatoes!! Noodles done we drain them and add Goya!! Adding butter from the kitchen plug we had, noodles are perfect! Fish goes on next filling the top of the bowl with meat. Potatoes next! Cutting the potatoes into squares we divide them equally between our two bowls!! Cheese next!! Mozzarella! Cut into blocks! We place them on the top of the bowl!!

Squeeze cheese and Ranch laid across the top layer of the bowl!! Diagonal lines I watch as leebo makes the spaghetti look like a designer bowl! Presentation was everything!! Earlier that day a group of young dudes was playing cards! Spades to be exact 3 of them were from Akron and one was from Cleveland!! They were all cool to an extent and playing cards this day showed me never get too comfortable with people! Playing cards they begin to talk shit! Back and forth! Clowning each other and then it going to the next level with the momma jokes! They gang up on the Cleveland dude and clown him out... now he feels some type of way and wants to fight! Get your bitch ass in this cell then! Let's really see what you talking about!

The Akron dude stands up and says I'm with the shit! The step in the cell and fight it out! First round they fight for a couple minutes! Get it off their chest! Then one of the Akron dudes try to go break it up and ends up jumping in!! This shit crazy I'm just watching it all from the next table! Looking over my shoulder making sure the police aren't coming I see the Cleveland dude call the other one who tried to break it up into the cell!! Yea YOU!! He points to him and points to the cell!! Get the fuck in there bitch I want work with you now!! They go in and the Cleveland dude wins the second fight! Pumped he gets to talking shit!! Today was different there was several beefs going on and I was aware of them all!! I paid attention to everyone and everything around me! I paid attention to body language! This was what allowed me to know if a fight was about to break out or if I felt in my gut something was about to pop off I put myself in position to avoid getting caught in the middle of it all!!

Another fight broke out! This fight was different two Cleveland dudes jumped a Akron dude! They were all young! Under 20! They fought early in the day! This was over a gambling debt! Reminded me of when my dad said stay away from the three G's!! I seen plenty of times people get into fights from not being able to pay debts or not wanting to pay out.

I watched the person who got jumped all day! I knew his background and his history!! I knew he had been to DYS... a juvie institution!! A violent one at that!! His body language told it all!! Waiting on his victims to slip he waited!! The whole day I watched them avoid him and be in their toes... until night time!! At the table I'm watching the pod as I drink my foxy and eat my fish spaghetti at the table up stairs!! I can see the whole pod from where i am sitting!! I watch him catch both people lacking!

First I see him run in the cell with the first person! It was so quick and so accurate I respected it! Nobody seen it coming! You hear sneakers squeaking on the floor and the metal rack hitting the wall!! He walks out and straightened his shirt! One victim down! One more to go!! The night goes on... playing cards up stairs I lose my hand if domino's and stand up! One of the people who were involved in the fight was standing up stairs as I get up he falls!! It was all in one motion! It was a blur until I really seen what was going on! The last victim gets caught lacking! Knocked out cold I watch as the person who knocked him out runs down stairs!! Sleep on the floor we clear out and go about our business!! There was no way we were getting blamed for this!! As we go downstairs the person who knocked the kid out upstairs doesn't know the person he just knocked out is apart of a gang! Big mistake!

I watch Ron Ron slide down the wall and catch the Akron dude slipping!! I never heard someone's jaw crack like I heard this time! Immediately he falls to the ground not expecting the punch! These were the worst types of knockouts because they didn't expect it!! He falls to the ground and he stomps him out!! Blood everywhere I'm watching from the table as I see the bloody scene going down right in front of my eyes! Signal 3 J BLOCK! Signal 3 J BLOCK! I hear the loudspeaker ring!

Lockdown I hear the guard yell!! Cell doors open and shut!! Medical comes and puts the victim in a wheelchair!! Bloody and injured he holds his jaw and groans through his clenched teeth!! The block had been shaking with fights and extortion for a few weeks after this and then they shut the compound down! SRT came through and did a sweep! SRT aka MEN IN BLACK was the SWAT of prisons... when you seen them they moved in big numbers and they were coming to shake some shit down! Tearing the blocks up lookin for contraband and illegals they made sure they came aggressive!

Every time someone seen them they would echo it through the pod! Men in black coming! Everyone knew and could get ready for the shit that was coming next!! This was the prisons way of cleaning up the violence! Clearing out the blocks with the known gang members and active members they shipped them out! Tearing the blocks up they found contraband and put those people in the hole and also rode them out! It was strict and a tight ship with all the violence going on!

Chapter Thirty Eight:
BARBER SCHOOL

The next week Cam comes to my room and tells me he got me in Barber School!! I asked him what he meant and he said it again!! You gotta cut you're dreads tho bro!! That's the only downfall to this whole thing I know you had your hair for a while you might want to consider it tho! Your hair grows not everyone gets this chance...

Thinking to myself I don't need any time to think I wasn't going home with dreads anyways so this was a easy decision!! He tells me Friday we will cut them, he gets me a pass and we goto the barbershop! I had my hair for 2 years! Dreads for a year as he cut my hair I felt my head getting lighter and lighter!! Air hitting my head I feel the hair stand up on my head!! I did it! I didn't care I needed this opportunity and I wasn't letting it pass me by...

A few weeks later they brought sergeants in and read peoples last name and last 3 digits of their prison numbers off!! Everyone was dead quiet wondering what was going on and why they were calling names and numbers off!! Sheffey... 115

We all report down stairs and they give us instructions that we were moving to the CAMP! I thought to myself damn I'm comfortable where I am at! Everyone knows me and knows how things move! But now I have to pack up and move my shit again!! I hate moving my shit! But this is their world I'm just living in it TEMPORARILY!! I pack my shit up! The process is annoying!! Metal cart with everything I own laying there!! Sad! I own none of this stuff sitting on this cart! Everything belongs to the state outside of my commissary and the boots I bought! Blankets.. Sheets... State Blues... plastic mattress... Everything is the states!! I HARE IT HERE!!

Moving into the camp was a total different transition!! Going from a Cell block to a dorm was always different, just like going from a cell would be different if you weren't used to being in a cell! Walking my property following the others going to the camp!! I remember thinking how this transition would be! Wondering if I was going to have to worry about simple things like someone going into my commissary while I'm not there! These were things you didn't worry about once you we're comfortable in your block or pod!

Going into a new environment a new living area you don't know who steals or who is watching you!! Especially on a open dorm with 350 people it's hard to point the finger at one person and say you stole from me if you didn't see it!! You can't be at two places the same time but one thing you knew was how much commissary you had or where you put things in your area at! Barber school had started and they literally moved me to Marions Camp a week or so later!! Cam was in J BLOCK, he was my mentor on the barber side! When I wasn't in my books reading about this new career I was about to take on I was watching him cut!

Asking questions to make sure I got the idea and concept down!! Now I could only learn from him at school!! It's life though and this is their world I'm just living in it! There was no saying I wanted to stay in J BLOCK, they said move and that was that! Either go to the hole or go to the camp!! I chose the camp and it paid off!!

Walking through the gates into the camp it was a 5-minute walk from the main compound to the camp! I had to walk this same 5-minute route everyday to go to barber school!! 1800 hours I needed to graduate!! Walking inside the gates I see two handball courts! One nice sized softball field! A big set of pull up and dip bars! Another pull up bar was standing alone in the cut!! A full basketball court! This yard was smaller then the main compound obviously because there was less people on this yard! One lap around the main yard was a mile! 6 laps around this yard was a mile. Big difference.

It was nice outside 75 degrees no wind!! People hooping and working out!! You could tell the people who had been down for a long time by their routine when it came to working out! The new people down didn't have the drive or experience! They just followed what they seen others do!! Working out at the camp became a regular thing to do!! With 2 years left on my Sentence I start to take things more serious!! School is first! Nothing is messing that up! My biggest focus was on school, because I knew once I secured that everything else would fall in place and help me get my mind right!! The main compound we wore state blues meaning blue pants and blue button down shirts!

At the camp we wore tan pants and tan button down shirts! People got extra just like they did on the streets! Creasing their pants and getting their blues washed a certain way so they looked like "stone washed jeans" I seen it all!! The older dudes always made sure their blues were on point and they had their smell good!! Never know when a female guard will show up they use to always say! Tryna knock a female guard was one of the biggest things you could do in prison!! This put you on another status! Obviously the female guards weren't messing with everyone because peo-ple talk to much! Never get it twisted though the female guards definitely loved Felons!

In a environment full of men this was something that happened on the regular in prisons all over the world! Put a female inside of a male prison and I guarantee if she's not happy at home she will end up talking to a inmate! Shit some females were married and still fucking an inmate!! They would never find out unless they were caught red handed, anyone could make a rumor up but getting caught in action was another ball game!! Ms. KING was the eye candy of the compound!

Her and a Few nurses had the juice and they knew it! Ms. King was tall and light skin! Jet black hair! Everyone liked her! The nurses were rare because they rarely came out but when they did they had tight nurses scrubs on so their bodies looked 10x better! Being away from females and not being intimate made us look at females different! I love women so this was definitely hard for me... going from being with a woman damn near every day to not being with a female for YEARS!! That made me think... ALOT! I HATE IT HERE!!

The Camp was a sweet bid... meaning I looked at it like this was where I was going to be for my last 2 years and this was where I needed to be to let my time wind down!! The movement wasn't controlled meaning once they cleared the 4:00 count we could go to rec without anyone telling us the yard was closed! We could goto the weight room how many times we wanted without someone telling us we had already been in too many times in a week! Commissary ran different! They had their own commissary store! (This eventually changed) although the pods held 300-350 people there was only two pods! MCC and MRC!!

Basically, MCC was the hood of the camp meaning all the older people and people doing programs were on the MRC side! MRC side wore tan on tan, MCC wore blue state shirts with tan pants!! MRC was bullshit in my eyes I never moved over there because it just wasn't something I was into! I went to barber school and worked out! If I wasn't working out or in barbershop I was cooking or getting my mind right!! It was simple I stayed in my own lane! When I first got to the camp there was no cameras! Tobacco was the bread winner in this camp! Going left and right it was easy to flip money with the tobacco game! There was so much people were giving away dumb amounts just so they could get rid of it! $25 a pouch was the lowest I ever seen the tobacco prices drop to! When there was a high deman on tobacco but a low supply them prices went through the roof!! $50-75 a pouch if you catch the right person willing to pay! The tobacco smokers were some times worse then dope fiends!! Paying whatever to smoke! Going through withdrawals and crashing out for their smokes! To them it was a necessity!

The Camp moved different! This was the Money Block! 90 percent of the contraband came from the camp until the guards caught wind and shut everything down!! Everything got sold!! Everything had a price! Nothing moved into the compound unless the camp already had their hands on it! Outside of tobacco and drugs there was too many hustles at this camp! This is where my life turned! I made the most money in 2 years at the camp then I did my 4 in the main compound! Cooking was a hustle, do it good enough and you could survive from people paying you to cook!! I seen it done! Making candy! Taffy! Suckers... Fudge!! Everyone who had a sweet tooth would turn down fudge that looked how these people were making it look! Some shit that should be in a prison Rachel Ray book!

Laundry porters got paid to bleach clothes! Iron man got paid to put crease in peoples shirts and pants! Store man gave you anything you wanted plus his tax!! This was also called a commissary flipper!! Shoe man, cleaned, fixed and sold shoes! Ticket man ran sports bets! 3 way man got paid for 3 way phone calls! BARBERS ate good off their clientele!! I ATE GOOD OFF MY CLIENTELE.

It was a mutual thing kind of like I scratched your back you scratch mine! I made them look good going on them visits and they paid me in commissary... There was too many hustles I can sit here all day and keep going about the different hustles there are in prison! So being broke or asking for money was slow for me ESPECIALLY ONCE I LEARNED HOW TO CUT HAIR.

I fell in love with cutting hair! I went to sleep thinking about it, woke up and wanted to cut!! The thrill of cutting a new type of hair everyday made me want to keep going! Like I said before in prison you see all different types of nationalities... You couldn't pick your barber unless you paid!! Another hustle inside the barber school!! Someone working the desk would get paid to let someone slide and g oto their barber or the barbers they thought were top of the class!! We cut everyday 8 in the morning we clock in to get our hours and we clock out at 1030. We have to be back to our blocks so they can count and we can eat lunch aka Chow!

12-3:30 we were back in the shop clocking out at 330 was the end of our day! From there we would go back to the block so we could do Standing Count. After that we eat chow and you go about your day until it's time to lockdown or g oto your bed area!! That was Monday through Friday! Obviously weekends we were off as well as any holidays or fog counts... fog counts happened a few times not on the regular but I witnessed a nice amount of them! This was when the fog was too thick for the guards to walk the perimeter of the prison "perimeter check"

This along with all the guard's reporting their numbers to the main booth on the compound is what cleared count! If numbers weren't right the guards had to re count which took forever!

Guards walked the perimeter checking for contraband or anyone trying to escape! Each guard had their own block they had to account for and they were responsible for! Count times they had to walk down each row and count person for person and then report those numbers by phone to the main booth aka CENTRAL! Count would then be cleared after perimeter check was finished and all numbers were reported! Yes this was every count! Annoying I know imagine being told to go to your bed like a little boy and told you couldn't move or go anywhere until they said so!! Mentally prison gave me trouble NOT PHYSICALLY!!

The camp had its own barn! They had their own classes on agriculture and allowed them to do real farm work instead of mopping halls!! Of course, we were inmates and always had to make the best of our situations, at the end of the day they weren't going to feed us! They didn't give a fuck about us! They were there to do 8 hour shifts and make our life hell if possible in between those 8 hours!

So we finessed and made our own way! Tobacco moved like crack in the 80's!! As soon as count would clear you would smell the tobacco and bible paper burning! Disrespectful but true the Bible paper is thin and often was compared to Ez wider joint papers! On the handball court you see people smoking and you see someone 6'5! This is when you look for the guards while your people smoke or fight! Fights happened but obviously not like on the compound! This is a privilege to a lot of people because they had it rough on the compound so they became comfortable with living a certain way!

The guards knew that and would threaten people by saying I'll move you back in the walls!! Meaning back on the main compound! This had a lot of people shook! Not everyone could handle the pressure of that living! Fight or Get beat on I always called it! Them being scared to go back they fold and fall in line and answer to the guards like little kids! It was sick to watch how a guard can break a man down that quick and then look down on them...

My first time going on the block I wasn't sure how the mail worked! So I walked up to the desk and asked if they had a mail list!! The guard looked at me and said no I don't have any mail for no heartless felon! I look at him like he is dumb as fuck! Starting at him I laugh and simply tell him I'm not in a gang! He says that's not what my computer says!! Fuck! That's when I knew I had a gang tag! Just from hanging with a group they classed me as belonging to that gang! There's no lies in this book! If I was apart of a gang I would say it.

I laugh and walk away showing him he can't break me like the rest... he wanted me to spaz out and get disrespectful!! I knew the mind games the guards and other people would try to use on me.. I paid attention! Never let them see you sweat... but deep down I knew how I really felt, bottle that up.. this is their world I'm just living in it!! In prison you would think there's just all scum bags and murders but I was able to meet some solid dudes who just simply were in the wrong lane or was in too many lanes at once and crashed out!

People who lost a lot of years behind those prison gates!! Some of the people had more memories inside the prison than outside! Some met people and those people became more solid and trustworthy than blood family members!!

My family was my backbone! Without them shit would have been 10X worse! My bid would have probably went different.. the phone calls and pictures kept me sane!! Many nights I couldn't g oto sleep so I looked at pictures and read letters only to get angry at myself for leaving them out there!! Why? Why would I do that? Not thinking! Young and Wild! 6 years was the perfect amount of time I NEEDED in order for me to see life how I see it now!! 2 years was not enough time and four years would have been close but those 6 years was a lot of weight on my shoulders!! But I stood ten toes down with that weight and I made it home untouched!! How did I end up in the worst county in OHIO not getting into one fight!

Going to commissary and cashing in and watching other people get extorted is beyond me. I never want you to think I'm bragging I'm getting to my point...

I was on a prison yard at 20 years old no facial hair. Barely any muscle because I was just partying all the time wasn't working out or keeping up with my health!! So I was skinny as hell!! Until I started doing my pushups, my pull ups and my dips!! Now we're talking about another monster!

Workouts became addictive! MANDATORY! Couldn't sleep right if I didn't work out! This was farther on in my bid, I know you are thinking I'm probably crazy for saying any prison time was what I NEEDED! But if you don't get it than you don't really understand how wild or young minded I was!! This prison sentence saved me!! I would have NEVER got my barber license on the streets!! That was last thing on my mind and going at my rate who knows if I would have even made it to see 21 on the streets! KARMA IS A BITCH! I got a clean slate when I came home and I made sure I kept my karma good! Because that bad side of karma isn't a joke at all!

23 months it took me to get my barber license... 1800 hours of hands on cutting experience!! I can't tell you how many heads I cut while in that

prison!! The number would blow your mind!! Daily cutting and improving my skills and learning new techniques.. even when I was watching other people cut I would add tips they used into my skill set!! It was a learning process and I soaked it up! Cam was a Student Aid "Tech Aid" they called us!

Once you graduated and of the teachers approved you became a Tech Aid! Cam was going home soon so I only had a few months to learn from him!! But it was enough time for me!! He made sure he helped me out the most because he seen how dedicated I was!! Sometime I would get mad in my head because he would put the most difficult haircuts in my seat When I was beginning to learn! I use to always say damn why you put this long hair cut in my chair!! It paid of in the end! He was my barber and gave some of the best fades I ever had to this day!! School was all mental for me!

There were multiple personalities around you at all times! Weird people, Tough acting people, talkative people, obnoxious people just too many emotions and personalities in one room daily!! You had to deal with these people and learn in the process! School on the streets is way different!! How many times has a barber on the street cut someone's hair doing DOUBLE LIFE!! You fuck that haircut up and you had to deal with the problems that came with it!! Talking about pressure!! Taking about being focused on a haircut!! Wanting to bless them so they don't put bad papers on your name.

That's all you needed was someone saying you were a shitty barber and the whole compound would know!! Too many times I heard people say I'm not going to such and such he shitty!! Wasn't always about speed! In barbering you have to have consistency and accuracy!! Classmates fought and Classmates got kicked out of school! That was just how prison went!

Some people went to school and don't even use their license!! Shit blows my mind how someone can just waste their time faking like they wanted to be a barber only to hit the streets and work for someone else in a factory!! It was competitive! There was a handful of people I looked as competitors everyone else was learning and or just didn't have it!

Some just wanted to go to school for "Good Days" and others just went to school to hustle! They knew the pack was going crazy and there was only one way to get it!! Find a Camp Plug! Good Days were a big deal! Some people got 5 good days a month! Meaning as long as they were in a program and not in trouble they would get 5 days knocked off their original sentence for good behavior!! Others got 1 good day a month! I personally got 1 good day a month! Once your MANDATORY time is up you can start receiving good days... I knocked over two months off my sentence!! School was fun at times and it was prison so it had the rough mental times as well.

Cutting hair became second nature for me. I loved it! I breathed it! Studying was even fun for me!! Because I had a goal at the end of the day! And hitting my goal was MANDATORY!! As I began cutting and began getting good at it my name started holding weight! Meaning people wanted me to cut their hair over most of the class! Like I said there was competition in the shop it was just all about who was really into it or was serious about it and you could tell who was serious and who wasn't.

My guy Ahmad was top of the clsss with me! He was the only one who beat my score on the written test! I got a 96% and he got a 98%!! We always tested each other and paid attention to each other's cuts!! My graduating class had 6 from our school and 3 from another prison barber school! Our School was new and we were the very first class to graduate from this school!! So we had to show up and show out! I took an Afro as the haircut I would be performing on test day.

We prepared for weeks to get our timing and techniques down!! You had a hour and a half to do a shampoo, blow dry, haircut razor shave and a facial!! Then you took a 50 question mutliple choice test!! We tested and we all passed! Ahmad, Ty, Danny, Lotion, Free and myself all passed and graduated! Graduating was so important to me because I needed to

Pain So Deep

graduate because I only had a year left after I graduated so it was crunch time!! I remember almost not graduating because of an ankle injury I received playing basketball the week of testing!!

Outside playing basketball not thinking nothing of it I land on my ankle and I immediately feel the pain shoot through my body!! Ahhhhh I yell as I goto the floor and grab my ankle!! Feels like my foot just snapped!! I hop u stairs to get to my rack, a injury was one thing they had to move you if they found out you had an injury because climbing stairs two flights of stairs was not good for any leg injury!

Avoiding getting sued they moved you as soon as possible... I put ice on my ankle and went to sleep I rolled my ankle plenty of times this one want a big deal! The next morning I couldn't move it, FUCK! I say in my head as I clinch my jaw!! I look down at my ankle only to see it is purple, Blue and Green! Standing on it felt impossible!! But getting to school was mandatory!! My dude J gave me a ankle brace and I put it on!! A ace bandage wrap along with the brace kept my ankle i tact and allowing me to move freely.

I tightened the ace wrap around my ankle then tied the brace up as tight as I could take! Putting my boots on I tightened them All the way ! Shoes tied tight I feel like I can move again, I don't know how I'm going to stand on my two feet and cut hair!! I walked to school jaw clenched every step I knew it was getting worse... I could feel the pulse in my foot throbbing!! I needed these last two weeks of hours to graduate! Otherwise I would have to wait until next class to test!! Suck it up! I went and walked on my ankle until I got my hours! Massaging it in free time I brought my ankle back just in time to take my State Boards Test.

I hadn't seen my mom or family in 5 years!! Last time I seen them was in 2011 when I was in the county!! And even then, I didn't get to touch them or kiss them... visits were through a glass window!! Imagine that... I was always thinking about them literally there was never a day I didn't think about them.. it got to the point I had to tell myself to let them live their life! Take a break from calling home! Slow up on writing! It hit me different because when those 15 minute phone calls end they always cried!!! Especially my grandma, she was the worst at this! At the end of every phone call I could hear her break down.. REAL TEARS!!

This shit broke my soul... hearing them all say they love me crying and sniffing that shit cut me deep.. sometimes I would have to sit for a couple minutes after they hung up to collect myself... anyone who really had a loved one out there they cared about knows this feeling!!

Anyone who wanted better for their families than to get a 15 minute phone call understands what I mean.. if you ever had a loved one locked up you feel my pain having to communicate and hear emotion through a 15-minute phone call!! Then click........ not knowing if you will talk to them again!! That was one of my biggest fears was not knowing if I would talk to my grandma again... idk she was just one person I really worried about because I knew how hard she would stress, on top of her age it just didn't sit right... of course I worried about my other family members but she is the backbone to my family a lot of people love her and she impacted a lot of people's lives!

Seeing her and my mom in the court room eyes bloodshot red from crying, hearing the judge snatch the breath from their bodies I hear them gasp. Loud cries follow sending chills down my spine I clinch my teeth head down I shake my head as I leave out the court room!! So yeah, my family means a lot to me!! They were there through thick and thin! Real Solid Shit!

Those friends that said they going to ride till the end, those same friends smiling in your face going to be the SAME friends leave your ass for dead in there only answering your phone calls and behind the scene dicking down the same girl phone you calling at night!!

It's a cold world it gets ugly! Pay Attention the streets are rigged and only last for temporary people! Meaning if you have a temporary thinking mind state you are simple minded and are not built to last!! You can't be built to last and have a temporary thinking mindset that will never work!! You can't keep up with someone who is built to last they are built for the LONG RUN!! Meaning temporary things don't impress him/her because they understand there is a bigger picture that has to come together first!! Following me? Pay attention if you think like a clown but dress like The Smoothest GQ model on this earth we stand on, Guess what? You still a Clown!! I learned in prison there's a lot to life... I watched them play chess and I watched game after game smart decisions... smart strategy!

I watched and I sat and thought on those moments I walked that yard by myself listening to my jp4 player!! They make it sound so good it's sick how they use technology to make it feel comfortable for people to come back... really sick if you think about it!! I learned a lot about myself in prison but knowing I WANTED LIFE was my main goal!

I seen people fighting for their life trying to get a chance at life just one more time.. I seen grown men the toughest people you would think never to break... I seen them break coming back from that court room!! I had no type of connection with these people but it sent chills down my arms to just hear them lose it in their cells!! Crashing out!! Hands punching their doors as they yell from frustration and pain!! Standing there I just listen and clench my teeth..... I HATE IT HERE!

I graduated from barber school June of 2016. It took me 23 months to get all my hours and take my test.. but I was focused and I made sure I handled my business all the way from the day I started barber school to the time I tested out!! Top 2! In score and time!! I took a Afro and my dude Ahmad was my competition. But it wasn't just at test time it was throughout barber school we pushed each other!! He had a technique of his own and so did I! We both had our eyes on the prize and we hit our goal! Everyone in my class that took their test and I give credit to where it's so but everyone in that class knows how competitive it was and they knew me and Ahmad were always trying to master our craft! It was like they could sense we were on to something with the clippers!

So we went to school and grinded daily, haircut after haircut we stood in the shop... every block in the prison and in the camp had a chance to get a haircut when the guard posted a sign up sheet! It was simple sign the sheet we send a pass for the following week rotating all different combinations of blocks and the camp a separate day!! I tested out with a 96 on my 50 multiple choice test! Ahmad got a 98!! I was laughing when they read our scores and we looked at each other and dapped up.

I knew I beat him in the haircut time, and I was ok with the 2 point defeat on the test side I got what I wanted and we worked hard for what we just got!! A few weeks later we have graduation! This was a little mush-fake bullshit graduation ceremony that they got funding from the government so they put it together to make it seem like it's for the inmates but really it's for that bag... ima tell it like I know it.

They let you have 2 visitors coming and I shot my shot with my mom! I NEVER wanted her to get on a routine for coming to see me!! I hated the process of getting to see them! I hated seeing them leave and me not laughing and going with them! There for a hour just to be gone again! Driving 3 hours from painesville to get to the prison to see me for a hour and then driving another 3 hours back home just wasn't no solid shit for me to put my family through.

My mom went to school and worked a job, shit, probably a couple jobs. She adapted to that I DONT GET TIRED mentality!! And I loved it still do!! So I asked my mom I remember the phone call she might too... excited to tell my mom the news I jump in the phone booth and close the window door behind me.. she answers feeling like a kid I can't wait to tell her!

I got my barber license mom!! She immediately says congratulations I love you, I told you that you could do it! I tell her thank you and tell her how it went... test scores she was shocked how well I did!! You really wanted this huh she asked. Yeah mom, I can't wait to come home and cut hair.... I love it for real.

She hears the passion through my phone call!! I tell her we have a graduation if she can make it if not it's ok... she says they will be there just get her on the visit list.. I tell her we were allowed 2 but they had to be over 18 and my sister tati was the only one at the time old enough and the only one I felt could really deal with seeing me like that!! It was tough they were holding tears as I walked in that room to see them.

I hadn't seen these beautiful people in YEARS!! Their faces had grown and matured into women! My sister was not a baby no more!! Sick to my stomach I wasn't there to help her in life!! Only talking to her for a couple minutes at a time as they passed the phone around the room so everyone had a chance to speak!!

My sister Jordyn barely talked.. she still barely talks she's just not a talkative person!! But she still managed to tell me she missed me and how proud she was of me!! Sitting there looking at them I can't stop staring they were grown it was weird because they looked different but there eyes were just you could see the pain!! The love!! It was all there focused in!!

I stare into their eyes... they stared back not budging not moving!!! Just watching me!! We hugged for the first time and their perfume hit my nose and I immediately felt calm and out of the room for a second... everything quiet! Room standing still in slow motion I hear a female voice, my mother's loving soft voice... I love you baby!! That moment both hurt me and helped me in such a way I don't think a lot of people understand... that pain of hugging your mom behind those walls in ANY JAIL OR PRISON is a different type of pain!!! That pain is something you don't forget that feeling in your stomach, looking around as you see other families sitting and talking with their loved ones.. some laughing others crying!

Always mixed emotions in the visiting room!! The room slowly gained sound again as I kissed her cold cheek her tears hit my lips I love you more I told her, my sister was grown now I smiled as she said what up Bro!! We hugged and I smiled the entire time!! I took a deep breath... after

5 years of not seeing them this moment was huge!! If I told you it wasn't a little different for me I would be lying... it was different in a sense I hadn't been around anyone I loved, anyone I really cared about and especially not these important people who are sitting in front of me!! I was 19 years young last time they seen me in person! A little ass boy! I was grown now! I grew into the man I am today because of the HARDSHIP I MADE IT OUT OF!!

After this visit they came to the ceremony which was held inside of the prison!! Another hard task to ask my mother and sister to do for me!! But they did it. We got our certificates and they stood there and clapped for me when they called my name.. walking past I couldn't do anything but smile from the time they arrived for the visit! After the ceremony they gave juice and cake and let us visit with our families for a few hours this was another reason I asked my mom I knew it was worth it now! I could visit them in morning then they could see me get my barber certificate and then get a visit for a few hours after!! It was all good vibes in that room!! Blessed to have them by my side! Blessed to see them still smiling with all the pain we been through.

Guards yell times up they walk the visitors after we say our last goodbye, I say see you soon!! My sister loved me we always had a different type of bond, but Tati was just so much like me in so many ways it was crazy!! And then her coming to this prison made it so much more of a bonding moment!! I hated telling them goodbye, but I only had 15 months left and I was a free man again...

Chapter Thirty Nine:
WALKING OUT NOT LOOKING BACK!!

Time passed I got "promoted" from a student to a Barber Tech Aid... I received 1 good day a month like I had been receiving when I was in barber school so no real promotion there but I was glad I still received them... with a little less than a year on my sentence now I can knock off a little less than 2 more weeks off my sentence!! And I do! From the day I started school till the time I finished I received good days! Grinding daily!! Weeks passed and I grew more anxious as time passed, waiting on my turn!! Seeing people leave made me even more anxious, I was bidding off of them meaning I knew people who were going home 3 months before me so I would wait on them to leave and when they left I knew I was next... if you been locked up you look at time differently... of course there is still 24 hours in a day but me personally I break down my day in time slots... after I wake up and get myself together I start my day and break it into time slots throughout the day!! Making sure I stay busy one thing I know is your day will pass you by if you aren't busy!! My workout changed! I became more hungry to workout.. adding jump rope and a Cross for training class my dude Lee ran! Lee was a psycho when it came to working out he would always push you to go that extra mile!! I love it because I seen the results!!

I was working out 3 times a day!! People knew I was in my mode I barely talked and majority of the time I had my headphones on!! Calling home just to check in on everyone they had a idea of when I came home but with my good days I had a surprise in store for them... only a few would be in on this secret!! Guards and inmates try you when you get closer to going home, some people simply are miserable and want to drag others down with them!! Guards randomly tearing my area up saying someone said I had a cell phone!! I knew what it was! Someone was trying to get me out of my hookup!! I stayed solid and laughed it off!! I got 60 days left of you think you bout to find a phone in my area you really got me confused with one of these goofies!! I tell the guard as he searches... just doing my job that's all!! Wasting your time and mine is all your doing right now... mad at the fact I gotta clean everything up he tearing apart looking for this phone!! They find nothing... 30 days left!!

My last 30 days in prison was the slowest part of my entire time being locked up!! It moved in slow motion! No matter what I did no matter how busy I stayed time just wasn't moving for me! I was thinking too much!! Working out and keeping myself together I made sure I was on point before I left those gates!! Deep waves and weighing 190 pounds solid I was looking the best I ever looked in life... prison preserves you! Meaning you drink water majority of the time and you working out so you are healthier than people on the street because all they wanna do is smoke and party... when I first got locked up I was 155 pounds I added 40 pounds and made it look good! Healthy and String I was ready! Mentally I was ready for the world.... I had been here too long! 6 years I had slot of time to think!! And I did! Business plans wrote down!! Connects I needed for those businesses!! Cooking with a couple for the last time before I left we made different breaks.. I cut hair until the morning I left! I gave my commissary away splitting it up between people I know didn't have money or food like that!! I made so much money of my beard trimmers!! I passed those on too, I wasn't going to take them home!!

Passing blessings was something I was good for! Even in a cold prison I still did some good!! The last week leading up to me going home was starting to get to me!! Stomach turning, I was really about to be free!! Going to take my pictures and release medical records I jump through all the prisons little hoops knowing they want me to stay and continue to get paid for me being there!! It's all good I know what I'm about to do and that's leave this hell hole behind me and not looking back! Success was my next move!

The night before I went home I stayed up all night just thinking I know my eyes had bags under them I was up late !! Just thinking of where I was just at for 6 years! Thinking back on all the foul shit I seen! I really made it out!! In 24 hours I'll be back reunited with my family!! Wow! It's really here.... I barely went to breakfast but this morning you better know I was there! Eating my cereal I pass the rest of my tray to someone else, leaving I go grab my locker box and sit in the hallway waiting on my name to be called to go home!! A couple of the people I kicked it with were sitting by me and talking to me, asking me if I'm ready and sharing jokes!! Good vibes from good people! I took their names and numbers down and would write them when I got home and got situated!

"Sheffey", the guard says you ready and I say hell yeah... I dap the few people I was talking to up and they tell me keep my head up and I tell them to do the same!!

Walking to the main compound I feel my chest pounding!! This is it!! People I see in the hallway see me and ask if I'm leaving today and I say yeah!! Before you leave everyone has to dress out meaning they switch you from your state blues to your going home outfit!! This outfit was a Grey Jogging Suit!! If you seen someone in this outfit you knew they were a free man!! The feeling felt different I never felt this way my whole time! I'm here, the time is now!! I'm anxious! Hungry to get home and get to business!! But I'm patient I know my success will take time and I know the real world is a lot similar but very different than prison!! I've been in hell for 6 years it was time to see a different lifestyle!!

As I sit in the waiting room staring out the window I had NEVER seen this part of the prison! I came in the back door like a slave and they walked me out the front door like I was a guest!! Talking nice and clear I paid them no attention I knew it was fake love!!

Time passed by and I grew more and more anxious! Where were they? Wondering when they were gonna pull up to get me out of this hell hole I waited patiently!! They couldn't just let me walk out and wait outside? I am a free man? No it's against the prison policy because they were technically still reliable for your life if something was to happen!! And then I see it... My oldest brother in his strong army walk!! My younger brother looking grown as hell I hadn't seen him since he was a little boy playing sports... my heart instantly raced!! My sister Tati and Imani all smiling and crying!! They had bags in their hands!! They walk in and we all hug for what seems like forever!! I tell them I love them and miss them.. holding the tears in was stinging my eyes!! My throat was tight and felt like in a knot the love was so pure and raw!

Love I missed for so long!! They hand me the bags and inside I see a pair of all white forces, a blue Nike jumpsuit, polo boxers and polo socks!! They got me together real quick and I was so in a rush to get home I kept the socks and boxers I had on and put everything else on! I was ready to leave I looked in that mirror before I walked out!! Took a deep breath and walked out!! Signed the papers the guards asked me to and got my money in a little Manila envelope! Inside this envelope was money I had saved up from not having to go to the store and the $75 you get when you leave prison... they give you $75 to get on a bus and get home! If you have a ride then you still get the $75 you just keep it so that's what I did... I would be damn if I was riding a bus home!! Someone was coming to get me for sure... I waited too long for this!!

We walk out those gates and that sun beams down on me!! Like god moved the clouds and sent a beam of light to hit me!! Glowing I taste the air!! It's different on the other side. Smells different! The wind blows different! As soon as I stepped out of that prison and hit the pavement to freedom all my pressures and all my dead weight had been lifted from my shoulders!!

Feeling like I was carrying a ton of bricks on me at all times had just been cut and now I feel normal! I feel human! Treating you like a dog or a slave inside of prison makes you look at life and living differently.... I didn't look back at that prison once we pulled off and that part of my life will always be remembered but that life is dead to me!! I won't put my family through that pain again! And most importantly I won't put myself through that pain and suffering again!! Mentally and Physically I changed!! Riding in that car I just stared out the window for a few moments taking a deep breath and really understanding I made it home and am now with the people I really love! My family! My family means everything!! Fuck a friend I'll never put a friend over my family again I did that once and look how they left me for dead... no letters and when I did talk to them it was because I reached out to get in contact with them!!

So as far as I'm concerned I'll say hi and bye but I owe nobody that wasn't there for me that said they would be there any loyalty!! Fuck them because at the end of the day that's what they said about me!! Out of sight out of mind! If you aren't present you will only see Facebook statuses saying FREE PYRO! But you won't get any money or letters from these same people who post the status!! Why did I have 100 people saying they missed me and loved me but not even 5 people wrote me? Is that love! Or is that loving someone when it's convenient for them!! Fake love is what I call it!! But I'm free and open minded! I see clearly and I understand how life works now! I needed to see the real and prison will show you every-one's true colors and will open your eyes if you let it...

Chapter Forty:
FAMILY!!

September 30, 2017 was the ending of my time in prison!! Maxed out! No early release or judicial! No halfway house!! 2,190 days straight! Living in hell! Listening to another man tell me when I had to shit shower or eat!! Being around human beings who don't take care of their hygiene! Being around ignorant people! Seeing the violence up close and personal I stil could smell blood and pepper spray in my nostrils... so much pain in that lifestyle I just left behind!! Everyday waking up not knowing if you would make it home or if you would lose a loved one while you were locked away! Not being able to see them one more time!!

That shit haunted me but I fought those demons daily and I won every fight with those demons!! In real situations they show how solid you really are!! Anyone can fold up and give up but who is going to remain solid and handle their business like a man?! That's the question! And that was me! 10 toes down I stood day for day blow for blow in that ring!! Eating the bullshit food! Listening to the guards degrade us by telling us SQUAT AND COUGH!!! I'll never forget what that last guard said to me before I left!!!

"I'll see you soon with more time than you came in with, you are just like the rest!"

That comment sits in my head to this day as MOTIVATION!! I laughed in his face and said I'll be making more money than you and living a better life than you by the time I'm 30 bet on that!! And I left him standing there looking puzzled and stupid!! One thing you can never do is put me in the category as the next man!! I'm not built like most people my age or younger! I'm rare! I see life through a tunnel vision and my mind is made... THOSE STREETS ARE DEAD TO ME!! the most money in the world doesn't add up to doing time in prison it's just simply not worth it! And if you are reading this I just hope you understand and grasp what I wanted you to get from this book... streets are good for two things ending you in a Cell or in A Box!

It's a temporary game that is called a trap for a reason!!

Trapping you in a mentality that you can't shake! Trapping you in a cycle you can't get out of! A lot of people go to prison come home and go right back to what they know... the easy route if you ask me!! The route I took and am taking to this day is the hard daily grind! But at the end of the day my goal is to have a beautiful family and put us in position to WIN!! And I will achieve that goal!!

My mother and Grandma thought I was coming home Monday! I got out on a Saturday!! So you know I had a trick up my sleeve for them! Without them this family wouldn't be what it is to this day!! Those Queens deserved this and I made sure they would NEVER FORGET THIS MOMENT...

My brother took me to the iPhone store and got me a 7plus! I never had a iPhone before this time and I was LOST in the technology.! I had no clue how to work this phone I felt like a old man!! Everything had changed! The touch screen was so smooth and glided when I scrolled! The last phone I had before I left the streets in 2011 was a T-Mobile side kick 2! It had touch screen but it was a vibrating screen when you touched it this was a different level!! They helped me set it up and showed me SNAPCHAT INSTAGRAM AND FACEBOOK like I was a old man.

I slowly was workin my way through the phone! It took me a long time to figure it out! Months before I really got the hang of it!! But I was in love with this phone! The pictures were pure and me coming home having my glow was something the camera caught perfectly!! Waves beating!! That's all I would do in my free time was brush my hair!! Weight healthy I worked out non stop!! Skin clear from taking care of my hygiene and drinking lots of water had my skin glowing!

There was a few new members of the family I needed to meet! Family members I heard of but never met because of where I was!! My youngest brother on my moms side had a babygirl and I couldn't wait to meet her! Seeing the pictures in prison only made me want to see her more!

We pull into this house I had never seen before! We lived in EUCLID,OH at this time! The house was beautiful I just remembered thinking how proud of my mom I was! Look how far she came look how much hard work she put into this family!! We use to share rooms now everyone got their own room!! Chris walks in first! His army tactics on point as I follow behind him and he directs me through the kitchen!! My grandma is up first....

Sitting in the upstairs living room she is making signs for me! WELCOME HOME SHON! I read the sign she is writing and decorating and it gives me goosebumps and my heart speeds up as she doesn't notice me enter the room behind her!! Chris stands in front of her and I walk up to her... I say something to her but she is so focused on the sign she doesn't notice who is talking to her she just talks as she keeps working!! I say hey and she looks up at me and looks at Chris thinking I was my younger brother she said she didn't notice it was me until she took a hard look! I looked her in her eyes and she immediately started jumping up and down as she cried hysterically!! Good tears!! This is the way I wanted to see my family cry when they were happy not seeing me behind locked walls and in handcuffs!! We hugged tightly anyone who knows my grandma knows she gives those tight hugs that take your breath away! 4'11 her power was so strong!! She cried in my ear as she kept repeating "Thank you Jesus" you brought him home to us... "Thank you Jesus" my grandma would always tell me she was worried about me and praying for me!!

I'm glad I was able to make it home to her and my family!! As long as she was at the house she wanted me next to her! Sitting on the couch she would hold my hand and just look at me!! Staring at me she said I love you baby and started crying! I missed you so much she continued... Many nights I didn't sleep because I was worried about you in there!! Every word hitting me harder and harder... tears of joy stream my face as I wipe them away!! You don't know how many nights I prayed to see you again!! We hugged and I let her know how much I love her and missed her!!

My mom went out to the store a distraction my brothers and sisters put together so we could surprise both of them at separate moments!! My mom was next!! She went to the dollar store to grab more decorations and markers!! Walking in the house everyone was sitting in the downstairs living room!! She walks downstairs and they tell her to grab the sign to start working on it was around the corner in the living room... just as she was walking over to get it I walked out!! I watched her eyes glow and get big!! Staring me in my face it hit her!! SHUT THE FUCK UP!! Omg SHUT THE FUCK UP!! Those were her exact words of excitement... she couldn't believe I was standing in front of her free!! We hugged and she balled her eyes out!! Sniffing and crying she said she missed me so much and loves me!! I say it back and we just stand there hugging and holding each other for a long time! This wasn't like the visit this was real, I was really home and free and around nothing but love and family!! Family Is All You Need!!

Everyone so happy and at peace we were a whole family again everyone home and breathing!! We talked and laughed and I met my Niece Gia!! Jayden my youngest brother on my moms side was the first one to have a kid! Beautiful babygirl! I fell in love with Gia from the first time they let me hold her!! It had been so long since I held a baby!! But it was like riding a bike you don't forget!! Staring in her eyes I told her I loved her and we connected! She loves her uncle and I would play her favorite music and we would dance and laugh!! She changed my life and she didn't even know it!!

Everything was going smooth! Family was all here and happy and I loved that! One of my close friends one of the only friends who kept their word Taylor bought a section at a club in Downtown Cleveland we were suppose to go to... I never made it!!

Prior to me getting released from prison they told me I had a few fines to pay in lake county for an old case! 2011 let me remind you is when this case was from. I specifically asked if I needed to pay money or was there more to the case, she told me just pay the money owed!! This case was from when me and mike went to jail at his house party and never made it to court!! I got locked up before I could make it to court there was no way I could have went! I was in another county looking at 17 years fuck that little ass money they wanted... Something told me to wait until Monday...

Me trying to be on the positive side and wanting to make sure I was on the right track I went on Saturday the very Same Day I got out at 3:00 my brother Chris took me to the County to Pay my fines!!!

Should have listened to my gut!!

We walk into the county jail and I immediately don't like it! Some-thing isn't right! We go to the desk and I tell her I just got released from prison and am there to pay off fines for a old 2011 case! She gets on the phone and say hang on for a second someone will be with me!! We stand there only to see when I turn around two sheriffs trucks pull up... I already know what's about to happen next!!! They walk up and say SHEF-FEY?

I say yea that's me I'm here to pay a .... they cut my sentence short take their handcuffs out and say YOU NEED TO COME WITH US!!

Handcuffs tight on my wrist I feel the blood circulation getting cut off!! Sitting in the back seat of this Sheriff Van this has to be a dream........

MAYFIELD HEIGHTS POLICE DEPARTMENT
WITNESS / VICTIM STATEMENT

Report number: 11-09556

Name: Janelle M. Dowdy
Age: 20
Sex: F

Address: 672 N. State St.
City: Painesville
State: OH
Zip: 44077

Race or Nationality: Blk (non-hispanic)
Marital status: Single
Cell phone number: 440-221-4048
Work phone number: Mentor Kohls

do hereby give this voluntary statement concerning Robbery which occurred on Tuesday (10-30-11)

At approximately 8:30am *Thursday morning* I drove to Concord. Gerald and Shon were there sleeping. They woke up, got dressed and explained their plan of robbing Howard's jewelery store. Shon had a tazer but that wasn't enough. We left the place in Concord at 9:30. Shon said we had to get his friend from Euclid because they needed another person. I picked him up on the street at about 10:00. They discussed how they needed guns to dri, and how he had someone to get them from. We then drove to Shoregate towers to pick up the guns, but the person didn't have them. At about 10:15 they instructed me to go to the Walmart in Eastlake where they stole 2 bb guns. These would be the tools used to rob the jewelery store. Nina - a friend of theirs, used to work there and told them how much money could be in (the main register) and that it is a Howards policy not to hit the distress button until after a robbery accured. (9:30am) I told Gerald how scared I was, but he kept explaining to me how we wouldn't get caught and everything would be "ok". He told me to have a couple shots 3:10am They instructed me to park in the back of the plaza to calm my nerves

continued on other side: [Page 1 of 4]

The undersigned affirms, under penalty of law of falsification, the above statement is TRUE.

Signed: Janelle M. Dowdy
Witnessed:
Date: 11/21/11 Time: 2:00 PM
Witnessed:

MAYFIELD HEIGHTS POLICE DEPARTMENT
WITNESS / VICTIM STATEMENT

Report number: 11-09558

I, _____ Name: (print all information clearly) _____ Birth date: _____ Age: _____ Sex: _____ Social Security number: _____

Address: _____ City: _____ State: _____ Zip: _____

_____ do hereby give this voluntary statement

Race or Nationality: _____ marital status: _____ home phone number: _____ work phone number: _____

concerning, _____ which occurred on _____ at _____
Crime or incident: _____ Date: _____ Time: _____

Going on and why. They said that they robbed this Jewlery shop and they did it with two bb guns and a tazer. It was Gerald Murphy, Andre McMorris, Shon Shezzy, and this girl named JnaL. This exactly how I was told bout wat happened, they pulled into the back of the store and they ran in threw da front and layed everyone dwn and a girl tried to run out so Andre threw her on the Floor, and Punched sum girl for not cooperating with him. Gerald was In da back Grabbing Jewlery and those diamonds. They Grabbed money Jewlery and I think dats it. When they left JenL (dA driver) sped off and Shon said dat they took A picture of the car but he wasn't sure iz dey was able to see da license plate number, they took Andre to Euclid and then Kame back to my house in concord. That's wen they must have hid everything Kuz they came over like nothing and got me outta bed that day. I was home sleep, babysitting Taylor's Kids. After dat We went out. But ~~Sunday~~ Saturday came and my door got kicked in and da police found da diamonds there @ my house. Me, my brother and Pyro went back

continued on other side: [Page 1 of 2]

The undersigned affirms, under penalty of law of falsification, the above statement is TRUE:

Signed: _____ Witnessed: Det. _____ D37

Date: 11/14/2011 Time: 350 AM/PM Witnessed: _____

MAYFIELD HEIGHTS POLICE DEPARTMENT
WITNESS / VICTIM STATEMENT

Report number: 11-05558

I, _____ Name: (print all information clearly) _____ Birth date: ___ Age: ___ Sex: ___ Social Security number: ___

_____ Address: _____ City: _____ State: ___ Zip: ___

_____ Race or Nationality: ___ marital status: ___ home phone number: ___ work phone number: ___ do hereby give this voluntary statement

concerning, _____ which occurred on ___ at ___
Crime or incident: Date: Time:

to my house to see what was missing and he said the bb guns tazor and diamonds was missing. I grabbed clothes and left. Saturday night Shon She77y brought two guns we all split up and went our ways but met up at da hotel to smoke and shit. They also rented a partybus for Gerald Murphys b-day kuzz they did all this for his b-day weekend. Neena Waybrant tld them about how to do it and all. I didnt know that ~~xxxxxx~~ they were goING to do dis till after da police went in my crib.

END
D27

continued on other side: [Page 3 of 3]
The undersigned affirms, under penalty of law of falsification, the above statement is TRUE.
Signed: __23   Witnessed: DET. __ D27

MAYFIELD HEIGHTS POLICE DEPARTMENT
WITNESS / VICTIM STATEMENT

Report number: 11-09558
#3

Name: (print all information clearly) _____ Birth date: _____ Age: __ Sex: __ Social Security number: _____

Address: _____ City: _____ State: __ Zip: _____ do hereby give this voluntary statement

Race or Nationality: _____ marital status: _____ home phone number: _____ work phone number: _____

concerning, _____ which occurred on _____ at _____
Crime or incident: Date: Time:

That was the last time I saw them that day. They had a party the next day, Friday, I showed up there at about 10 o'clock, the cops came for a noise complaint at about 12:30, they made everyone leave and arrested Mike and Shan, and Gerald kept saying "we got bail money, it's nothin'." I don't want to make it sound like I didn't do anything serious, I committed a crime and I shouldn't have let anyone influence me. I am a smart girl and I'm very happy to have all this finally be over. By making this statement I feel my conscience is clear. I would like to say sorry, I'm sure it doesn't mean much but I do sincerely mean it and will take full responsibility for my actions.

continued on other side: [Page 3 of 3]

The undersigned affirms, under penalty of law of falsification, the above statement is TRUE.

Signed: _____ Witnessed: _____ 11/21/11
Date: _____ Time: _____ AM/PM Witnessed: _____

MAYFIELD HEIGHTS POLICE DEPARTMENT
WITNESS / VICTIM STATEMENT

Report number: 11-09558

I, Jorge R Jimenez Rodriguez, [redacted] 21 M [blank]

concerning A Robbery which occurred on _____ at _____

Thursday→ First Pyro stayed @ my house for a while and then got kicked out. Wen he came back to stay kuze he didn't have no where to go he spent da nite there. And den left in da mourning While I was asleep. Wen he came back he woke me up and told me lets go kick it Jen L and murphy was with him and we got drunk and went to da mall after dat we went back to Painesville and got ~~~~ in Brittanys car and we rode out to Beechwood mall and dey went shoppin dey brought mi food. On Friday they went shoppin again at Beechwood mall. We went and party at mike shears house dat nite Pyro went to Jail. On Saturday Pyro was out he already got a Hotel room and has been staying there. Saturday I found out wat they had done because the police went in my house and I've talked to my girlfriend threw text messages. I walk to painesville and went and got a ride from this girl named Brittany to da hotel room where they was @. Wen I got there Pyro and Gerald Murphy explained wat was really

continued on other side: [Page 1 of 3]

The undersigned affirms, under penalty of law of falsification, the above statement is TRUE.

Signed: [signature]   Witnessed: DET D27
Date: 11-14-2011   Time: 3:50 PM   Witnessed: _____

Mayfield Heights Police

Investigative Report **Title / Subject:** Follow Up

Incident Number
11-09558

was looking at me while he was telling me his side of the story. I then told Mr. Sheffey that I knew all about the robbery. I told him I knew he did the robbery with Mr. Murphy, Mr. McMorris and that Janelle was the driver. When I said this to Mr. Sheffey he put his hands on the desk and lowered his head onto his hands so he was no longer looking at me. I told Mr. Sheffey that I knew that it was Mr. Murphy's twenty first birthday this past Saturday and not Mike's. Mr. Sheffey stopped talking and would not answer any questions. When Mr. Sheffey put his head down I noticed his new tattoo was scabbing. This tattoo was on his left wrist area. Mr. Sheffey then asked for his lawyer. I then told Mr. Sheffey that he would be taken back down to the jail and that if he changed his mind and wanted to talk that he could ask for a detective. Mr. Sheffey was then taken back to his cell.

On Friday, 11/18/11 a subpoena was sent to T-Mobile with regards to Ms. Lybarger's cell phone ███████████. Subpoena's were also sent to T-Mobile for Mr. Rodriguez's cell phone (440-269-9523) and Mr. Sheffey's cell phone (440-231-9607).

On Sunday, 11/20/11 Ms. Dowdy was arrested on MHPD's warrant for this case.

On Monday, 11/21/11 Ms. Dowdy was interviewed in MHPD's upstairs interview room by Det. Steffey and Det. Oberdoester. Ms. Dowdy admitted to being the get away driver in this case and she identified Mr. Sheffey, Mr. McMorris, and Mr. Murphy as the guys she drove to Howard's Jewelry and Loan on 11/10/11 and that they committed the robbery. This interview was taped. See Det. Steffey's supplemental.

On Tuesday, 11/22/11 I spoke to Prosecutor Paul Myles and it was decided to file direct charges on Mr. Murphy and Mr. McMorris.

On Saturday, 11/26/11 I received a phone call from Communication Officer Menosky who informed me that Mr. McMorris had been arrested on our warrant.

On Monday, 11/28/11 I along with Det. Oberdoester interviewed Mr. McMorris in MHPD's upstairs interview room. I first read Mr. McMorris the Miranda warnings which he signed and said that he wanted to answer questions.

Mr. McMorris at first denied knowing anything about this case. Mr. McMorris then started crying and admitted to being involved in the robbery. Mr. McMorris said that on 11/10/11 Ms. Dowdy picked him up at his house with Mr. Sheffey and Mr. Murphy in the car. They then drove to Mayfield Heights where they robbed Howard's Jewelry and Loan. Mr. McMorris said that he did not want to do it but Pyro (Mr. Sheffey) wouldn't turn the car around.

I then asked Mr. McMorris why he pulled the customer back in the store and he said, "I was scared." I then asked Mr. McMorris why he pushed over the jewelry cabinet and he said, "Because I was mad." Mr. McMorris said that he did not get any money after the robbery.

I then asked Mr. McMorris why he threw his hooded sweatshirt out of the car on Babbitt Rd. and he said, " didn't want it anymore." Mr. McMorris said that after the robbery Ms. Dowdy drove him home first. Mr. McMorris hasn't seen or spoke to Mr. Sheffey, Mr. Murphy, and Ms. Dowdy since the robbery. Mr. McMorris then wrote out a statement to this report. I taped this interview and placed the CD in the case folder.

MAYFIELD HEIGHTS POLICE DEPARTMENT
WITNESS / VICTIM STATEMENT

Report number: 11-09558

I, Andre mcmorris, [REDACTED] 19 m
21930 ivan ave, euclid, oh 44[1]2[?]
216-731-4225 do hereby give this voluntary statement concerning,

I was at Home Sleep when I got a call from pyro He told me he hand a move for us I didnt no where it was till we got there But also it was 3 People in the car I only new 2 of the People name in the car there name is meech and Pyro so we went up to mayfiled at a store I put my mass on out side in went in with them I pulled a lady in from outside the Place I also Kocked something over thin I ran to the Back in got in the car thin they tuck me to euclid on a street called tracy I tuck off my hoody and left it there they tuck all the money home and kept telling me they were going to cull me and cut me in.

End D27

The undersigned affirms, under penalty of law of falsification, the above statement is TRUE.

Signed: Andre M
Date: 11/28/11 Time: 1:32 AM/PM
Witnessed: DET D27

MAYFIELD HEIGHTS POLICE DEPARTMENT
WITNESS / VICTIM STATEMENT

Report number: 11-09558

I, Jorge P. Jimenez Rodriguez [redacted] 20 M do hereby give this voluntary statement concerning A Robbery which occurred on

Thursday→ First Pyro stayed @ my house for a while and then got kicked out. Wen he came back to stay Buzz he didn't have no where to go he spent da nite there. And den left in da mourning while I was asleep. Wen he came back he woke me up and told me lets go kick it. Jen L and Murphy was with him and we got drunk and went to da mall after dat we went back to Painesville and got in Brittanys car and we rode out to Beechwood Mall and dey went shoppin dey brought mi food. On Friday they went shoppin again at Beechwood mall. We went and party at Mike Shears house dat nite Pyro went to Jail. On Saturday Pyro was out he already got a hotel room and has been staying there. Saturday I found out wat they had done because the police went in my house and I've talked to my girlfriend threw text messages. I walk to Painesville and went and got a ride from this girl named Brittany to da hotel room where they was @. Wen I got there Pyro and Gerald Murphy explained wat was really

continued on other side: [Page 1 of 3]

Date: 11-14-2011 Time: 3:50 PM

MAYFIELD HEIGHTS POLICE DEPARTMENT
WITNESS / VICTIM STATEMENT

Report number: 11-05558

to my house to see what was missing and he said the bb guns tazor and diamonds was missing I grabbed clothes and left. Saturday night Shon Shetty brought two guns We all split up and went our ways but met up at da hotel to smoke and shit. They also rented a partybus for Gerald murphys b-day kuzz they did all this for his b-day weekend. Neena waybrant tld them about how to do it and all. I didn't know that they were goING to do dis till after da police went in my crib.

END
D27

[Page 3 of 3]

MAYFIELD HEIGHTS POLICE DEPARTMENT
WITNESS / VICTIM STATEMENT

Report number: 11-09558

I, Andre mcmorris, Age 14, Sex m

Address: 21850 ivan ave, City: Euclid, State: OH, Zip: 44116

Home phone number: 216-731-4dds

do hereby give this voluntary statement:

I was at Home sleep when I got a call from pyro He told me he had a move for us I didnt no where it was till we got there But also it was 3 People in the car I only new 2 of the people name in the car there name is meech and pyro so we went up to mayfiled at a Store I put my mass on out side in went in with them I pulled a Lady in from outside the place I also Kocked something over thin I ran to the Back in got in the car thin they tuck me to Euclid on a Street called tracy I tuck off my hoody and left it there they tuck all the money home and kept telling me they were going to call me and cut me in.

Evo
D27

continued on other side: [Page 1 of 1]

The undersigned affirms, under penalty of law of falsification, the above statement is TRUE:

Signed: Andre M
Witnessed: DET D27
Date: 11/25/11 Time: 1:32 AM/PM

Mayfield Heights Police
Investigative Report — Title/Subject: Follow Up
Incident Number: 11-09558

I asked Mr. Rodriguez why he thinks they robbed the Mayfield Heights Howard's Jewelry and Loan store and he said," Because Neena Waybrant set it up." I asked Mr. Rodriguez who Neena was and he said that she used to work at the Mentor Howard's Jewelry and Loan store and she is friends with all the guys involved. Mr. Rodriguez said that Neena told them how they could rob the place, that she knew they could get real money (a lot of money), and she knew that they wouldn't call the police until after they got away.

I then asked Mr. Rodriguez how he knew so many details about the robbery if he wasn't there and he said that he spoke to Mr. Sheffey and Mr. Murphy this past Saturday night at the hotel in Mentor and they told him everything. Mr. Rodriguez kept denying his involvement in the robbery. Mr. Rodriguez kept crying and saying that he had no involvement with this robbery. Mr. Rodriguez said that yesterday while he was partying with Mr. Sheffey and Mr. Murphy he decided that he was going to hire an attorney and turn himself in to MHPD. I asked him why he would do this if he had no involvement and he said, "I knew I was getting arrested because you guys found that shit in my house." Mr. Rodriguez said that he wanted to turn himself in because he wants to clear his name. I asked Mr. Rodriguez if he wanted to take a voice stress analyzer test and he said, "I will take that mother fucker right now." I then asked Mr. Rodriguez if he would be willing to write out a statement to everything he told me and he said, "Yes." I then gave Mr. Rodriguez a few statement forms and he asked me a question. Mr. Rodriguez asked that I leave his name out of this case and I asked why. Mr. Rodriguez said that he was afraid of Mr. Sheffey and what he may do to his family. I asked what he meant and he said that Mr. Sheffey bought two real guns yesterday on the street. Mr. Sheffey bought a .40 cal and a .357 handgun. Mr. Rodriguez believes these guns are at the hotel in Mentor. Mr. Rodriguez then said forget it, they are going to figure it out anyways.

Mr. Rodriguez then wrote a three page statement with everything he just told me. I then called Det. Duffy (Lyndhurst P.D.) who informed me that he can do a voice stress analyzer on Mr. Rodriguez tomorrow morning. I then went back into the interview room and told Mr. Rodriguez this and he said that he wanted to take the test. I then escorted Mr. Rodriguez back into the jail and I told him that I would get him tomorrow morning for the voice stress analyzer test.

I then called Jordan Perkins about this case. Mr. Perkins told me that this past Thursday (11/10/11) he was at home and then left to go out with his mother at around 11am. I asked Mr. Perkins if anyone was home and he said, "Jorge." I asked him if he was sure and he said, "90 percent sure." Mr. Perkins said, "I'm pretty sure Jorge was home because my sister was working, I went out with my mother and Jorge is the only other person who watches the kids." Mr. Perkins said that Jorge had to be home then.

I asked Mr. Perkins where he was this past Saturday and he said that he left home around 3pm or 4pm. Mr. Perkins said that he left the house with Jorge and they walked to Painesville. Mr. Perkins said they walked for about an hour then he was picked up by his mother. I asked Mr. Perkins if they saw and police cars as they walked out of his development and he said, "No."

I asked Mr. Perkins what he knew about the robbery and he said, "Jorge told him about it yesterday (11/13/11)." I asked Mr. Perkins what Jorge said and he said that he was about to get arrested for something he didn't do. Mr. Perkins said that Jorge denied being involved in the robbery. I asked Mr. Perkins if he knew that there was evidence from the robbery in his basement and he said, "No, that's where Jorge's brother, Peter Ventura and Mr. Sheffey hang out.

On Tuesday, 11/15/11 at 10am, I along with Det. Steffey took Mr. Rodriguez to Lyndhurst P.D. so he could take the voice stress analyzer test. Upon arrival we met with Det. Duffy who then interviewed Mr. Rodriguez in Lyndhurst P.D.'s upstairs interview room. Mr. Rodriguez told Det. Duffy the same story that he told me yesterday about the robbery. Det. Duffy then administered the voice stress analyzer test which Mr. Rodriguez denied being a part of the robbery and being in the car during the robbery. Mr. Rodriguez passed this test with

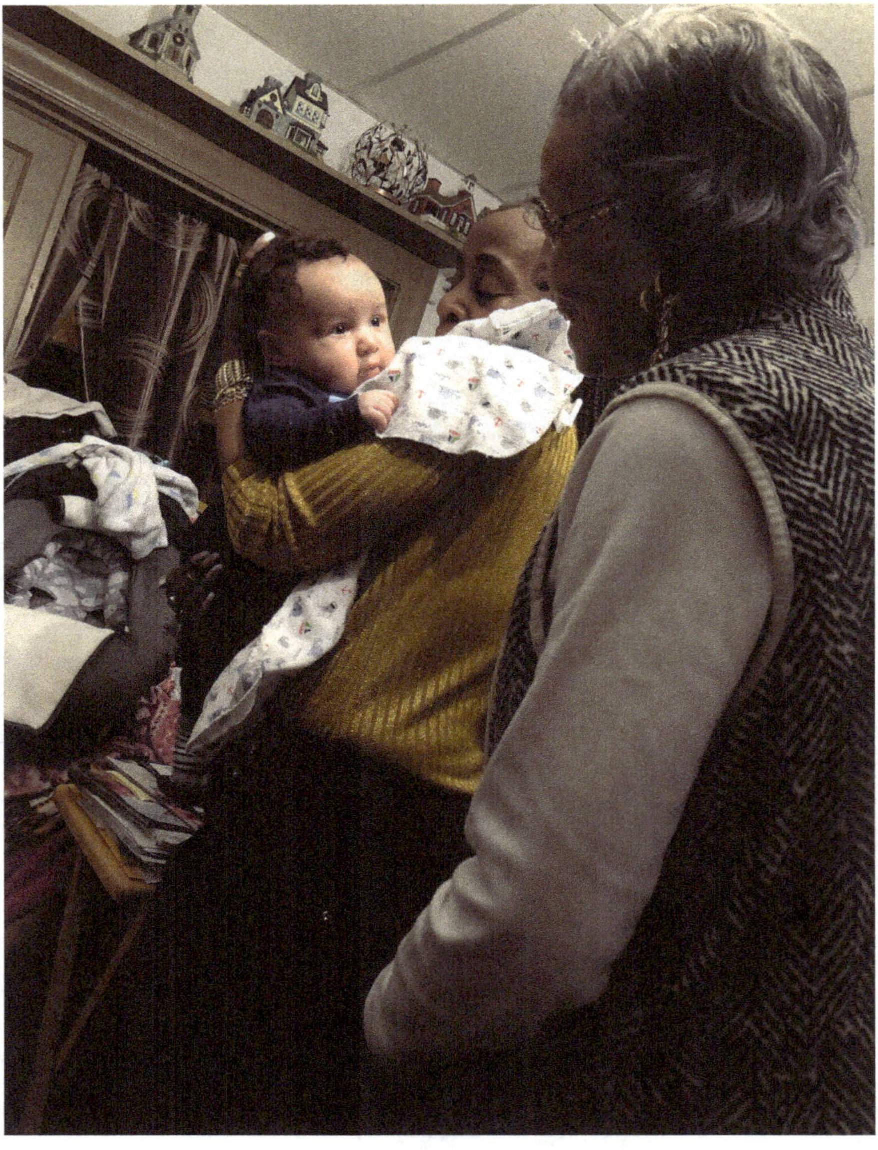

Pain So Deep

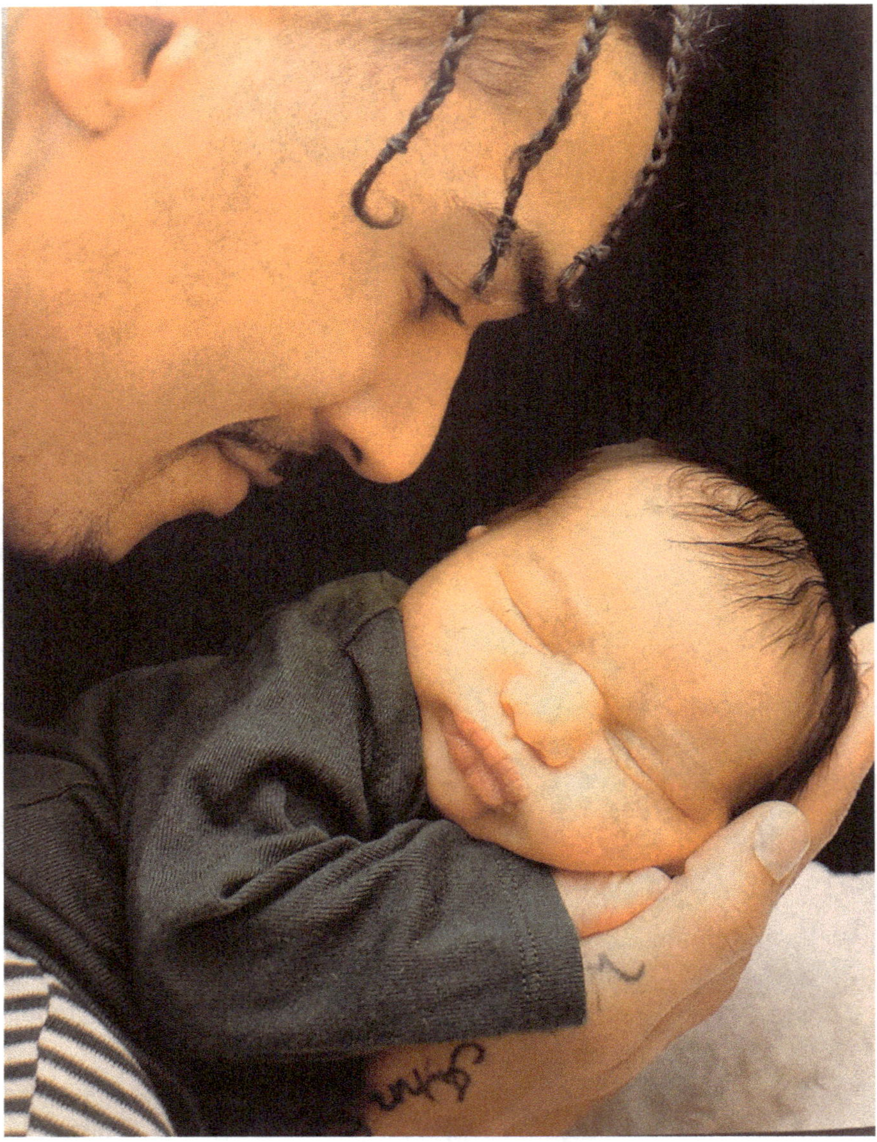

Pain So Deep

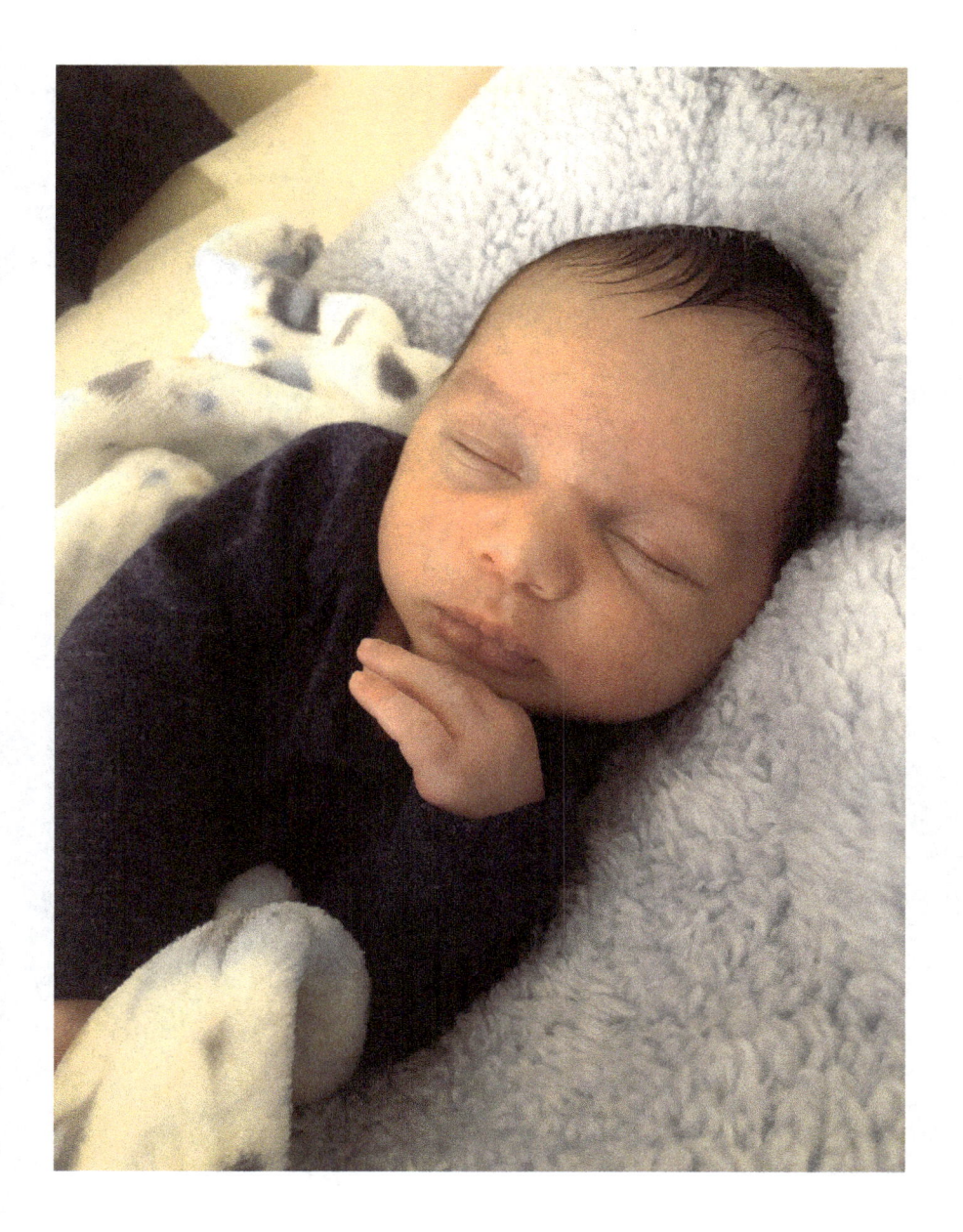

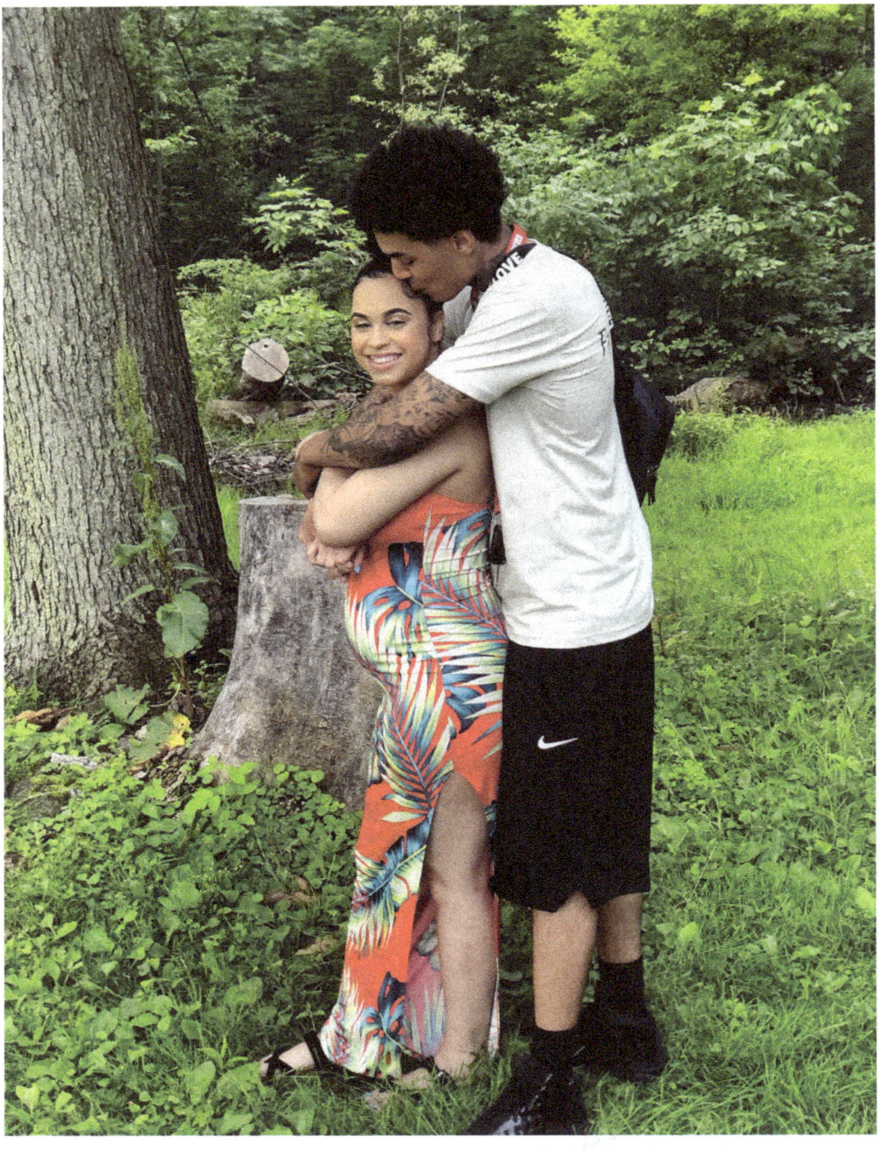

Pain So Deep

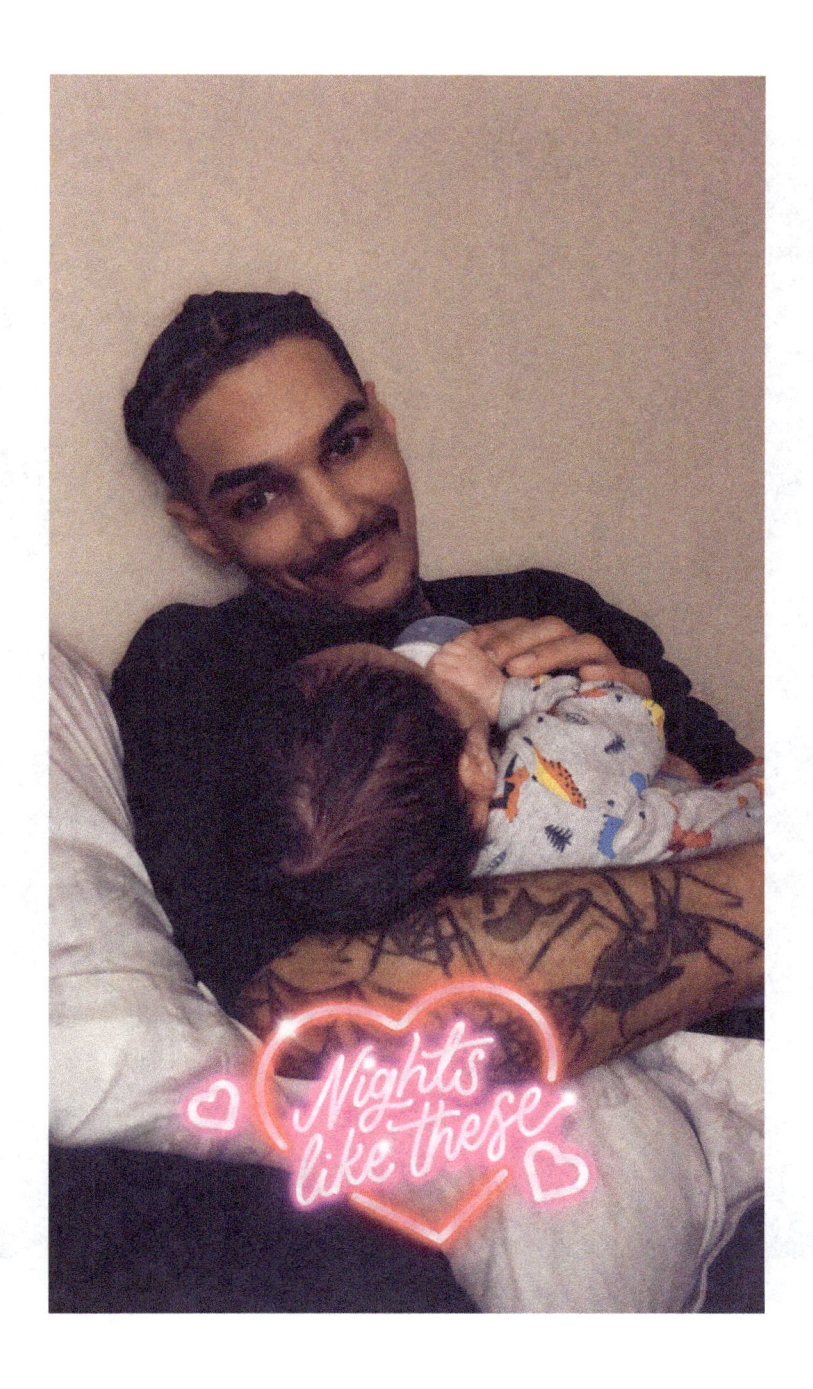

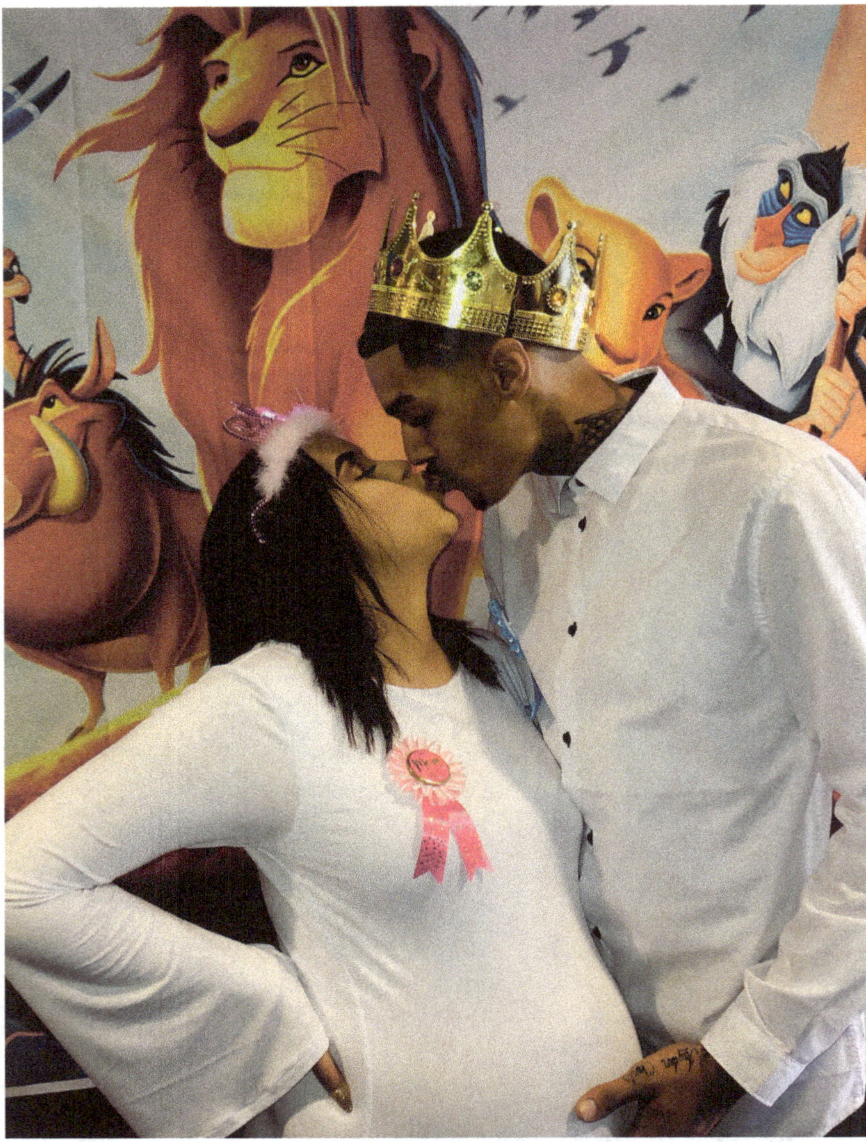

Pain So Deep

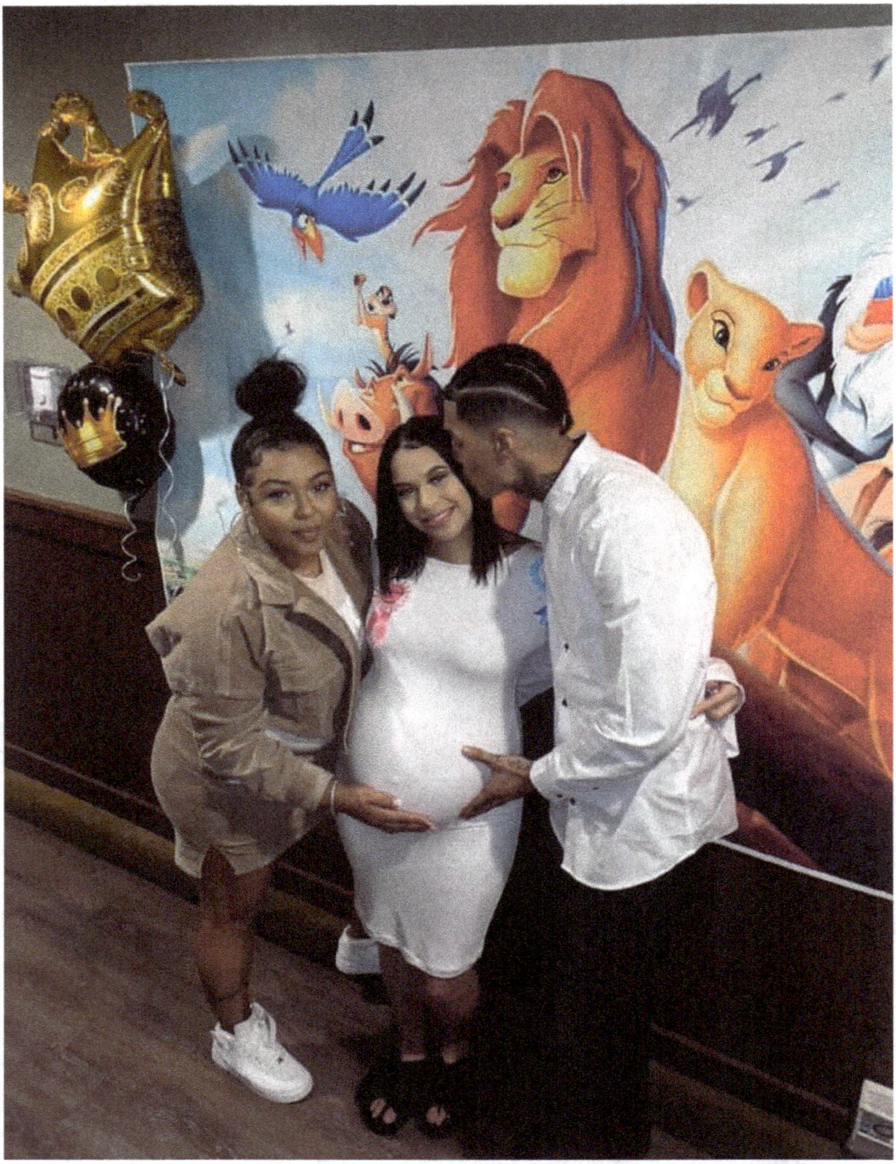

Pain So Deep

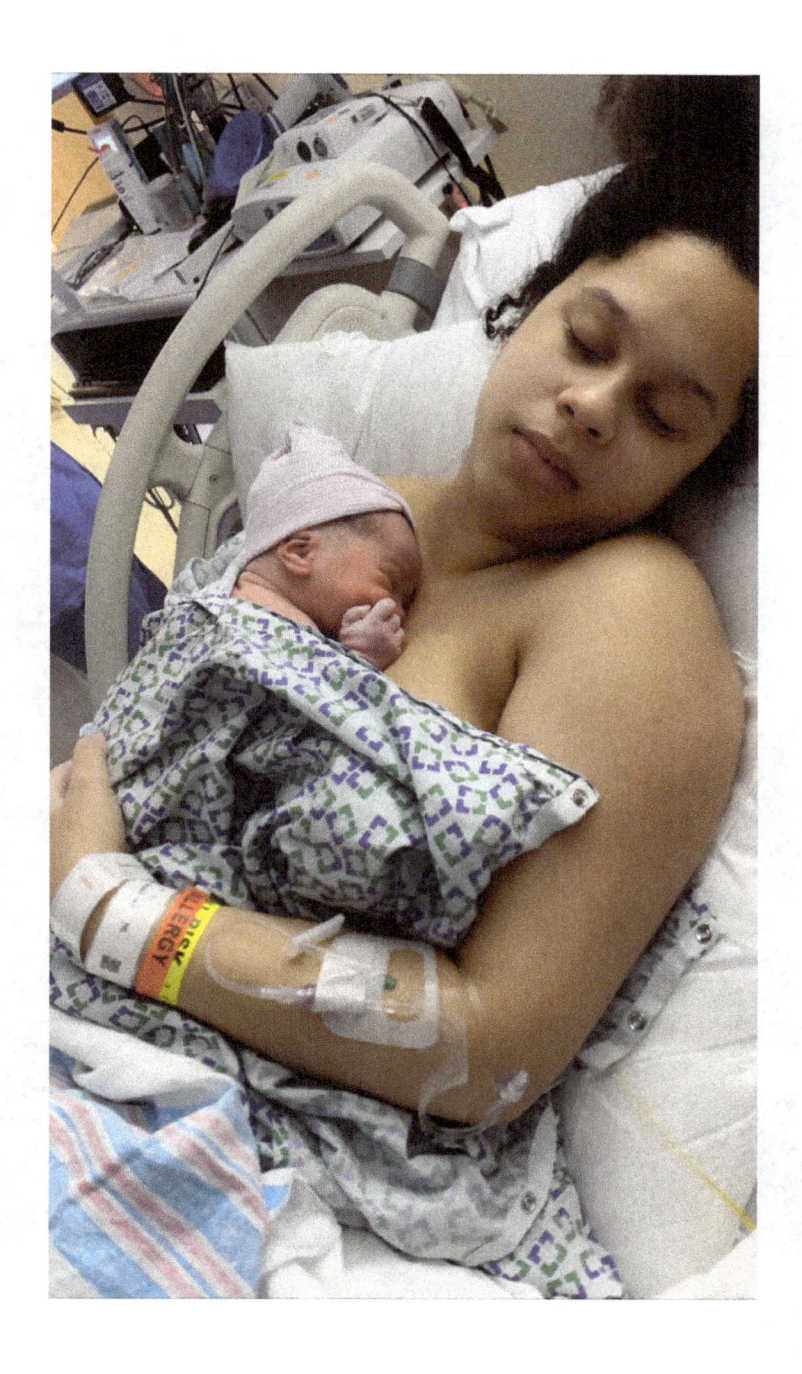

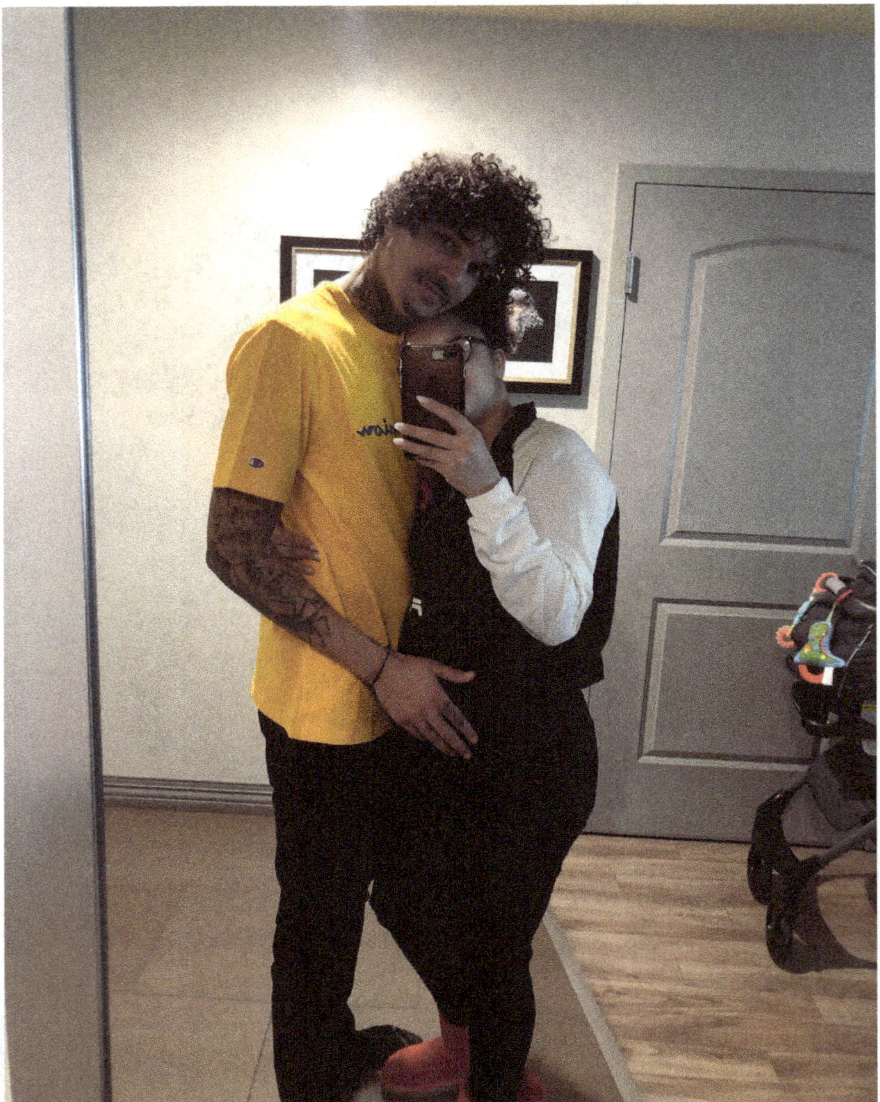

Pain So Deep

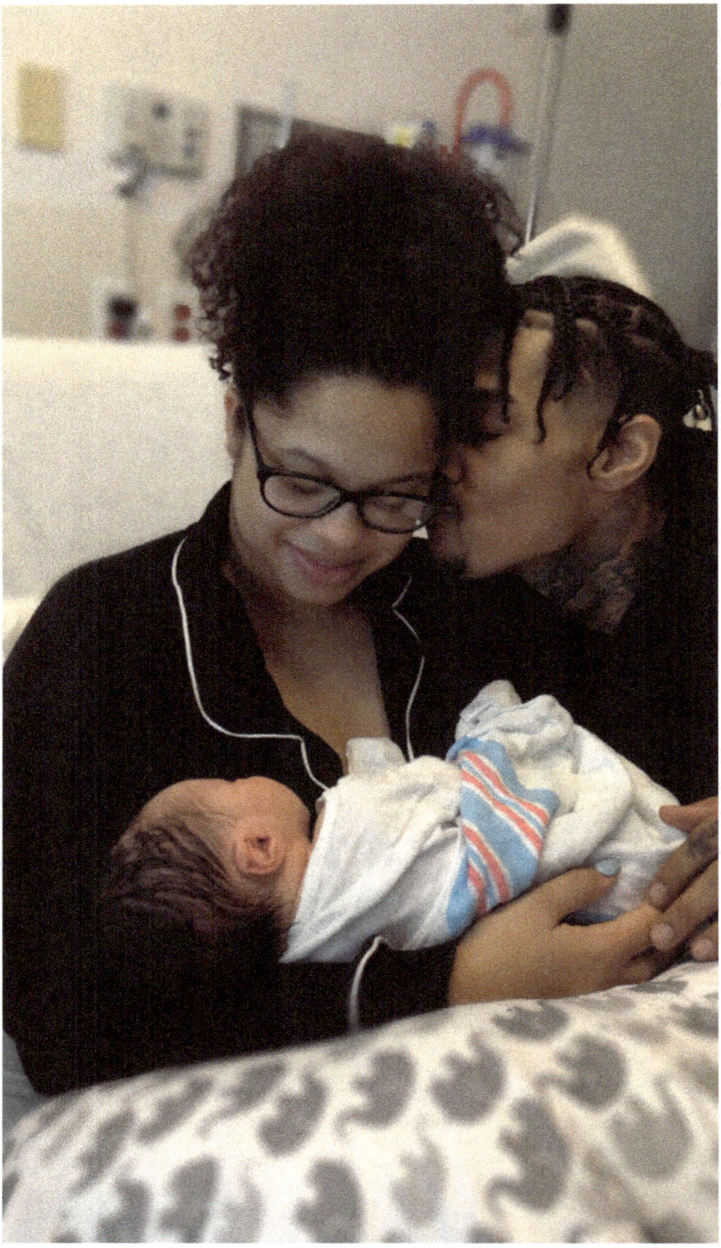

Pain So Deep

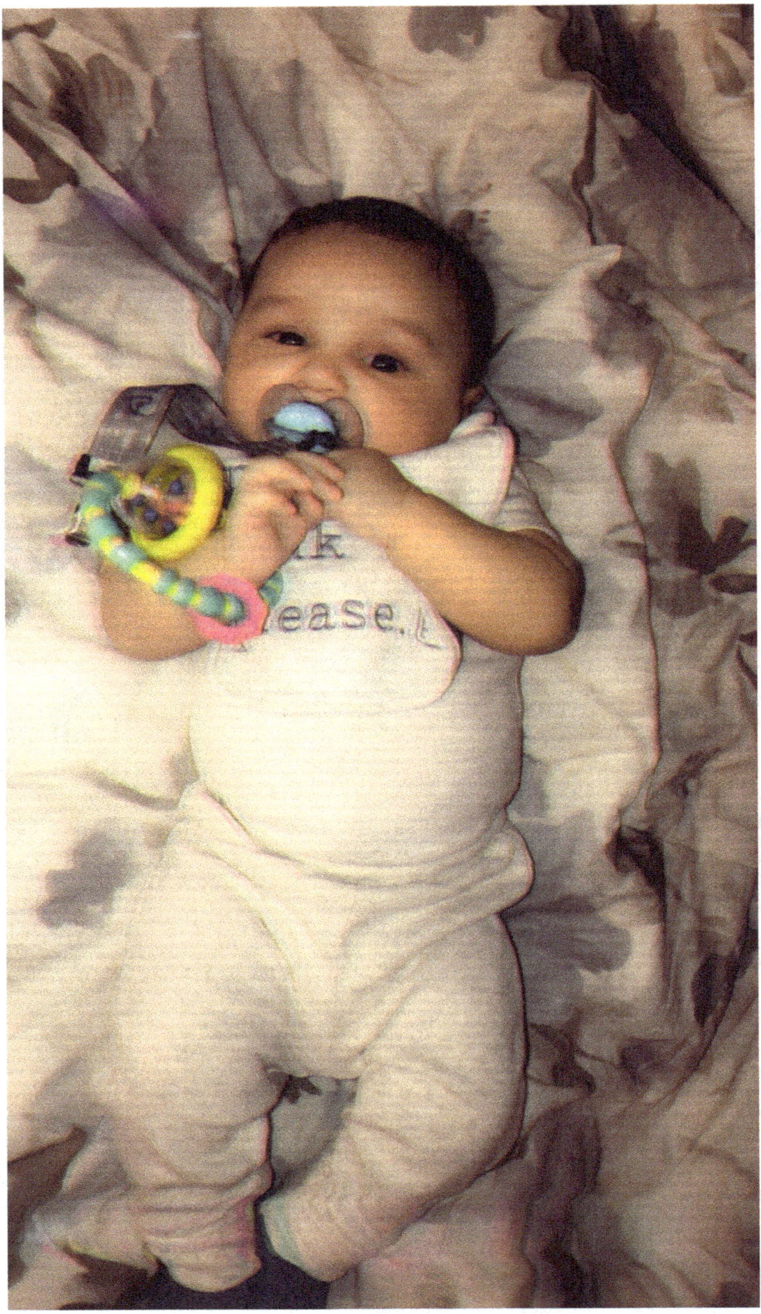

Pain So Deep

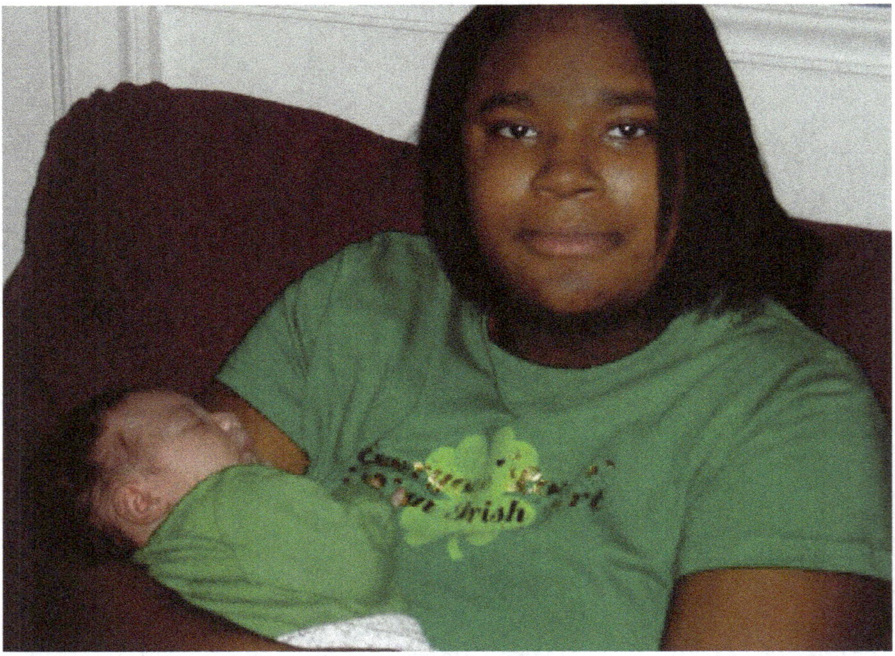
Irish

Pain So Deep

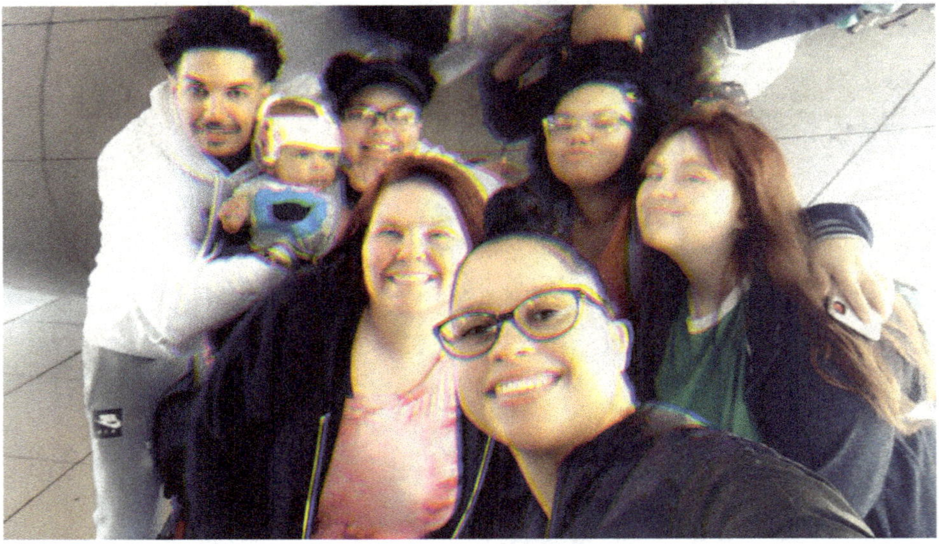

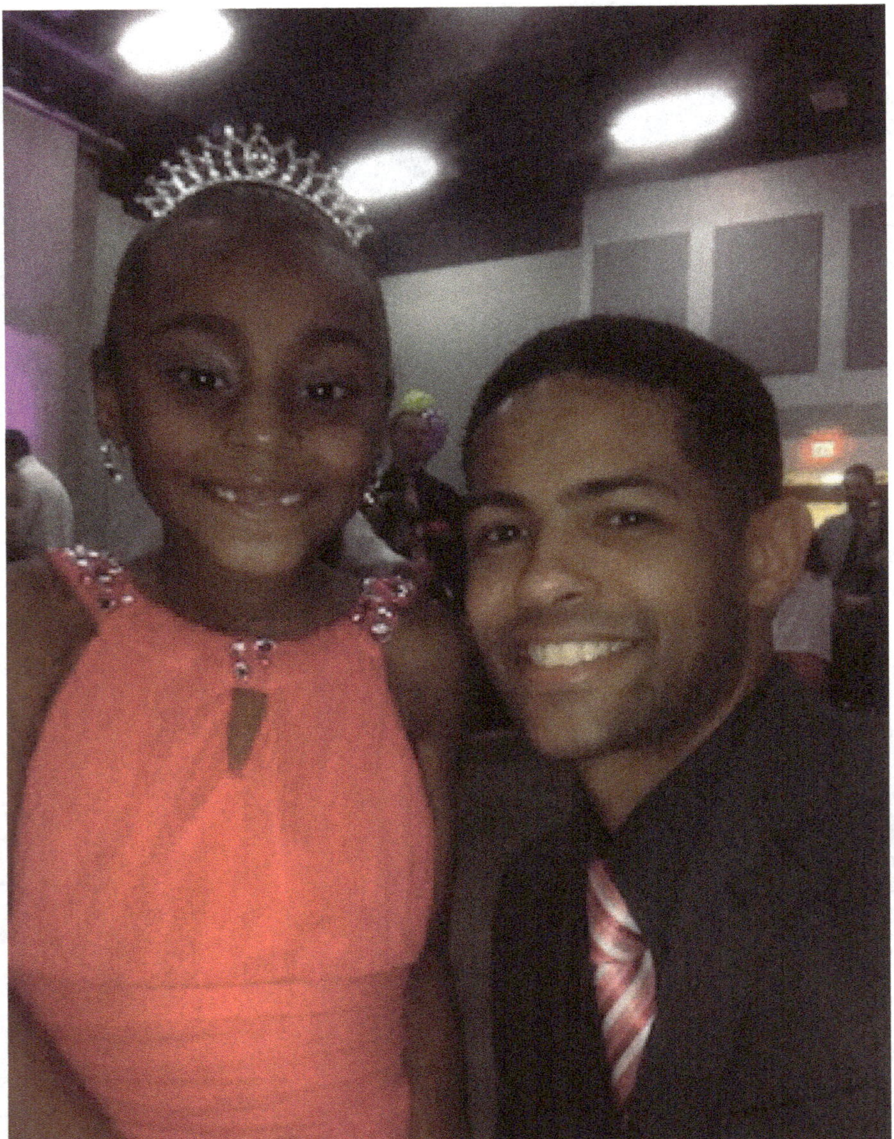

Pain So Deep

Shon Sheffey

Pain So Deep

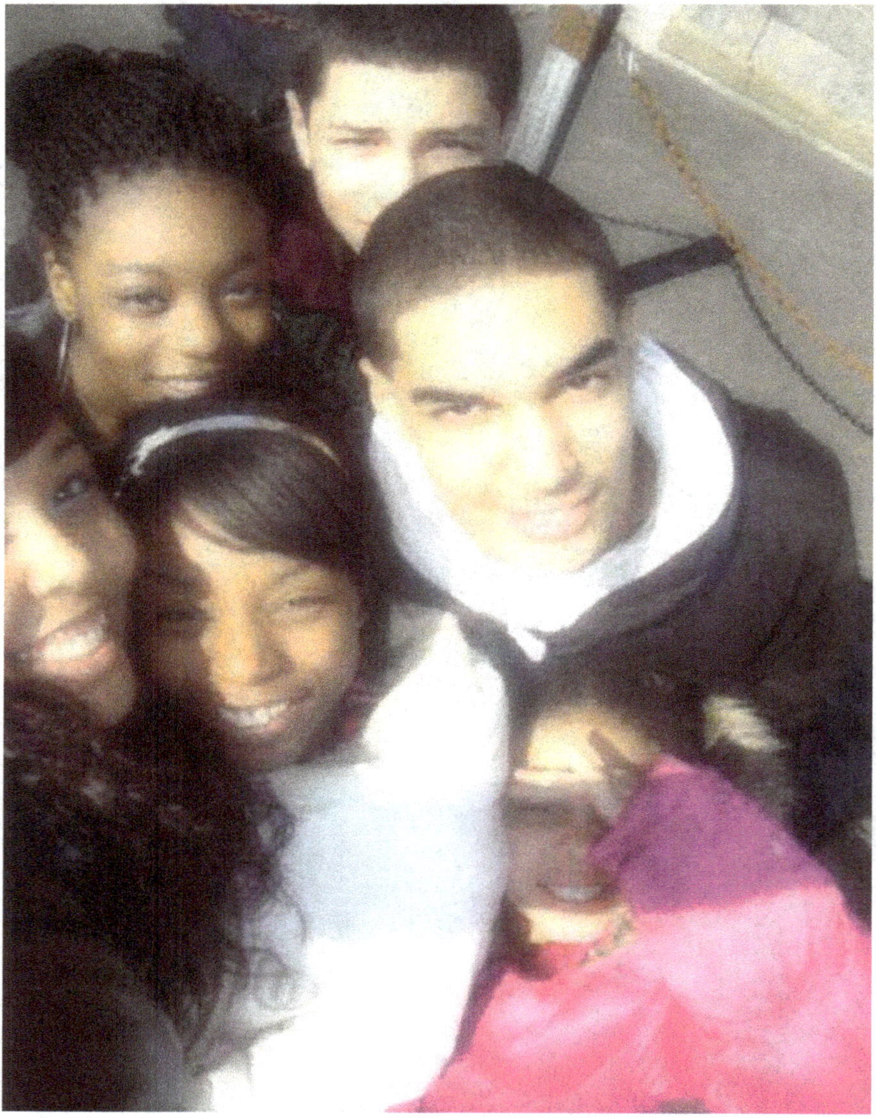

Pain So Deep

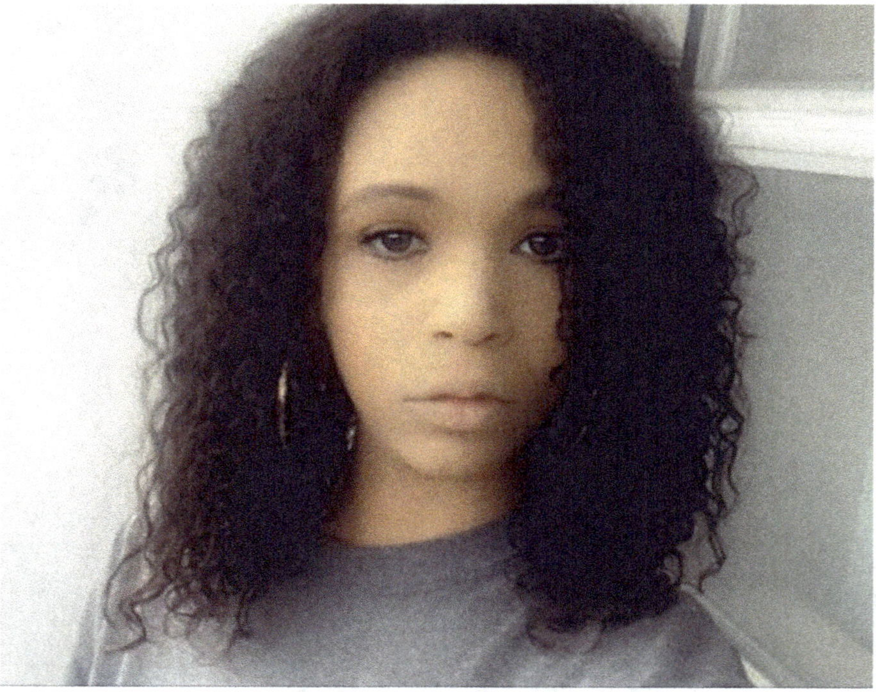

Pain So Deep

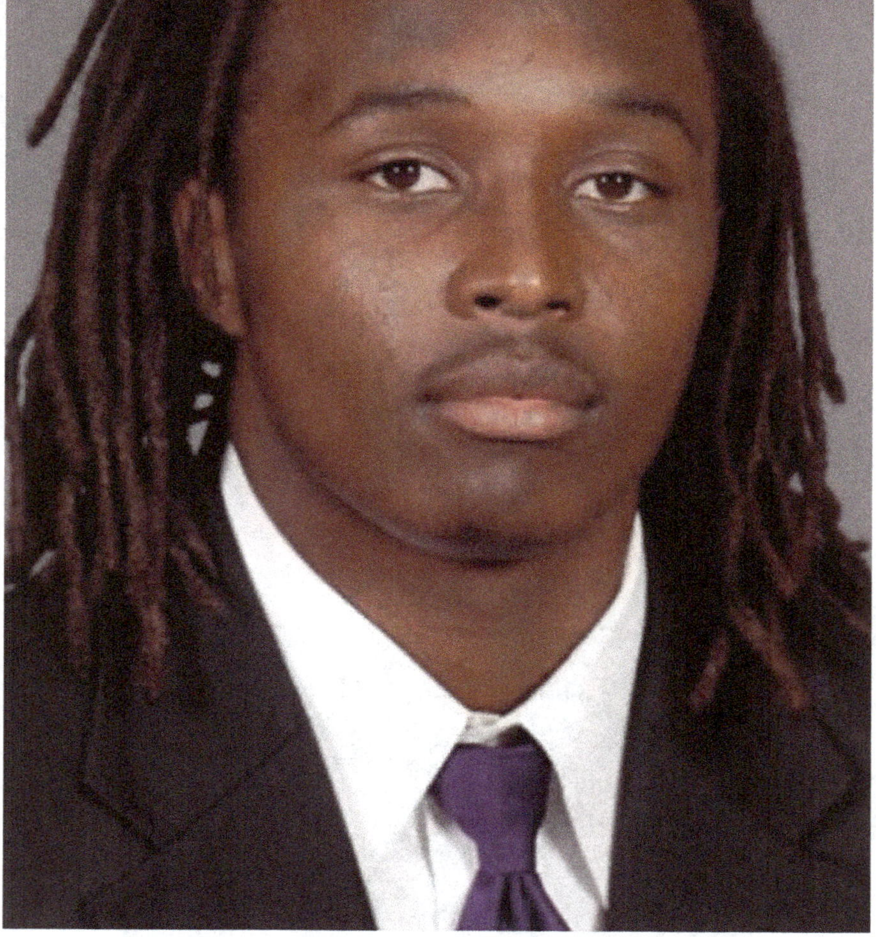

Pain So Deep

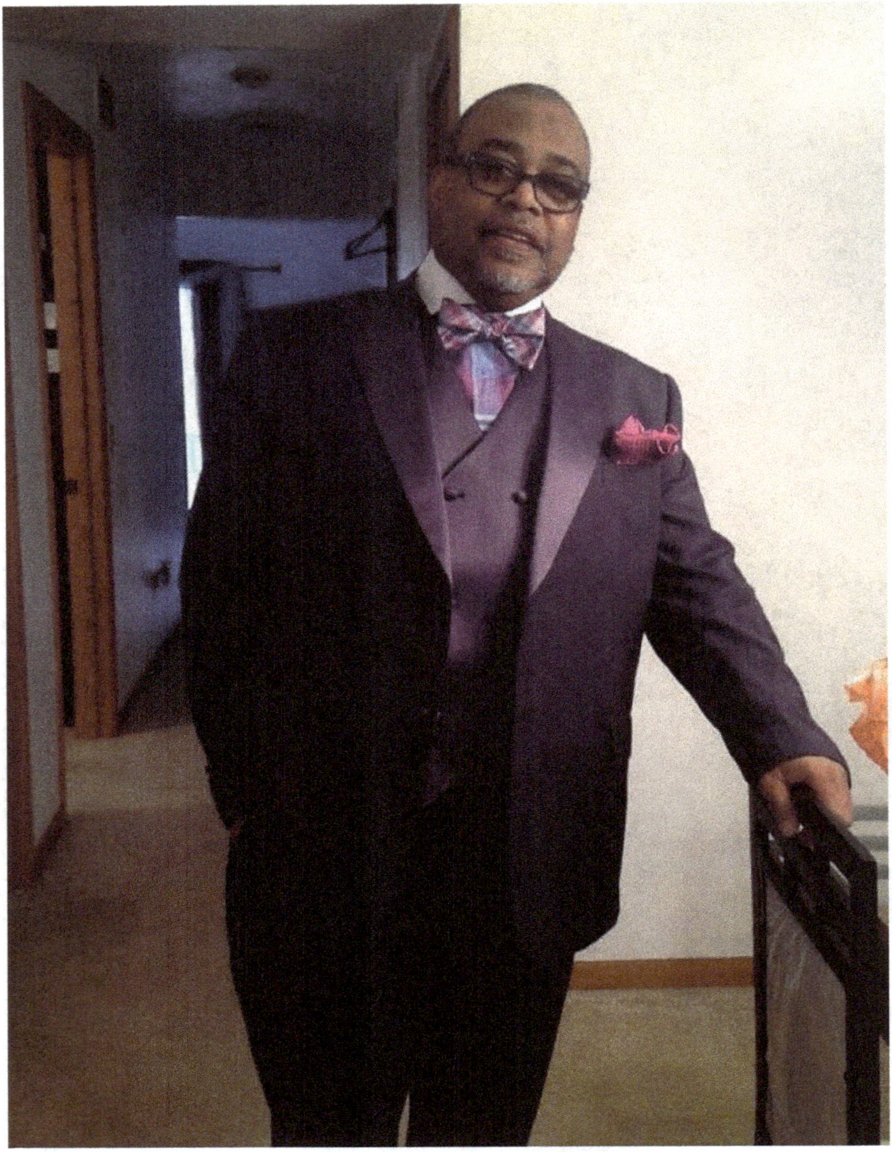

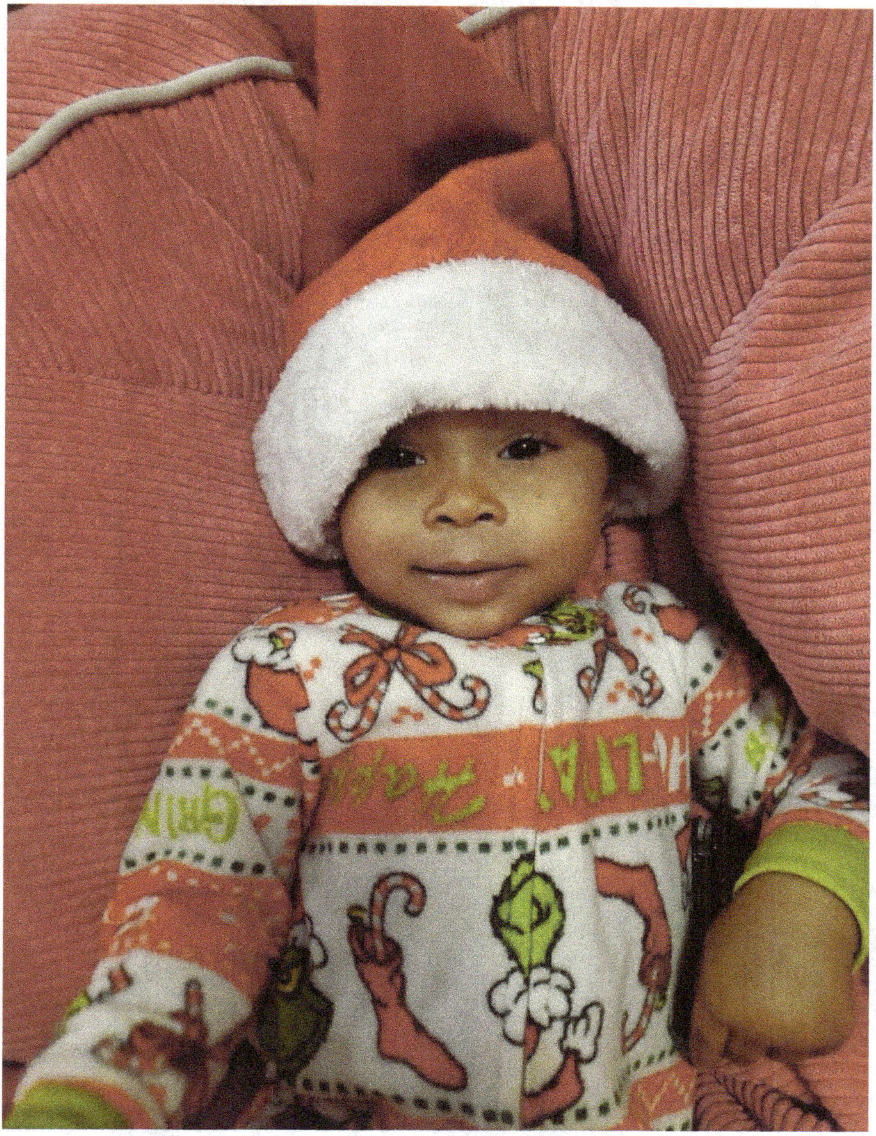

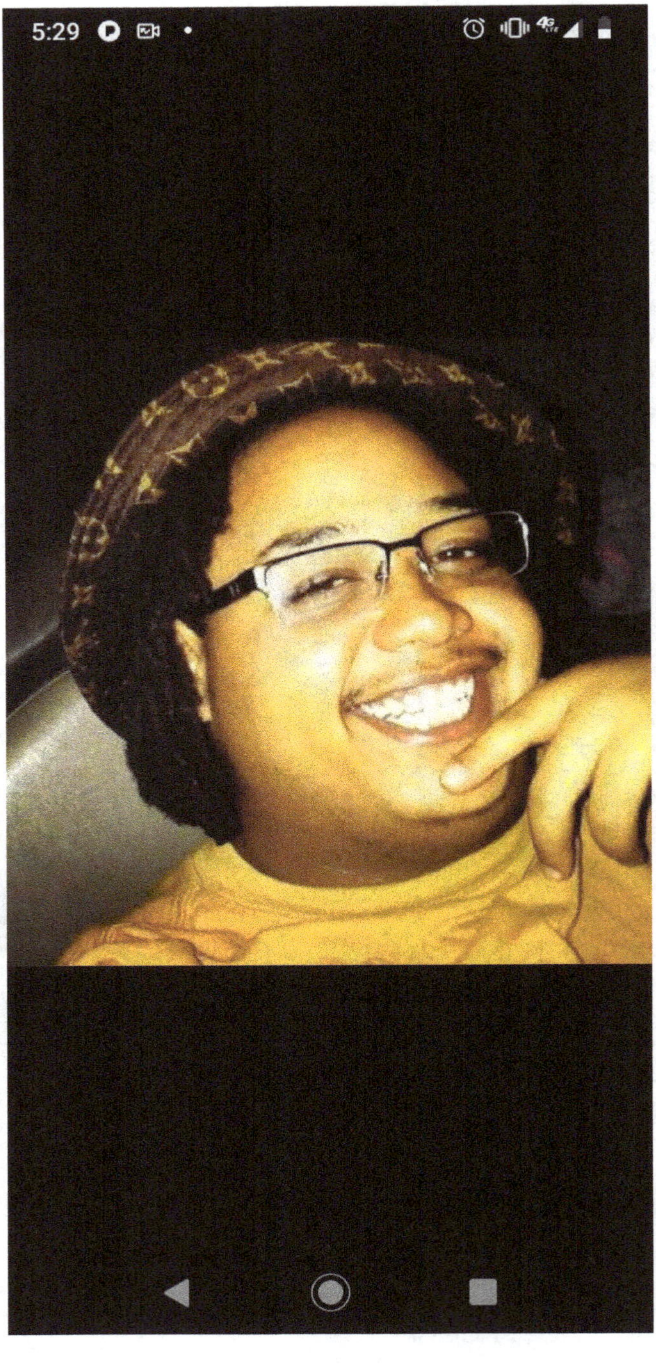
5:29

Pain So Deep

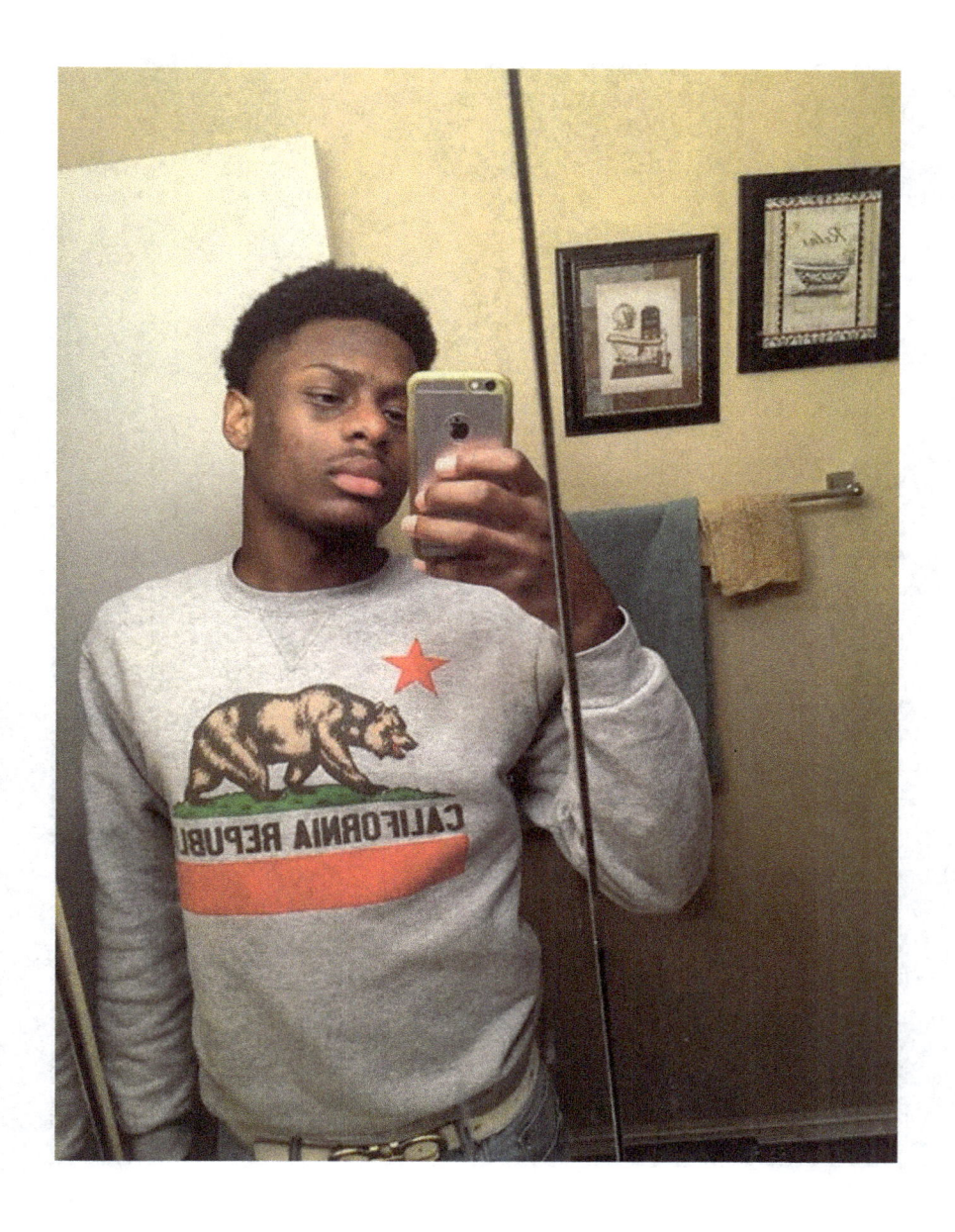

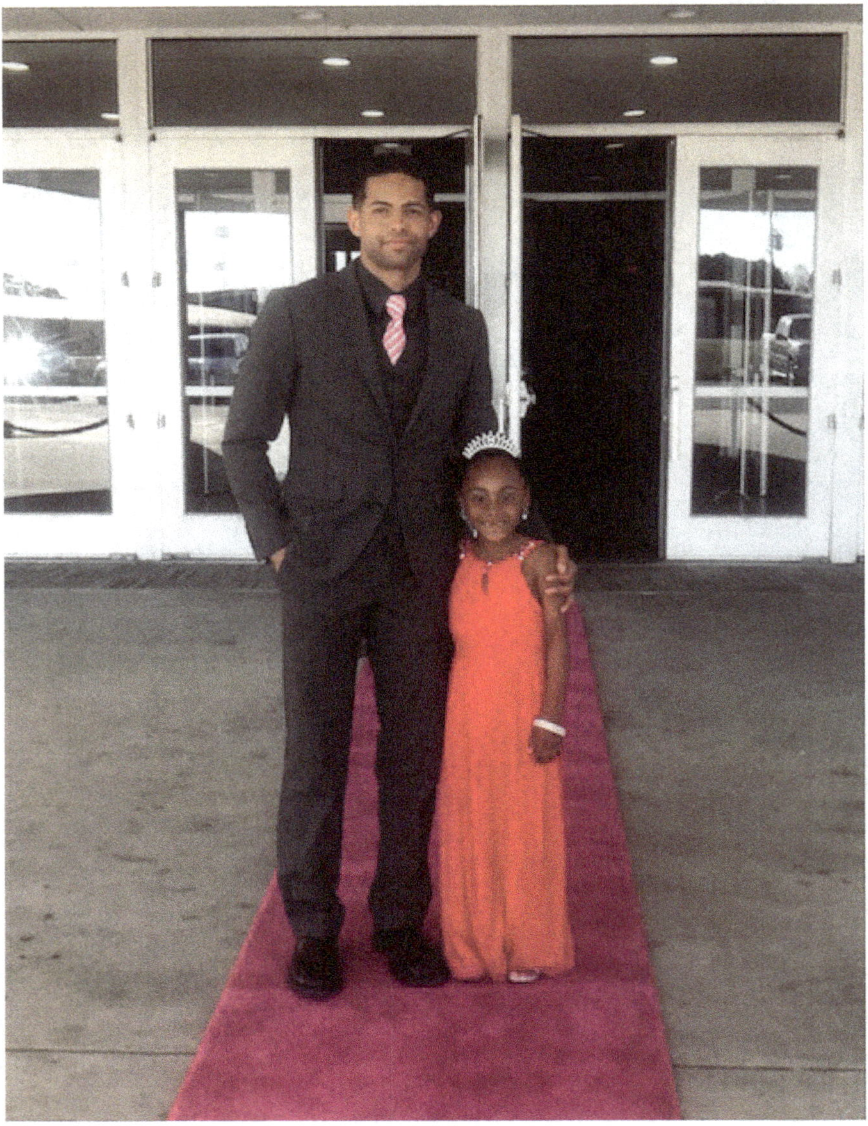

Mayfield Heights Police
Investigative Report
Title / Subject: Follow Up

Incident Number
11-09558

Pyro) was but isn't now." Mr. Rodriguez said that Ms. Perkins kicked Mr. Sheffey out last week. Mr. Rodriguez said that Mr. Sheffey still has his stuff in his basement. Mr. Rodriguez said that Jordan Perkins (Taylor's brother) stays there from time to time. When Jordan isn't there he stays with his parents.

I then asked Mr. Rodriguez what he knew about the Howard's Jewelry and Loan robbery and he said that this past Saturday he received a text message from Ms. Perkins saying that the police were at their home. Mr. Rodriguez wasn't home when the police were there. Mr. Rodriguez said that he was walking to Painesville with Jordan Perkins when the police were in his home. Mr. Rodriguez said that when he got to Painesville he got a ride from a girl named, Brittany (unknown last name) to a hotel in Mentor (Value) where Mr. Sheffey was staying at. At this hotel Mr. Rodriguez said that Mr. Sheffey told him everything about the robbery. Mr. Rodriguez said that he and Mr. Sheffey then went to Mr. Rodriguez's house and there they saw that the police had been there. Mr. Rodriguez said that Mr. Sheffey noticed that the diamonds were taken from the wooden box. The envelopes were taken and some of the clothes were taken. Mr. Rodriguez said that the ski masks used in the robbery were still in his house. Mr. Rodriguez said that he and Mr. Sheffey started freaking out. They talked about leaving the state and hiding for a while.

According to Mr. Rodriguez, Mr. Sheffey told him the following about the robbery this past Saturday (11/12/11) while they were at the Value hotel in Mentor. Mr. Sheffey said that he, along with Gerald Murphy, and Andre McMorris robbed Howard's Jewelry and Loan. Mr. Sheffey was wearing a ski mask with a joker face on the front of it. Mr. Sheffey had the stun gun during the robbery and that the stun gun did not work. Mr. Sheffey is the guy that punched the girl in the face (Ms. Reese) inside the store at the time of the robbery because she wouldn't get on the floor.

Andre McMorris was the guy that grabbed the female and pushed her to the floor as she was trying to flee the store through the front door at the time of the robbery. He also wore a ski mask and had a BB gun in his hand at the time of the robbery. Mr. McMorris lives in Euclid.

Gerald Murphy also robbed Howard's Jewelry and Loan by using a BB gun. Mr. Rodriguez said that Mr. Sheffey stole these BB guns from a Walmart.

Mr. Rodriguez then said that Janelle (unknown last name) was the get away driver. Janelle was driving her car, a four door Pontiac Grand Am. Mr. Sheffey told Mr. Rodriguez that Janelle took off her temporary license plates after the robbery because they thought the traffic light on Mayfield Ridge took a picture of her license plate. Mr. Rodriguez said that after the robbery Janelle dropped Mr. McMorris off in Euclid and then Mr. Sheffey came to his house.

Mr. Rodriguez said that this past Thursday, 11/10/11 he was at home with Jordan. Mr. Rodriguez said that Mr. Sheffey came over to his house early, sometime after 11am, and woke him up. Mr. Sheffey asked Mr. Rodriguez if he wanted to go, "Kick it." Mr. Rodriguez said that he, Mr. Sheffey, and a few others went to Mentor mall where they bought nothing. They all then went to Beachwood Mall where they spent a lot of money. Mr. Rodriguez said that he just got a bracelet while the others bought a lot of stuff. Mr. Rodriguez said that Mr. Sheffey and the others partied all weekend. He said that they partied yesterday by buying a party bus. They went downtown to Christie's and Hustler. Mr. Sheffey also got a new tattoo from a tattoo artist in Mentor. The tattoo was part of a sleeve Mr. Sheffey already has. Mr. Rodriguez said that they spent all the money from the robbery. I asked Mr. Rodriguez where Mr. Sheffey is now and he said, "At the hotel in Mentor. The room is in his name and he bought it for the week."

I asked Mr. Rodriguez where he was this past Saturday and he said that he left his house around 3pm or 4pm. Rodriguez said that he walked to Painesville with Jordan Perkins. When they walked out of their development they saw two police deputy cruisers pulling in. Mr. Rodriguez didn't think anything of it and kept walking to Painesville. This is when Ms. Perkins texted him that the police were at his house. Then Mr. Rodriguez got a ride to the hotel where he spoke to Mr. Sheffey.

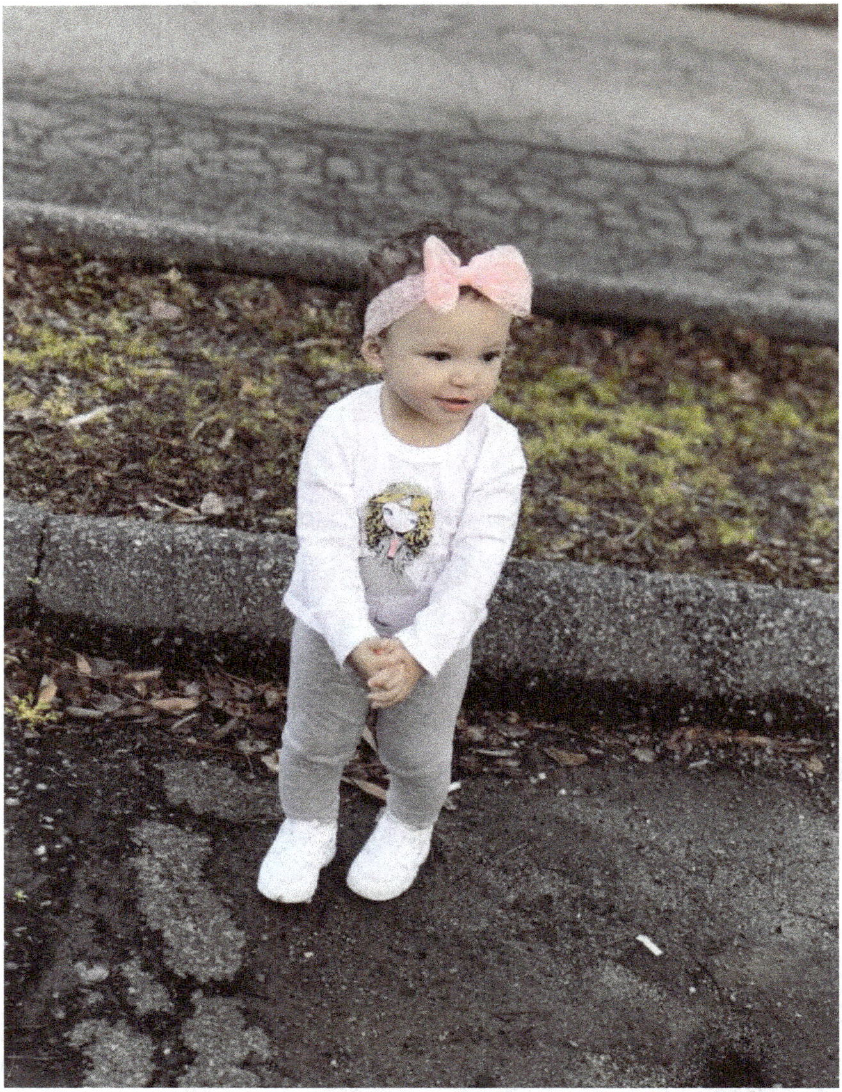

Pain So Deep

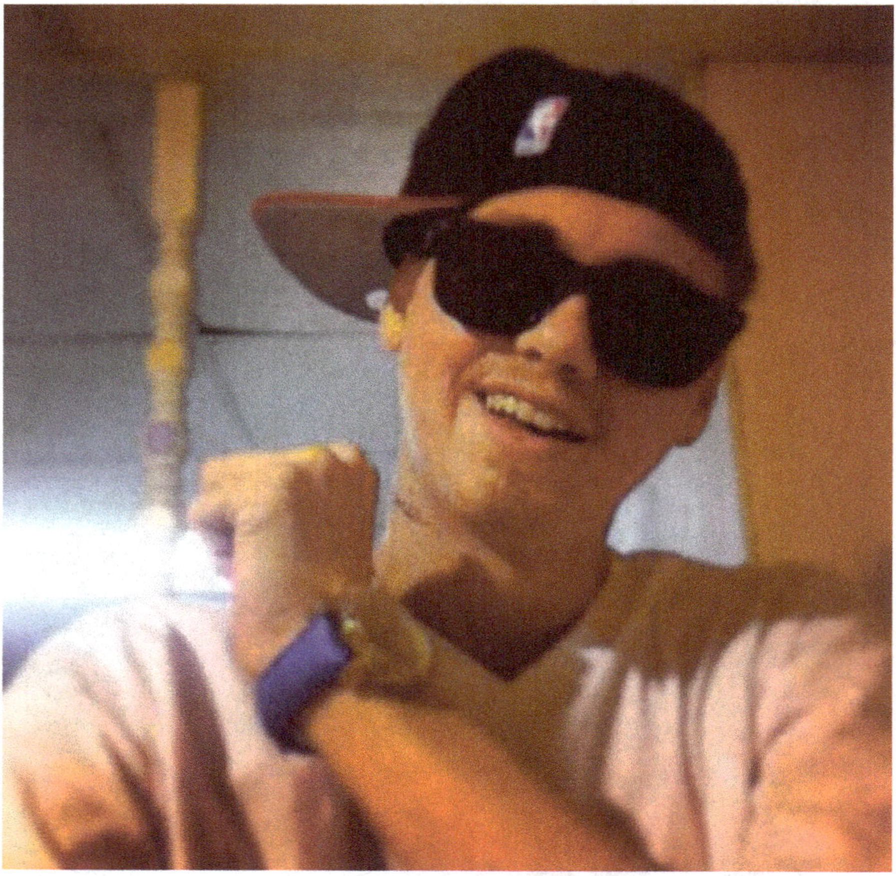

Pain So Deep

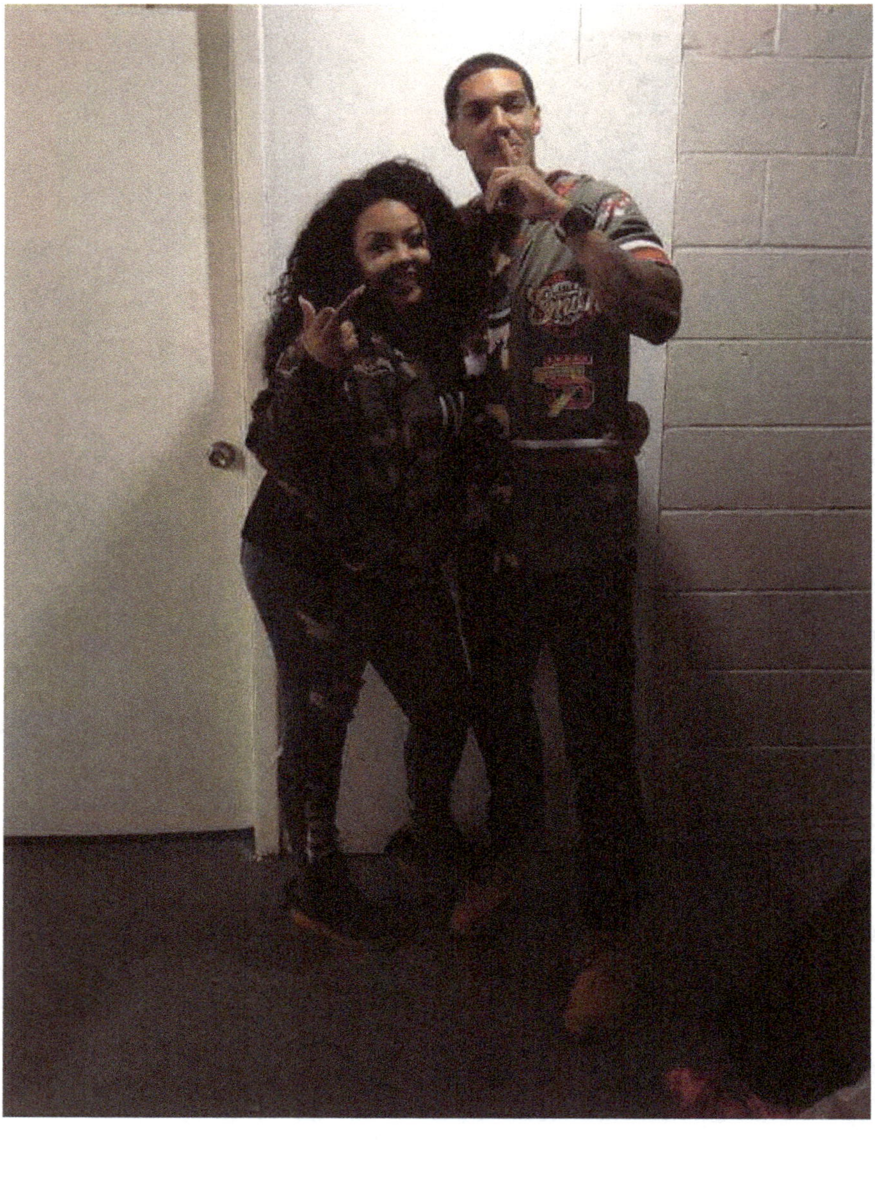

Pain So Deep

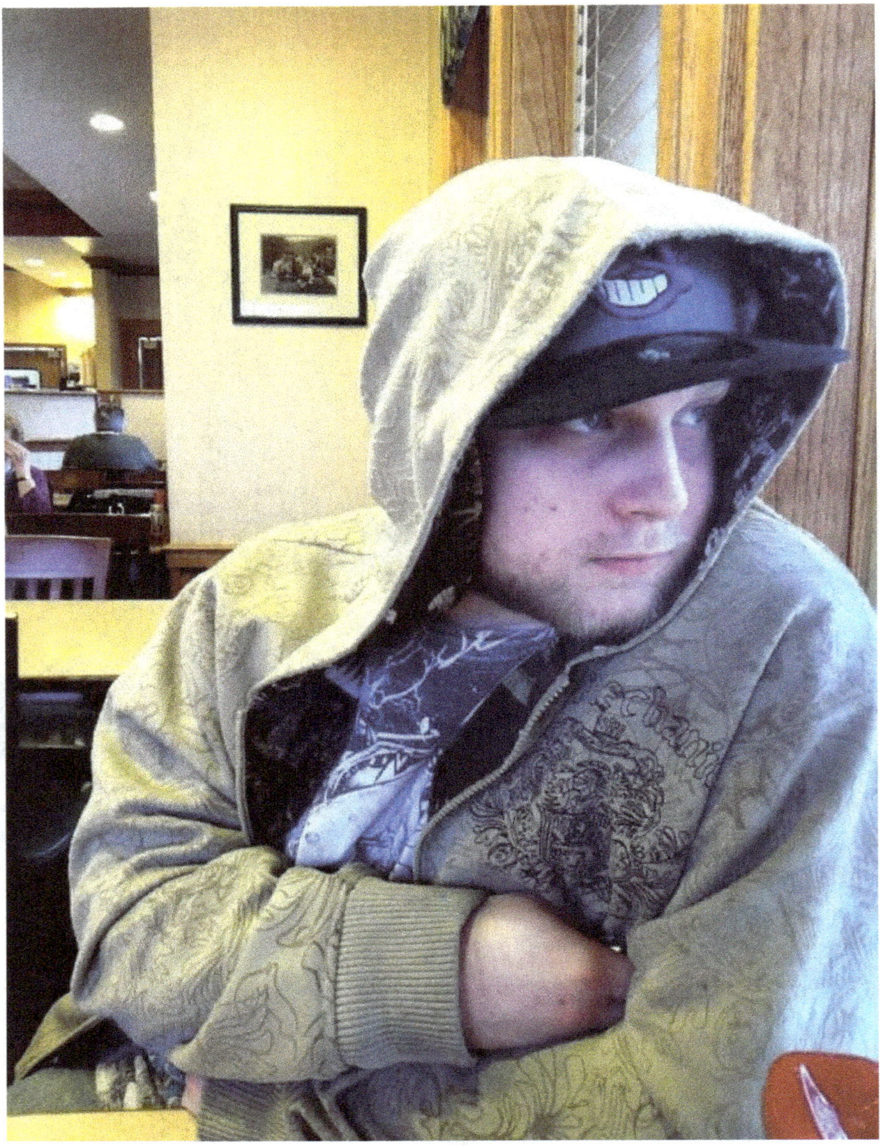

Pain So Deep

Tribute Wall

Freddie Jean Washington
1956 - 2018

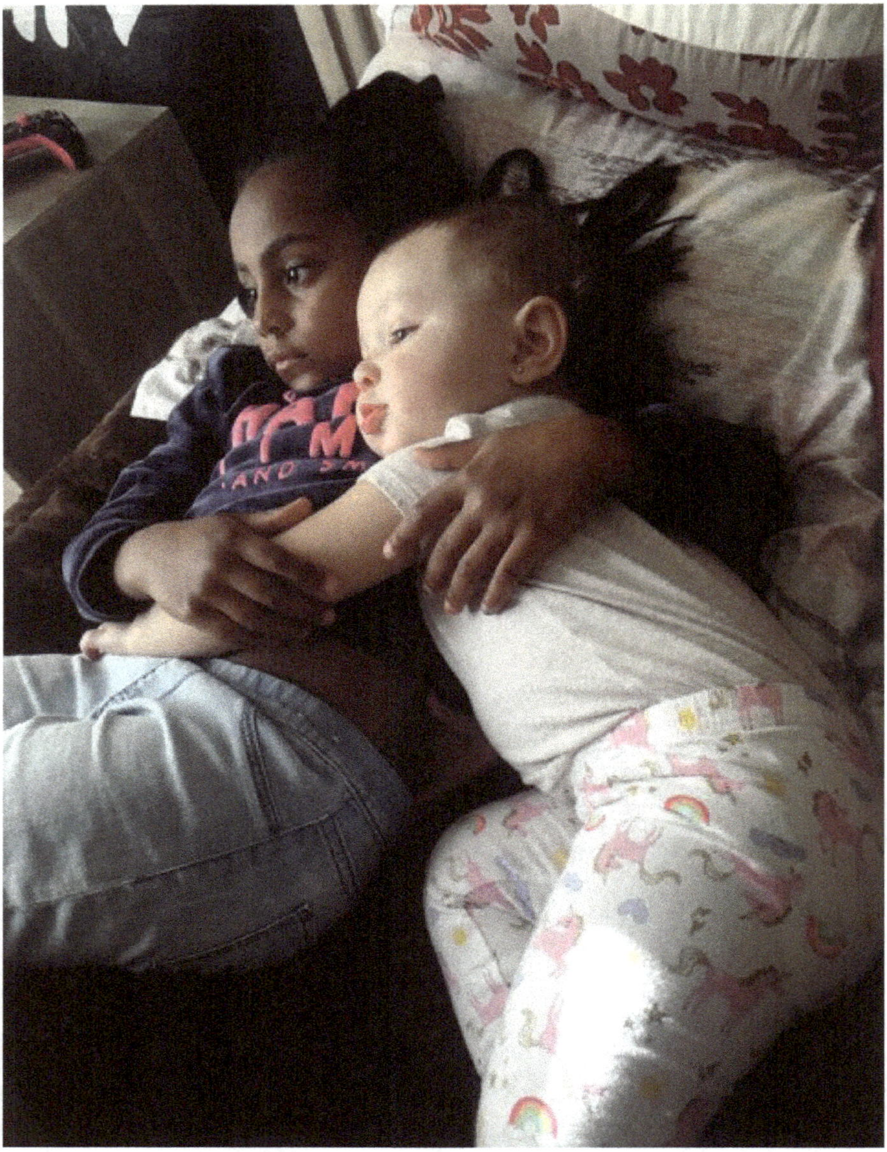

Pain So Deep

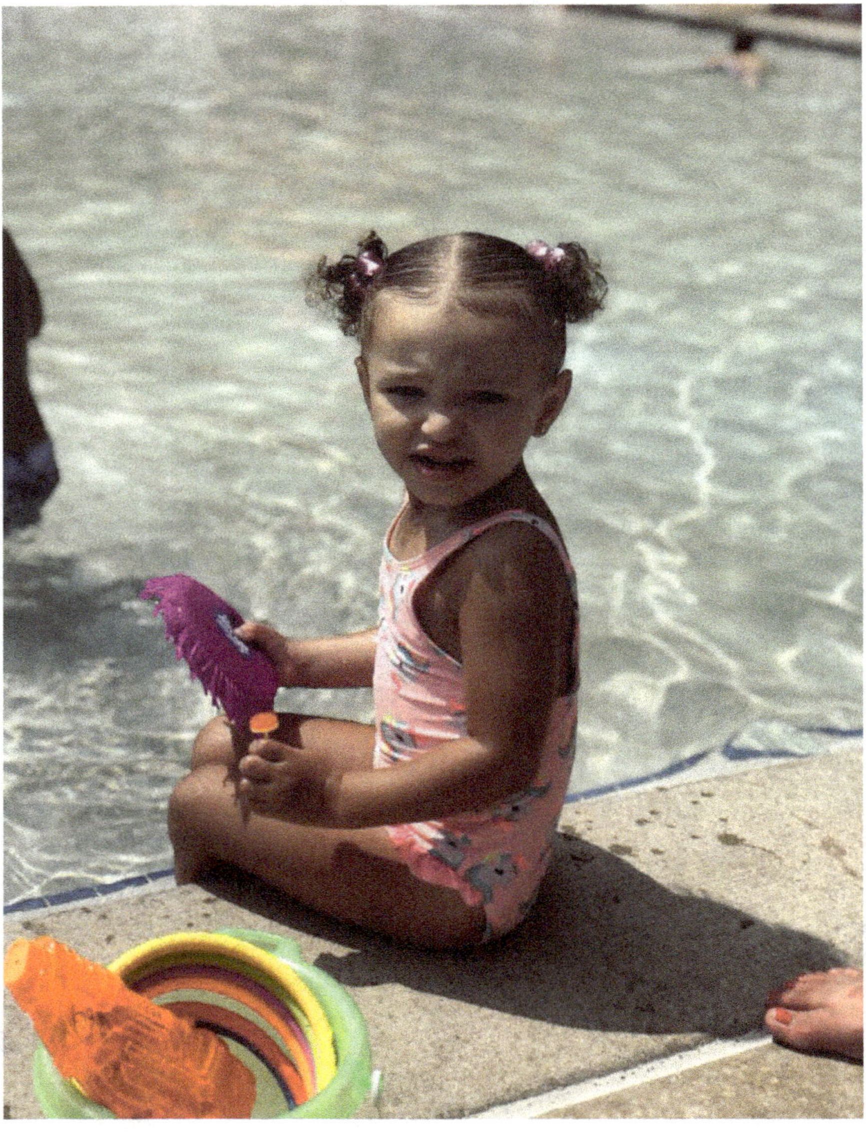

Pain So Deep

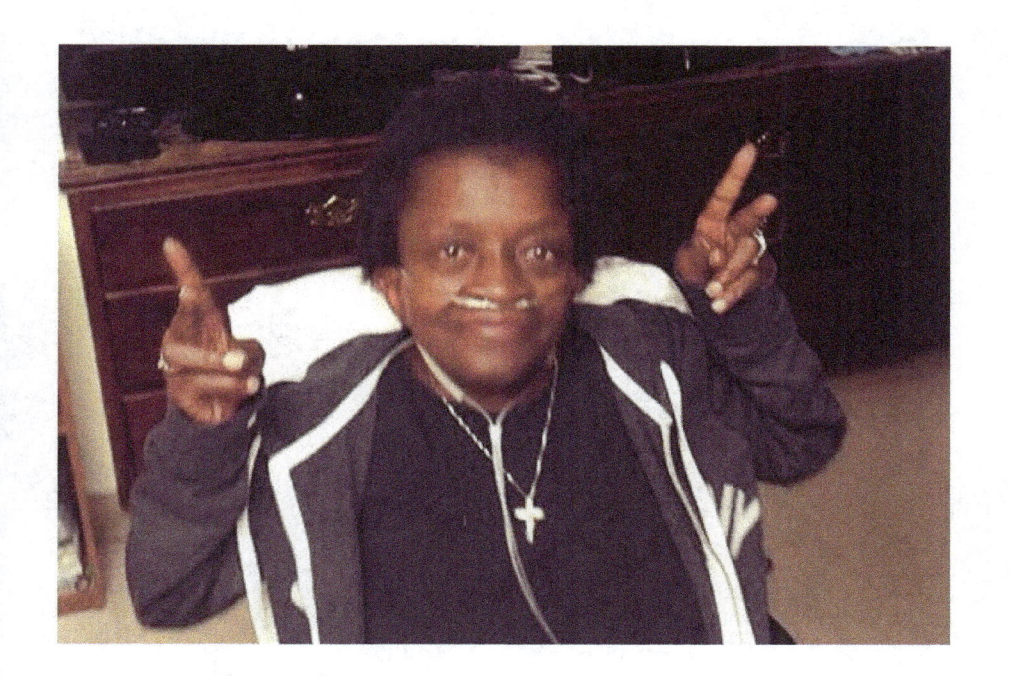

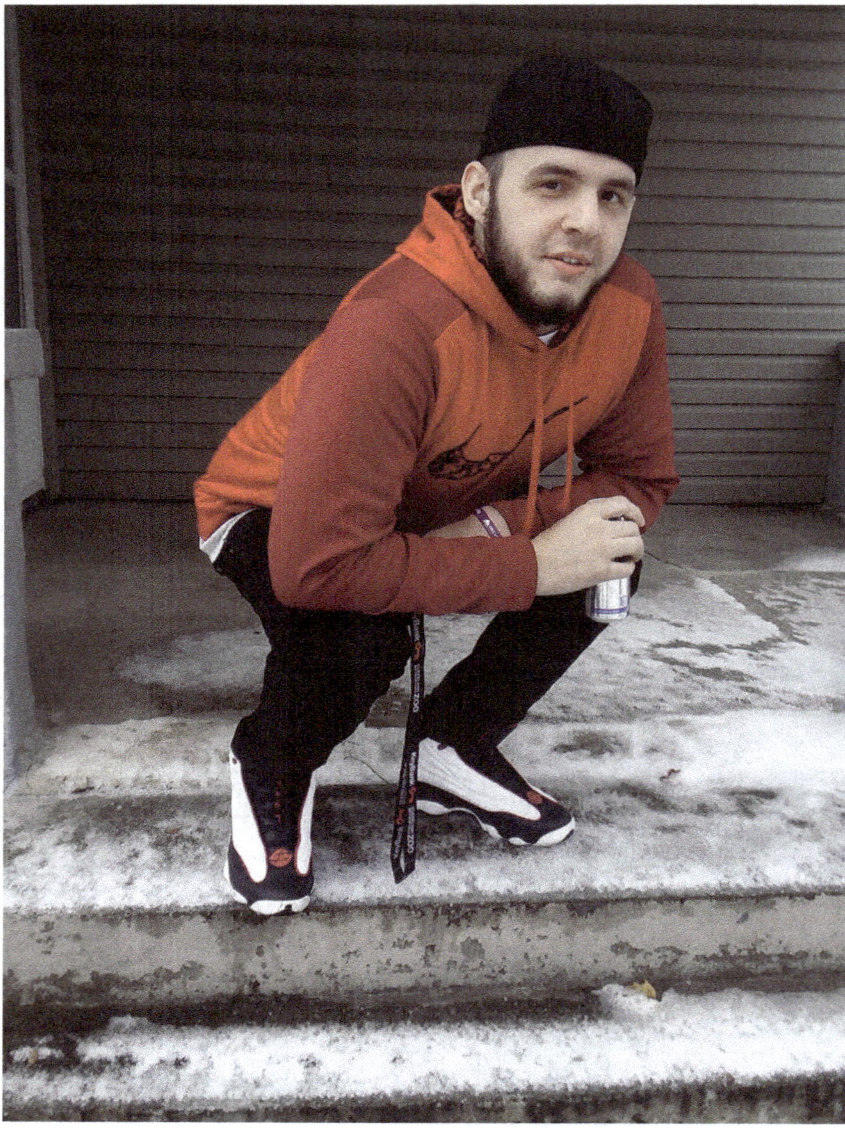

Pain So Deep

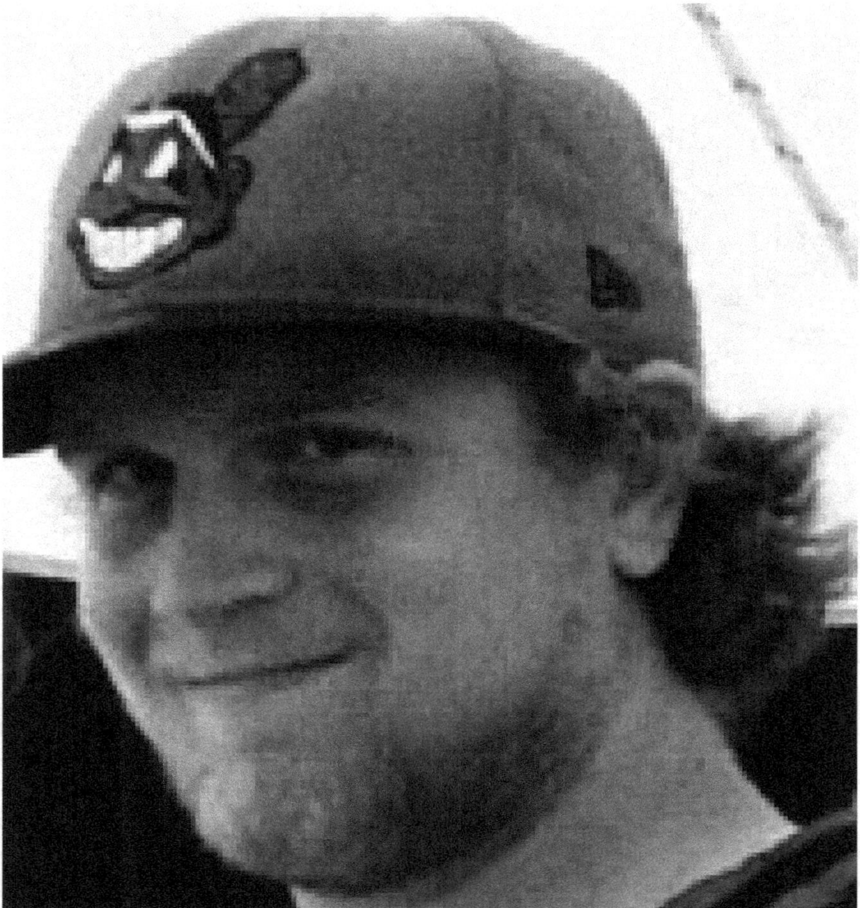

Pain So Deep

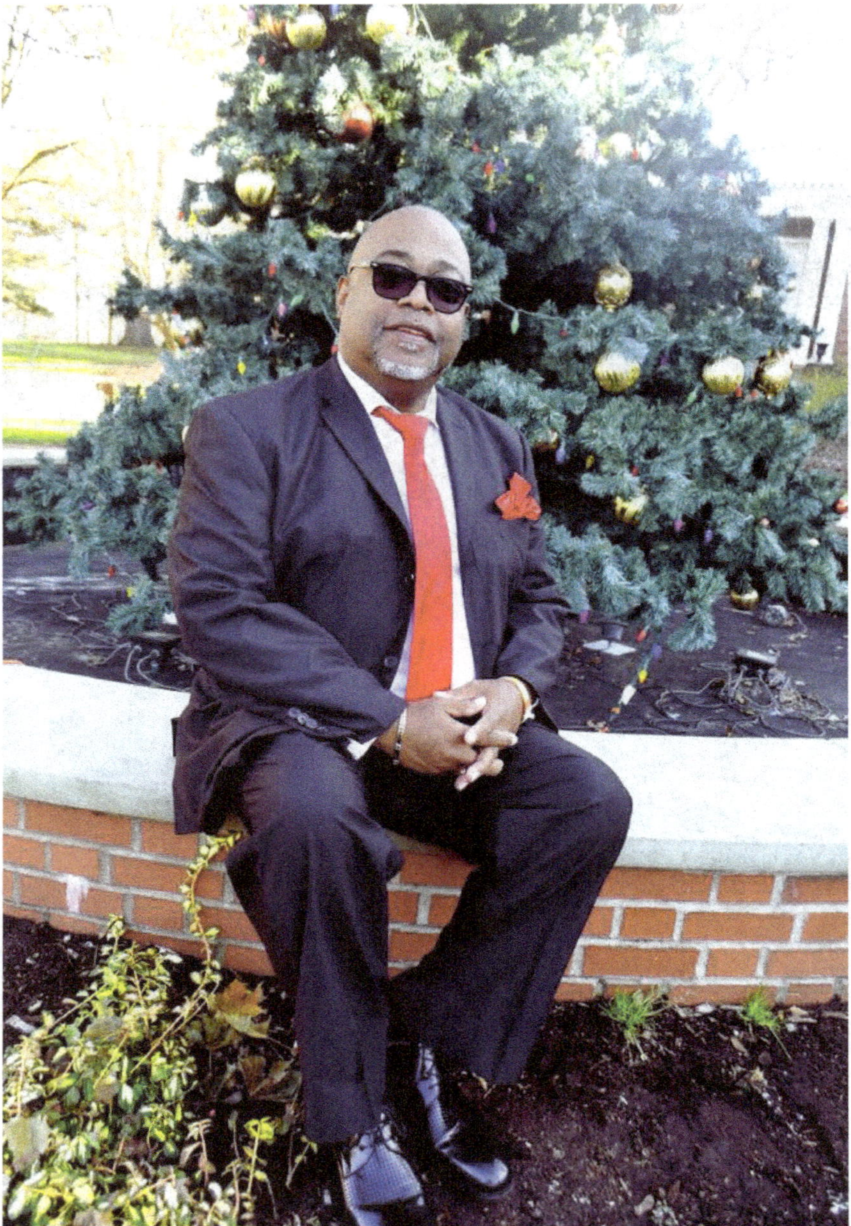

Pain So Deep

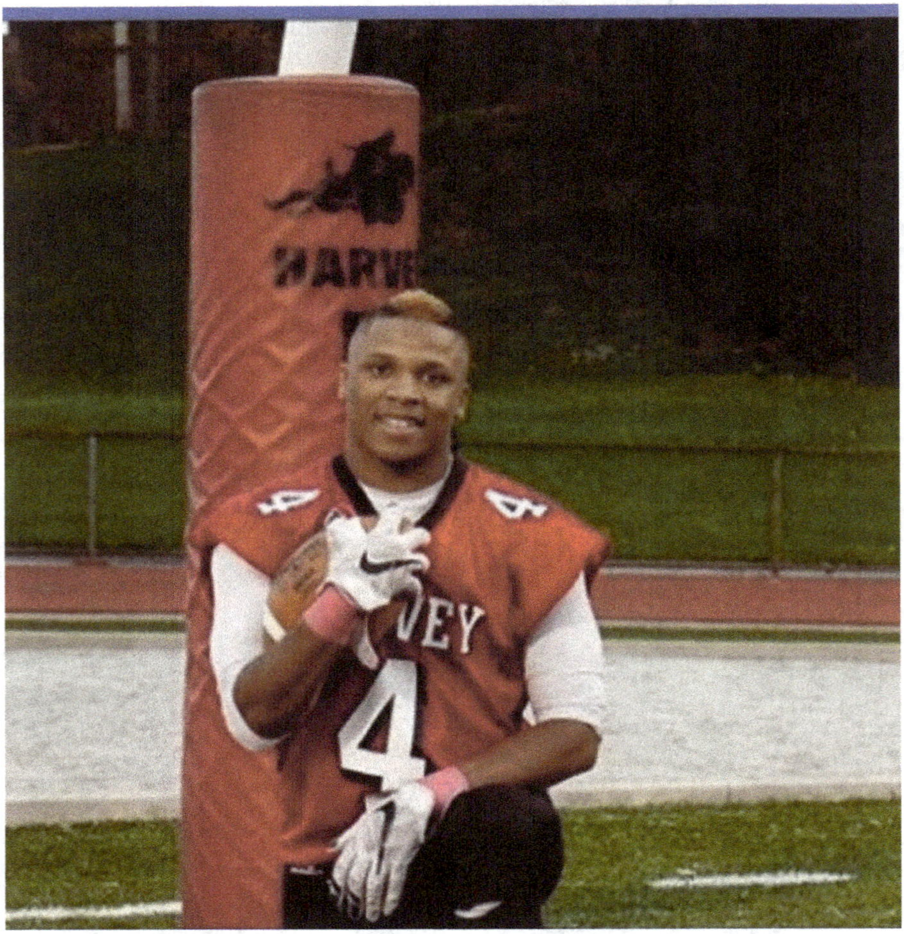
4
4
4

Pain So Deep

November Amor
MAR 11, 2018

Pain So Deep

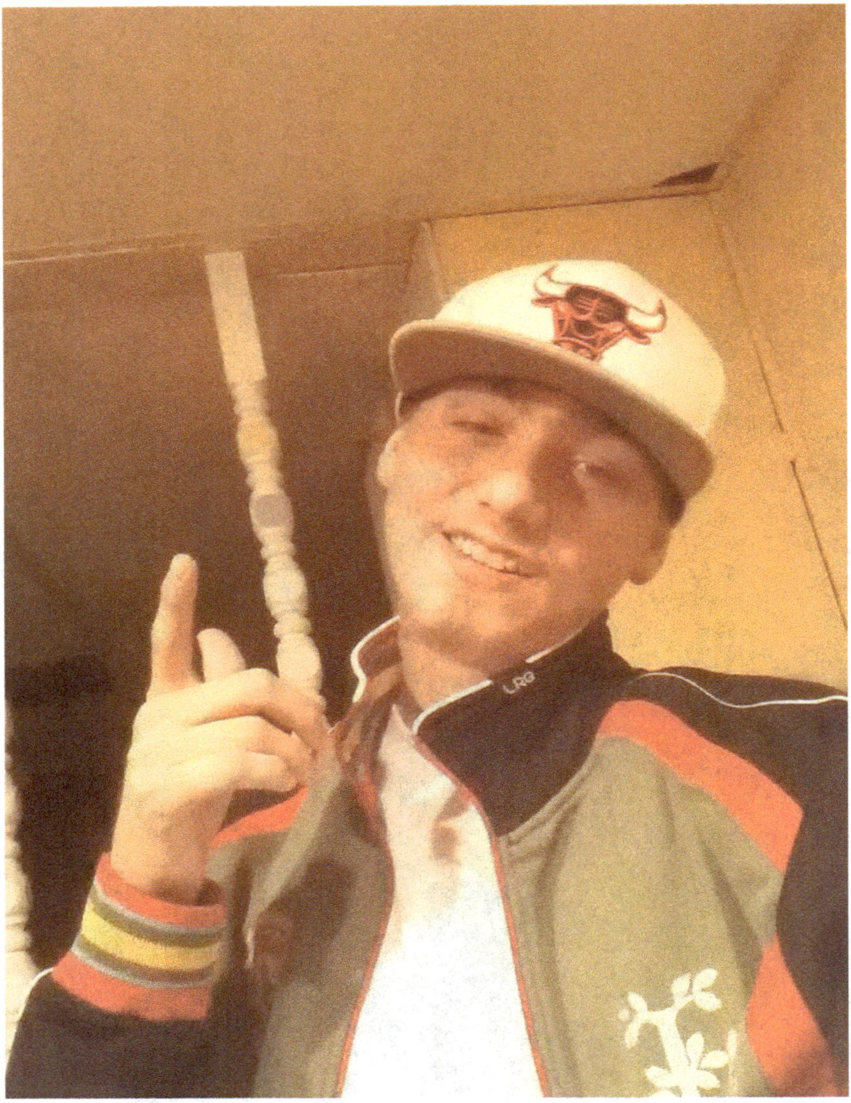
LRG

Pain So Deep

340

Pain So Deep

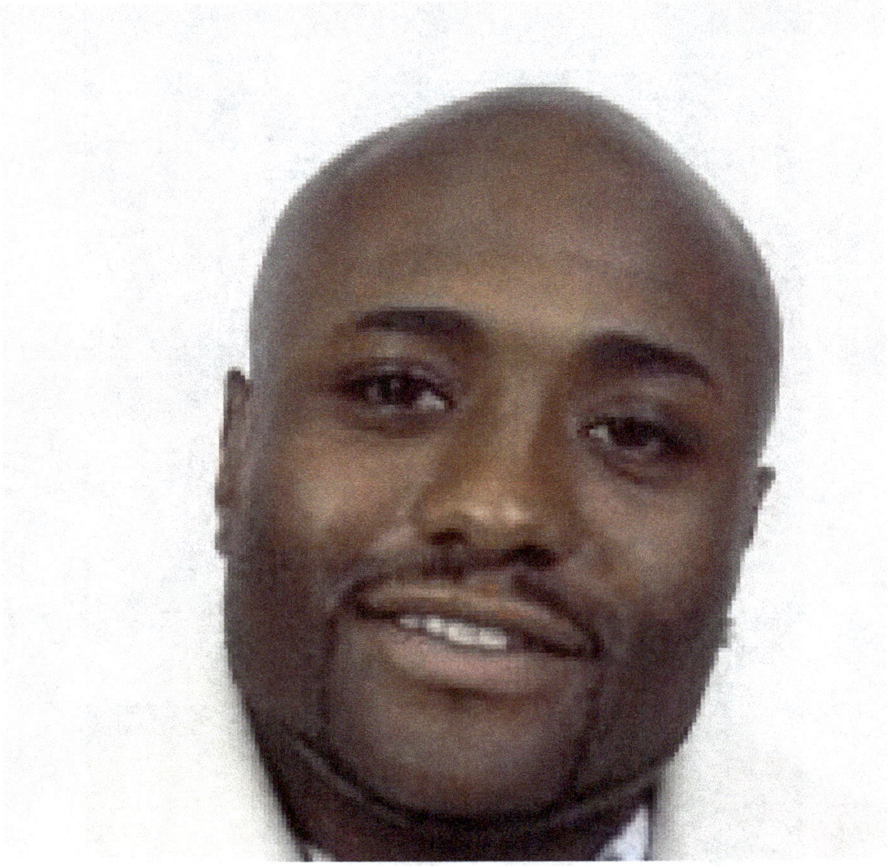

Pain So Deep

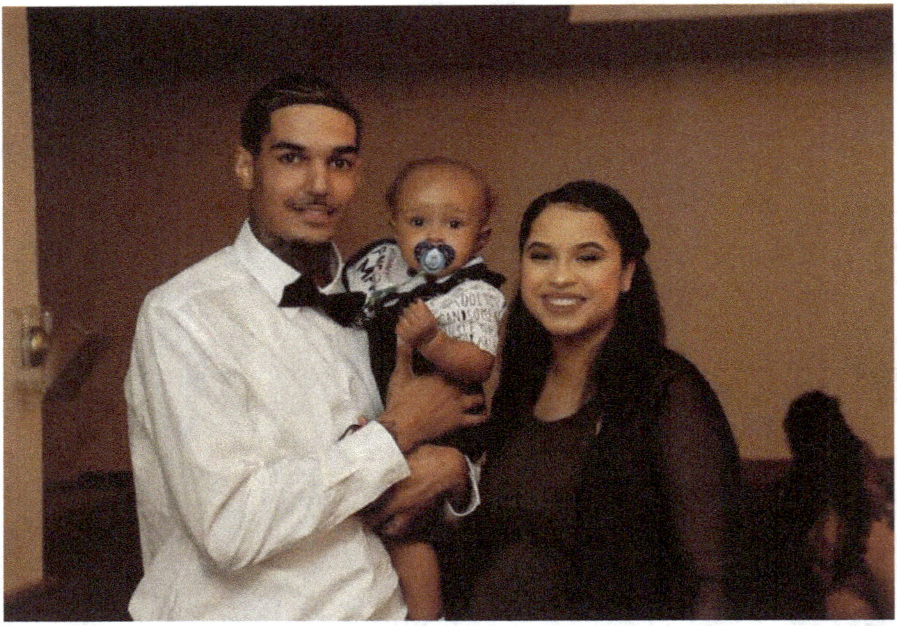

Pain So Deep

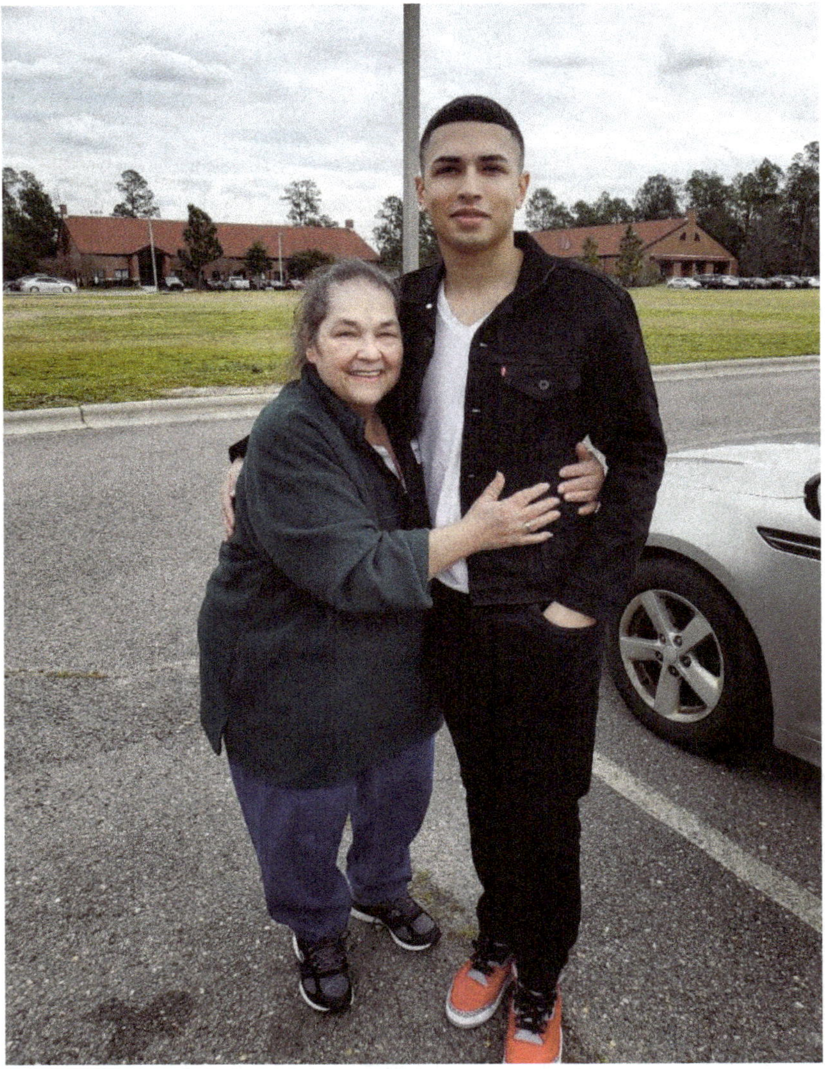

Pain So Deep

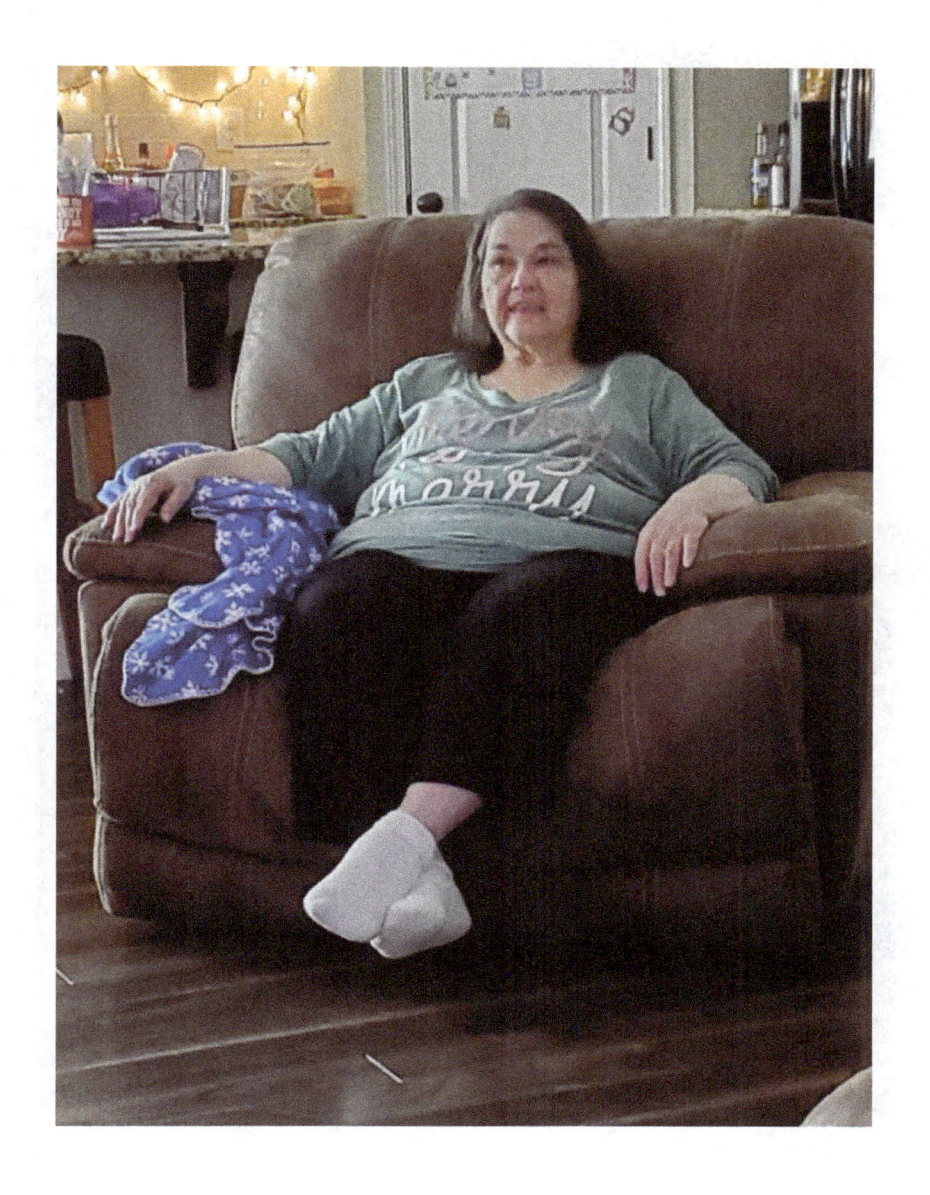

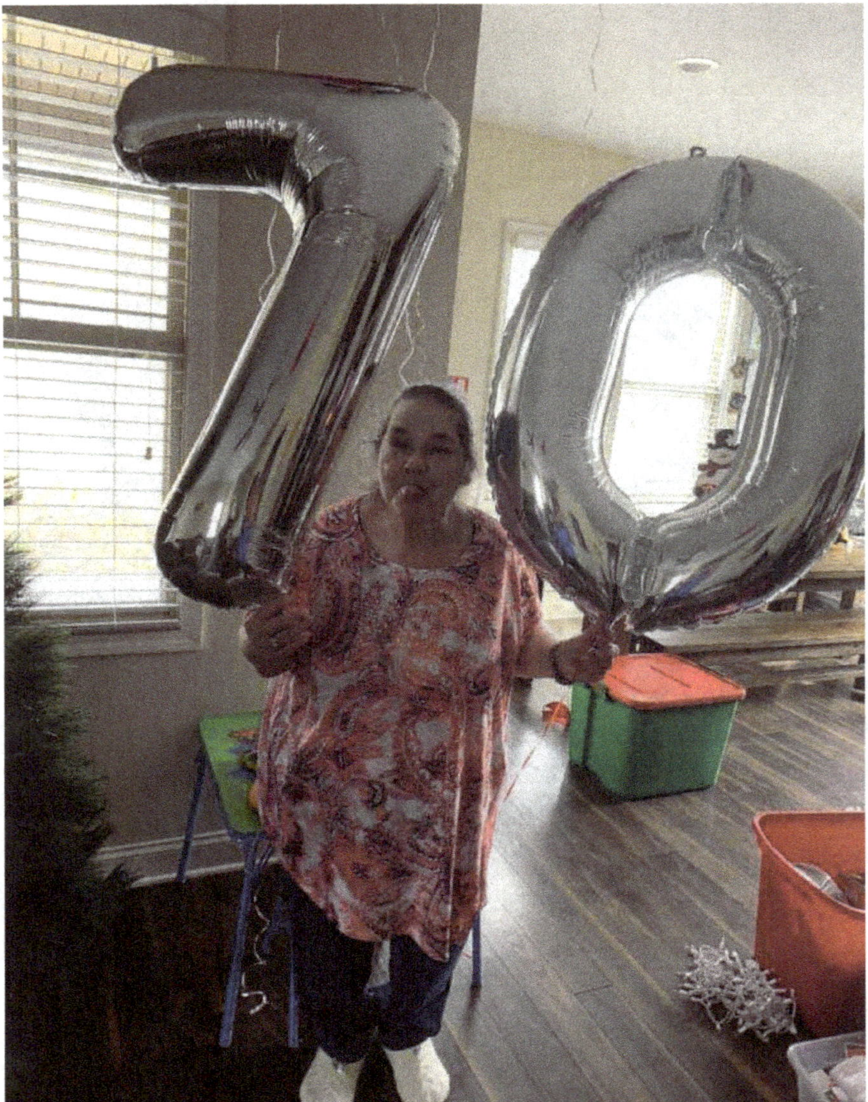

CPSIA information can be obtained
at www.ICGtesting.com
Printed in the USA
JSHW040914090523
41428JS00001B/2

9 781087 863146